School Leaders Matter

This book outlines practical steps that both government and schools can implement to significantly reduce the demands placed upon school leaders. It also provides highly effective tools and strategies to enable school leaders to reflect upon and improve their own wellbeing.

Packed full of research-led approaches, this book:

- Examines school leader burnout, what causes it, how to recognise it, and how to prevent it
- Reflects on why school leaders fail to prioritise their own needs and how this can be addressed
- Provides a comprehensive framework for schools to support leader thriving and resilience
- Shares effective, evidence-based coping strategies for leaders.

This is a must-read book for all school leaders and those looking to support and improve school leader wellbeing.

Helen Kelly is a researcher, writer, speaker, and consultant in the field of school wellbeing. As a principal, she led international schools in Bangkok, Berlin, and Hong Kong. Prior to this she was a solicitor in the field of health and safety at work.

School Leaders Matter

Preventing Burnout, Managing Stress, and Improving Wellbeing

HELEN KELLY

LONDON AND NEW YORK

Designed cover image: © Getty Images

First published 2023
by Routledge
4 Park Square, Milton Park, Abingdon, Oxon OX14 4RN

and by Routledge
605 Third Avenue, New York, NY 10158

Routledge is an imprint of the Taylor & Francis Group, an informa business

© 2023 Helen Kelly

British Library Cataloguing-in-Publication Data
A catalogue record for this book is available from the British Library

ISBN: 978-1-032-05633-3 (hbk)
ISBN: 978-1-032-05634-0 (pbk)
ISBN: 978-1-003-19847-5 (ebk)

DOI: 10.4324/9781003198475

Typeset in Dante and Avenir
by Apex CoVantage, LLC

To all the school leaders who have shared
their stories with me

To Dave for his support and patience

Contents

Foreword

Several years ago, I was fortunate enough to examine Helen's doctoral thesis. Now she has taken that learning, and her own deep experiences in practice, to write this book. Reading it, I was struck that many of the issues have not changed since I began to write about stress and leadership in the 1990s; but what has changed, I think, is a deeper awareness of the toll policy change and financial issues have had on leaders in schools. This can be seen both in educational writing nationally and internationally, and also in consultancy and expertise provided to schools. It is sobering to note that this huge body of work seems to be marginalised in the schools where it is needed most. As Helen says, school leaders matter, and it is a source of worry to me that successive governments have taken a "replace/disposable" attitude to school leadership, rather than looking at leaders' needs. Hopefully, this book will be used by school leaders to plot their own course through the difficult times that we live in and emerge the other side, thriving and with an extended capacity to help others with whom they work.

This book is well written, and, importantly, since the readers are busy people, it is structured in such a way that you are able to dip in and out of it, reading the parts that are most relevant to you at the time. The author's passion for the subject shines through, and her advice to leaders to listen to their bodies and take the time to reflect and regroup is something that school leaders find hard to do, because they are so keen to help others. This book is something that no school leader should ignore, as it gives them opportunities to see how they can balance life and work in a way that helps them both personally and professionally.

Given the COVID-19 pandemic, many school leaders worldwide have reached their own crisis point and understand that to live well is not to live for work all the time. I hope that the readers of this book will feel that they have an extra tool in their kitbag to help them with their leadership. Helen Kelly has taken her own deep experience of living with the stress of leadership and distilled it into a book that is readable for those who see themselves as time-poor. Reading this may be the start of a journey into the literature in this area, and an opportunity for busy leaders to take time to reflect and renew their spirit.

Professor Megan Crawford
August 2022

Preface

Midway through the school year 2018–19, I began to experience chest pain. At first, it only happened when I was at work and always in the head of school's office. If I am honest, the year was not going well for me. Although we were moving the school forward, there was conflict among the senior leadership, and I found myself becoming increasingly angry and frustrated. I lost my composure a few times in senior leadership team meetings and there were raised voices and tears. I felt a deep sense of unfairness that things were not going the way I wanted, and I began to doubt the merit of what we were trying to achieve as a school. I felt overlooked and disrespected, so I began to push myself harder to gain recognition elsewhere.

I was already a regular presenter on the regional conference circuit, but I signed up for more engagements, wrote articles for key publications, and began to offer wellbeing workshops for school leaders. I was receiving a lot of attention and praise but, by the spring, I was also becoming increasingly overcommitted and exhausted.

As the academic year neared its end, I found it hard to keep my resentment in check and my cynicism began to grow. The chest pains became more frequent, but I dismissed them as anxiety. It was only when the twinges began to occur in the evenings, at home, that I knew I had to take them more seriously. My father had died from a heart attack at 54, exactly the age I was then. I knew that stress was related to cardiovascular disease and my stress levels were through the roof, so I decided to seek medical advice.

Thanks to private health insurance, I was able to see a cardiologist within 48 hours and he immediately booked me in for a range of tests. By the end of the week my results were in, and I was back at the doctor's office. The consultant was visibly shocked when he told me I had major blockages in two of my main arteries, something he did not expect to see in a slim, fit patient who had not eaten meat for over 25 years. As one of my staff later put it, I was not the typical poster child for heart disease. However, my family history and the effects of the stressful work I had been engaged in over the previous 15 years could not be completely mitigated by a plant-based diet, yoga, and regular exercise. I was completely devastated. I had spent my whole adult life managing my health to avoid this happening, but the one thing I had not managed was my stress.

Two days after the shocking news, I was admitted to hospital for an angiogram, where they would insert a camera into an artery to take a closer look at the blockages. If the blockages were as bad as they looked on the scan, I would need angioplasty to clear them and possibly stents. I had never spent a night in hospital. In fact, I had never been ill before, save for occasional flu and tonsillitis. It was daunting, and I was afraid. On the morning of the procedure, things did not start well. As they tried to insert the camera through an incision in my wrist, stress caused my arteries to spasm and constrict, and it took a while for them to get the camera inside. Once in, however, they found the blockages were only moderate to severe, which was less serious than expected, and I was informed I would not need to have further procedures. I felt a huge sense of relief but, as they prepared to remove the camera, my arteries went into spasm again, much more strongly than before, and the camera became stuck inside. The pain was extreme, and I cried out in agony. I went into tachycardia, where the heart rate increases to over 100 beats per minute. The team administered nitro-glycerine to relax the arteries, and the crisis passed.

When it was all over, and I was waiting to return to my room, the doctor looked down at me and said, "Helen the chest pain you've been experiencing is caused by arterial spasms, like the one you just had. These spasms are caused by stress. You need to re-evaluate your lifestyle and eradicate stress from your life." I felt like I had been punched in the stomach and I burst into tears. I thought they were going to fix me but instead I was being told that I had to fix myself.

I went home the next day, expecting to return to school after 48 hours of rest. During those two days, it became increasingly apparent that I could not go back to work. I couldn't sleep, I had no energy, my digestive system ground to a halt, and I was anxious and depressed. I was surprised to find I also had no interest in going to work. I wrote long emails to the cardiologist, in the middle of the night, insisting that these problems were all side effects of the medication he had prescribed to treat my long-term condition. The doctor was gently dismissive, suggesting my problems might be psychological, and he referred me to his colleague, a GP who deals with stressed executives.

It was hard for me to accept that my problems might not be related to the heart condition, but I made an appointment to see the GP. She was patient and sympathetic but also matter-of-fact. She told me I was experiencing an occupational burnout, which was likely the cause of all my symptoms, including the chest pain. I had pushed myself too hard and had become overwhelmed. She told me this was very common among executives in Hong Kong and signed me off work for the last two weeks of the school year. This would give me a total of nine weeks to rest and recover before the return to school in August. The doctor also offered me antidepressants and recommended I seek counselling as soon as possible.

I informed my closest colleagues that I was suffering a burnout, but the rest of the school community thought my continued absence was related to the heart problem. They were concerned and kind, filling my house with flowers, fruit, and cards. My team was shocked by my appearance and my lack of interest in the day-to-day running of the school, but they were extremely supportive and capable and stepped in to fill my obligations. They understood that I needed complete rest and could not be exposed to any stress. They were amazing and I was very lucky to have them.

Over the summer, on a long holiday to Spain, I took the decision to retire at the end of the next school year, to prioritise my health. I was only 55 but I felt I had no choice. Both of my parents died before they were 70 and I did not want the same to happen to me. On my return to work in August, I met with my new head of school and handed in my resignation, which she accepted with understanding. I wish I could tell you that after a wonderful summer spent in Europe, I had renewed vigour and was ready to enjoy my final year as a principal, but that is not how the story ends.

After two days back at work, I developed a headache that would not budge, the chest pain returned stronger and more frequent than before, a fatigue descended upon me, which did not improve with sleep, and I became wrought with anxiety. My team noticed I was struggling and began to worry about bringing problems to me, tiptoeing around me with concerned faces. I tried to manage my symptoms, leaving work early and only attending essential meetings, but towards the end of the second week, I reached a crisis.

It was lunchtime and as I was walking back to my office from the cafeteria, I began to feel very strange. My head boomed, my chest hurt, I felt nauseous and dizzy. I was convinced I was having a heart attack and I suddenly became very afraid. I went back to my office, grabbed my handbag, and told my colleagues I was going home as I was not feeling well. Irrationally,

I called an Uber and went into the city to the cardiologist's office, rather than to the nearest hospital. I was not in full control of my faculties by the time I arrived but, fortunately, the doctor was able to see me. I was hooked up to an ECG machine and informed that I was having a panic attack, not a heart attack. Nine weeks of rest had not been enough to recover from the impact of 15 years working in a high-pressure job. I was told that following a burnout it was common to become more sensitised to stress than before and that there was a high probability that if I continued in my current role, I would experience more panic attacks and become increasingly ill. I began to worry that I might not make it to the end of the school year.

My story is not as unusual as you may think. Occupational burnout has become so prevalent in recent years that in 2019, it was recognised by the World Health Organization (WHO) as a work-related condition. Burnout is not a single event but a process resulting from chronic workplace stress, which occurs over weeks, months, or years. The WHO defines it as being characterised by three dimensions: feelings of energy depletion or exhaustion; increased mental distance from one's job, or feelings of negativity or cynicism related to one's work; and reduced professional effectiveness.

The vulnerability to burnout of headteachers and principals has been acknowledged since the 1980s but, until recently, it was difficult to quantify the incidence of burnout among school leaders or compare it to other professions. Since 2011, however, large-scale studies of principals in Australia,[1] New Zealand,[2] and Ireland[3] have used the Copenhagen Psychosocial Questionnaire (COPSOQ II) to compare data from school principals with the general population. Results shows that school leaders in all three countries are at a much higher risk of burnout than the average worker. The Australian principal study,[1] which has been carried out annually over the last decade and has engaged over half of all senior leaders, has consistently found the burnout risk of participants to be around 1.7 times that of the average Australian employee.

Not all school leaders burn out, but it is important to understand that burnout is not a condition that is simply absent or present. Instead, it is a continuum along which an individual may move back and forth, depending on the levels of stress they are experiencing and how well they are able to manage that stress. Recent studies by foremost burnout researchers Leiter and Maslach[4] have identified five profiles of workplace experience along the burnout continuum. At one end of the continuum is *Engagement*, characterised by low levels of exhaustion, detachment or cynicism, and high levels of professional efficacy. In the middle of the continuum lie three profiles, where individuals are not currently experiencing burnout but might be moving towards it. They are *Ineffective*, displaying low levels of professional efficacy only; *Disengaged*, showing high levels of detachment or cynicism only; and *Overextended*, characterised by high levels of exhaustion only. Finally, at the other end of the continuum is the *Burnout* profile, where an individual experiences high levels of exhaustion and detachment or cynicism, together with low levels of professional efficacy.

Evidence suggests that, on average, 30% of all workers fit the *Engagement* profile and 55%–60% fit into one (or sometimes two) of the *Ineffective, Disengaged*, or *Overextended* profiles. This leaves 10%–15% of employees experiencing a full burnout situation.[4] This may not sound like a major problem, but 15% of school leaders represents 70,000 US principals or vice principals; 10,000 headteachers, deputy heads or assistant heads in England; and 3,000 principals or deputy principals in Australia. In addition, there will be considerably higher numbers whose unmanaged stress has rendered them *Ineffective, Disengaged*, or *Overextended* and are at risk of a burnout occurring at some point in the future.

So why are school leaders experiencing such high levels of burnout? During my first principalship, I began to think of myself as a plate spinner, the circus act that keeps plates of different sizes gyrating on poles. Plate-spinning involves running frantically between these poles, spinning each to ensure the plates don't smash to the ground. As a new principal, it was exhilarating watching how well I could spin the plates representing different aspects of my role. When things were good, I felt accomplished, but when plates began to wobble, I would panic, and if they fell and broke, I would beat myself up about my poor leadership. As my career developed and I moved on to a second principalship, I began to realise that I was not only a plate spinner, but also a ringmaster conducting proceedings, directing performers, and linking acts together to create a seamless circus performance. I was a tightrope walker and trapeze artist, taking crazy risks observed by onlookers, many egging me on to succeed but some willing me to fall. I was a clown, painting on a smile to mask my anxiety, while raising the morale of others. Finally, I was a lion tamer, putting my head into the mouth of the beast just to reassure others I was competent, in control, and fearless.

By the time I applied for my third principal role, after ten years on the job, I was a competent all-round circus performer. I remember spending months reading through the lengthy role descriptions and person specifications that accompany job adverts, feeling proud that I was able to tick so many boxes. It never occurred to me then that it might be unrealistic to expect one person to meet all these requirements. I loved what I did, I was up for the challenge and wanted to prove I was worthy. I relished being given the opportunity to make a difference in the world and to continue to learn and grow. I had no idea then that I was asking too much of myself, that the levels of everyday stress that come with the principal's role would affect my wellbeing so significantly that I would be forced to prematurely end the career I had spent so many years building.

I know from my own experience that burnout does not happen overnight, but instead it creeps up on us over a long period of time. As we move through the burnout continuum, from *Engagement* to *Burnout*, we are likely to receive warnings that all is not well. These warnings may consist of chronic fatigue that does not improve with rest, insomnia that gets worse over time, and increased vulnerability to colds, flu, and other infections. Warnings may also include headaches, digestive problems, dizziness, poor concentration, chest pain, or palpitations. These warnings are not only physical but may involve symptoms of poor mental health that begin with tension and may develop into increased feelings of anxiety, frustration, and anger, as well as a sense of detachment and cynicism towards the workplace. These issues can leave an individual prone to depression, isolation, feelings of pessimism, and decreased enjoyment of life. They may self-medicate by drinking more alcohol, eating more, spending more, or abusing drugs. These symptoms, emotions, and behaviours will likely affect an individual's effectiveness on the job and their professional and personal relationships. For some, this will lead to an eventual crisis, as happened to me.

When I realised that I had become so overwhelmed I had burnt out, my first feelings were shame and guilt – shame that I was not strong enough to sustain my leadership over time, that I had failed where others succeeded, and guilt that I had let my school community down. School leader burnout is not something to be ashamed of, however, nor is it a sign of weakness or an indication that the sufferer is not fit for the job. Most burnt-out headteachers and principals begin their leadership careers as strong, capable, and well-qualified individuals who have higher than average levels of drive and a sincere commitment to improve their schools.

Burnout researchers have found that, while personal characteristics may play a role in rendering one individual more vulnerable to burnout than others, burnout is not a problem of the individual. Headteachers and principals do not burn out because of flaws in their character or behaviour, or because they are weak or lack the resilience to manage the demands of their work. The increasing incidence of burnout among school leaders is rather an indication that the leadership role has become too demanding and that leaders are carrying a burden much greater than is reasonable. Headteachers and principals all over the world are working themselves into the ground physically, mentally, and emotionally and are becoming overloaded, exhausted, and depleted.

Cardiologists Friedman and Rosenman coined the term "hurry sickness" after noticing that many of their patients were involved in "a continuous struggle and unremitting attempt to accomplish or achieve more and more things or participate in more and more events in less and less time."[5] This describes the average school leader, who is conscientious and works hard but struggles to acknowledge the limits of what they can take on and habitually commits to more than they have time for. They are keen to meet the expectations placed on them, no matter how unreasonable. They are reluctant to say no, regardless of how overloaded and stressed they feel. They worry about how others may be affected if they take time off or how they will complete their work if they slow down.

So the demands of school leaders' work is placing them on the path to burnout, but does this matter to anyone except leaders themselves? I would argue that there are a host of reasons why the wellbeing of school leaders and the sustainability of their leadership should matter to others, to governments, to schools, to parents, and to society at large. Education is key to the success of any nation, and headteachers and principals are integral to school effectiveness. There is a substantial body of research to suggest that, after classroom factors, school leaders are the second most important school-related determinant of student achievement. Burnout affects the wellbeing and performance of individuals and reduces their ability to carry out their roles effectively. If school leaders are key to a country's success, then we need them to be at the top of their game, rather than overwhelmed and struggling to cope.

Burnout is also linked to poor job retention among school leaders, yet we need to retain headteachers and principals in our schools, and in the profession, more than ever. In 2005, UNESCO[6] published a report highlighting a crisis in global school leader recruitment and retention. In the decade and a half since that publication, the situation has not improved. In the United States, nearly half of new principals leave their schools within the first three years, and 20% of all principals leave their posts annually.[7] This is most noticeably a problem in schools with large numbers of students from low-income families – the schools that need effective leadership the most. Replacing those leaders is a constant struggle for many schools. In 2018, over three-quarters of UK schools failed to recruit, or had difficulties recruiting, a new headteacher in the previous year, while two-thirds experienced the same with deputy head or vice principal positions.[8] The financial costs of recruiting a new headteacher or principal are also considerable and affect the least wealthy schools most. In 2017, it was estimated that the direct economic cost of turnover of each Australian principal was in the order of AUS$200,000.[9]

School leaders are a valuable resource whose wellbeing and workplace effectiveness impact society. It is something we all need to take more seriously. Yet school leader burnout is a silent epidemic. Although the COVID-19 pandemic brought an increased awareness of the stress experienced by education professionals, the unique demands placed on headteachers and principals is still largely undiscussed.

While school leader burnout is not unusual, the frankness with which I share my story is uncommon. Leaders I have encountered in recent years describe my openness as "brave." While many struggle with the demands of their role, most feel they cannot be honest about their challenges. They fear being perceived as weak or not fit for the job. Women tell me that having spent years fighting to be taken seriously as leaders, they cannot afford to be candid about their vulnerabilities. So leaders hide the truth from those around them, preferring to soldier on alone rather than seek support, risking burnout which may destroy their careers and from which they may take years to recover.

I tell my story to set the scene for the rest of the book but also to destigmatise the experience of burnout in schools. As a confidante of hundreds of school leaders around the world, I feel a responsibility to encourage readers to be more honest about the challenges they may be encountering, to understand the warning signs, and to take steps to prevent burnout happening to them. This is not simply a self-help manual for school leaders, however, as placing the onus of managing stress and preventing burnout solely on individual leaders will have limited effect. This book is written for policymakers, those responsible for school governance, and individuals and organisations involved in the professional development and support of school leaders. It is also written for parents who should want the best for the headteachers and principals to whom they entrust their children. It addresses why the 21st-century school leader's role is so demanding and how we arrived at a point where so many are overwhelmed. It examines what can be done at the policy, organisational, and individual levels to create the conditions where headteachers and principals can thrive and experience *Engagement* rather than *Burnout*.

Notes

1   Riley, P., See, S.M., Marsh, H. and Dicke, T., 2021. *The Australian Principal Occupational Health, Safety and Wellbeing Survey 2020.* Sydney: Institute for Positive Psychology and Education, Australian Catholic University.
2   Riley, P., Rahimi, M. and Arnold, B., 2021. *The New Zealand Primary Principal Occupational Health, Safety and Wellbeing Survey 2020.* Melbourne: Research for Educational Impact (REDI), Deakin University.

3 Riley, P., 2015. *Irish Principals' and Deputy Principals' Occupational Health, Safety and Wellbeing Survey*. Melbourne: Research for Educational Impact (REDI), Deakin University.

4 Leiter, M.P. and Maslach, C., 2016. Latent Burnout Profiles: A New Approach to Understanding the Burnout Experience. *Burnout Research*, 3(4), 89–100.

5 Rosenman, R.H. and Friedman, M., 1977. Modifying Type a Behavior Pattern. *Journal of Psychosomatic Research*, 21(4), 323–331.

6 Chapman, J.D., 2005. *Recruitment, Retention, and Development of School Principals*. Brussels: International Institute for Educational Planning.

7 Levin, S., Bradley, K. and Scott, C., 2019. *Principal Turnover: Insights from Current Principals*. Palo Alto, CA: Learning Policy Institute.

8 National Association of Headteachers, 2018. *Recruitment and Retention Report 2018*. London: NAHT.

9 Hom, P.W., Lee, T.W., Shaw, J.D. and Hausknecht, J.P., 2017. One Hundred Years of Employee Turnover Theory and Research. *Journal of Applied Psychology*, 102(3), 530.

Acknowledgements

It is the fulfilment of a lifetime ambition to become an author. Writing a book is an intense experience that requires application, determination, and resilience. I would not have arrived at this point without the help and support of many people, who have smoothed my path over the last ten years. I give my heartfelt thanks to them all.

To the participants in my original 2016 research and the many school leaders who have confided in me over the last ten years and have given me a global perspective on the life of the school leader. I am grateful for your honesty and trust. I want to protect your anonymity, but you know who you are.

To my former team in Hong Kong who made me feel so cared for when I fell ill. Special thanks to DJ MacPherson and Zoe Heggie, who made it possible for me to take a step back when I needed it most, and Dr Jane Camblin, who gave me space and dignity when I was at my worst. To Winne "the machine" McCarthy, the best, and most caring, executive assistant in the world. To Dr Lisa Kipfer, Rob Grantham and Viv Wallace, part of the Sensational Six, without whom I might have fallen off a cliff earlier.

To CEO Andreas Wegener and my other former colleagues in Berlin who supported me during my Ed.D. research.

To Laura Liguori, who read my chapters and kept reminding me that this was an important book that needed to be written.

To followers on my social media and visitors my website (www.drhelenkelly.com) for their encouragement and input.

To Professor Megan Crawford, who was an early inspiration to me through her book *Getting to the Heart of Leadership*. I was thrilled and privileged to have her as the external examiner on my doctoral thesis, to receive her subsequent support and encouragement to take my work to a wider audience, and to have her read my manuscript and provide the foreword.

To my husband Dave Kelly who listened to my ramblings during daily lockdown walks while I formulated my ideas, who gave me "space" to write while living together in a campervan of 8 square metres, who was always ready to hold me to account if I drifted off into the realm of the fanciful and who read my early chapters and argued with me about my use of commas and semicolons.

Introduction

A growing body of research from around the globe confirms that school leaders are highly stressed and that much of this stress is related to their work. In 2019, three key reports were published on educator wellbeing in the UK,[1] Australia,[2] and New Zealand.[3] Eighty-four percent of UK senior leaders said they felt stressed, while the studies from Australia and New Zealand found principals reporting much higher levels of work-related stress than the general population.

The literature paints a worrying picture of the effect that work-related stress is having on school leader wellbeing. The UK study reported the overall wellbeing score for school leaders as significantly lower than that of the general population. A third of participants said they had experienced a mental health issue in the past year, with 40% attributing this solely to their work and half to a combination of work and home factors. Forty-one percent of participants showed signs of anxiety, and almost a third showed signs of depression. Over three-quarters said that in the previous year they had experienced at least one of a range of symptoms associated with poor mental health, including insomnia, irritability, mood swings, overeating, tearfulness, recurring headaches or migraines, and panic attacks.[1] In a large-scale study from Ontario, Canada, 30% of principals said they had experienced stress-related illness connected to their work. Nearly a third described their level of general or emotional wellbeing as "poor" or "very poor," while 41% reported "poor" or "very poor" physical wellbeing. Over a third of participants said the demands of their work had a "considerable" or "extreme" impact on their physical health, over half reported a similar effect on their sleep or diet, and nearly two-thirds a similar effect on their fitness.[4]

DOI: 10.4324/9781003198475-1

Studies from Australia,[2] New Zealand,[3] and Ireland[5] show that principals experience much higher levels of symptoms linked to chronic stress than the general population, including depressive symptoms and sleeping problems. They also have much lower perceptions of the quality of their health than average – a measure that is a valuable predictor of mortality, cardiovascular disease, hospitalisation, medication use, absence from work, and early retirement. In my own 2017 study of international school leaders, over two-thirds said work-related stress was affecting their health. One participant described the effect of their high stress levels.[6]

> Ambient stress has been higher recently. Health-wise my sleep has suffered. I have not exercised as much as usual and I have been sick more often. I have had colds and coughs that I do not usually get and they have been hard to shake off. My left eye has started to twitch over the last 6 weeks and my blood pressure has gone up. Those are warning signs. Either I am going to burn myself out or something is going to have to give.
>
> (International School Principal, Germany)

Stress not only affects school leaders' health but also their professional and personal lives. Forty-one percent of international school leaders say that stress affects their ability to do their job well.[6] A similar proportion of UK headteachers say that their work performance suffers because of work-related wellbeing issues, while 22% report an impact on their professional relationships.[1] Two-thirds of international school leaders,[6] nearly half of UK leaders,[1] and a third of Ontario principals[4] find work negatively affects their relationships with friends and family. Studies from Australia,[2] New Zealand,[3] and Ireland[5] have found that principals experience much higher levels of work-family conflict than the general population, due to having insufficient time and energy for their families.

> It's hard for my wife to understand why I need to spend time on my own at weekends, playing golf and decompressing when I haven't seen her all week because of the late work nights.
>
> (International School Principal, Middle East)

While some school leaders can draw upon active coping strategies to help mitigate the high levels of stress, a significant number are not coping well. Many turn to unhealthy coping mechanisms to manage the strain. In the UK, almost half of headteachers admit to overeating to help them cope, while a third abuse alcohol and a quarter turn to unnecessary spending.[1]

> I have piled on weight over the past year or so as I spend the evenings and weekends comfort eating. I can get through a couple of bottles of wine most Friday and Saturday nights and drinking on a school night has also crept up.
>
> (Headteacher, UK)

Across a range of studies, a worrying number of leaders report feeling overwhelmed or reaching a crisis point. Fifty-seven percent of Ontario principals say they often feel overwhelmed by their work,[4] while half of international school leaders say their job demands have brought them close to breaking point at times.[6]

> Things got really bad after the governor's meeting. I was up most nights worrying about school and had to drag myself through the days. I was often tearful and struggled to remain focused. I started questioning if I should be doing the job.
>
> (International School Principal, Thailand)

The annual Australian Principal Occupational Health, Safety and Wellbeing Survey produces an immediate alert to participants reporting signs of concerning stress levels. Principals who report thoughts of hurting themselves over the course of the previous week, those whose quality-of-life risk score is "high" or "very high," or individuals reporting very poor working conditions receive a "red flag" email to inform them that their scores give cause for concern and to suggest where to seek help. In 2019, 28% of participants received a red flag email.[2]

School Leader Burnout

While emergency service workers such as police, firefighters, paramedics, doctors, and nurses are the most likely to suffer occupational burnout, those in other people-centred professions like care workers, social workers, teachers, and school leaders are also considered high-risk. Since the early 1980s, studies from around the world, including the UK, United States, Hong Kong, Israel, Greece, and Switzerland, have identified burnout as a problem for school principals. While there were a small number of studies from the United States in the 1990s that showed principal burnout to be mostly at a moderate to high level, there was little other data available on the incidence of school leader burnout until a decade ago.

Since 2011, the use of the COPSOQ II scale in large-scale studies, carried out in Australia,[2] New Zealand,[3] and Ireland,[5] has enabled a comparison between the burnout of school principals and the general population. These studies assess burnout using a self-report tool to measure the degree of physical and mental fatigue or exhaustion of the participant. The average degree of burnout reported by the general population using this tool is 34.1 out of 100.[2] In 2019, New Zealand principals reported an average degree of burnout of 57,[3] while those in Australia scored 54.[2] In an Irish study from 2015, the average degree of burnout reported by principals was 60.[5] Higher degrees of burnout are reported by females across all three countries and also by participants working in isolated areas. Principals working in government schools report higher burnout scores than those in the independent sector.

Retention and Recruitment

Evidence of headteacher and principal retention and recruitment issues linked to the stressful nature of the work goes back at least three decades. A 1995 study from Colorado found that a quarter of participants did not plan on staying in the job until retirement age, due to the stress involved in their work.[7] A study from Canada, in the same year, reported that nearly half of participants had thought about quitting their job in the previous year because of high levels of stress.[8] Throughout the early 2000s, a multitude of studies from around the world highlighted difficulties in recruiting and retaining qualified principals, due to the stressful nature of the job. Recent studies show that the situation has not improved.

In 2019, two-thirds of UK senior leaders said they had thought about leaving the profession during the previous two years, due to pressures on their health and wellbeing. Leaders identified the impact of workload on their wellbeing and seeking a better work-life balance as the main reasons for considering leaving.[1]

Headteacher and principal turnover is associated with a range of negative effects for schools, including higher teacher turnover, loss of shared purpose and trust among staff, derailing of school improvement initiatives, and, most importantly, poorer student outcomes.

> It has been a tough and stressful year; I have learnt a lot. For me I need something else. I do not want to spend the rest of my life doing this, working with this amount of stress. I have to think about the next career stage or moving out altogether.
>
> (Principal, Australia)

Increasing school leader stress is a serious issue that affects leaders, their colleagues, families, and students, as well as society at large. It is something that needs to be addressed if we are to avoid these wide-ranging impacts.

Overview of the Book

This book provides an in-depth examination of school leader stress and burnout and considers how it can be addressed. It is written in two parts, with Part I examining the causes of school leader stress and burnout and Part II discussing how these issues can be resolved. I begin in Chapter 1 by considering the nature of the headteacher and principal role and how it has developed over the last five decades. I discuss the political and other changes that have created an intensification of school leaders' work and discuss how this has driven stress levels to become unmanageable for many.

In Chapters 2 and 3, I look at the demands of the school leader's role in more detail. Drawing on an extensive body of research, I begin in Chapter 2 with an analysis of the emotional demands that headteachers and principals encounter in their daily work, including the impact of relationships with teachers, parents, and supervisors. I also examine the effect that student-related issues have on leaders. I discuss the youth mental health crisis sweeping the world and the increasing demands on schools to meet students' special educational needs.

In Chapter 3, I examine workload and other related stressors that affect headteacher and principal wellbeing. I consider working hours, work pace, and work-life balance and discuss the implications of long working hours for health, happiness, and job performance. I examine a range of other workplace stressors that affect school leaders, including resource management, accountability, and statutory obligations.

It is impossible to write a book about school leader stress and burnout without discussing the impact of the COVID-19 pandemic. In Chapter 4, I discuss the effect of a school crisis on school leaders already experiencing high levels of stress. I examine the types of crises that schools encounter and the effect that a crisis has on a school community and on its leaders. I then draw upon my own research to examine the impact of the global pandemic on schools and their leaders. I discuss how headteachers and principals coped in the face of unprecedented demands and the huge effect that the crisis has had on many. I consider the potential long-term implications of the pandemic for schools and the profession.

The book draws on research and on the personal experiences of school leaders from around the world, working in a wide range of sectors. The themes discussed are intended to be universal and should resonate with headteachers and principals wherever they work. International schools, while not unique, do experience contextual and situational factors that distinguish them from schools in domestic education systems, however.

Chapter 5 examines the stressors of headteachers and principals working in international schools and highlights the specific challenges of leading them.

In Chapter 6, the final chapter of Part I, I take a deeper dive into the subject of burnout, drawing upon major research in the field to discuss the causes of burnout, the warning signs and symptoms of burnout, and burnout prevention.

In Part II, I move away from the causes and impacts of school leader stress and burnout to look at how these issues can be addressed at the policy, organisational, and individual levels. I begin in Chapter 7 by discussing what governments can do to reduce the demands placed on leaders and provide workplaces that are more conducive to *Engagement* rather than *Burnout*. I examine a range of political solutions, including reducing social disadvantage, reviewing education funding, and addressing high accountability cultures. I also consider practical solutions, such as revising the school leader's role, improving leadership training, development, and support, and tackling school leader abuse.

In Chapters 8, 9, and 10, I look at what schools can to do to reduce leader stress and provide working conditions that support leader wellbeing. In Chapter 8, I set out a strategic framework, the School Leader Wellbeing Framework, intended to drive improvement in school leader working conditions and make a real and lasting improvement to their wellbeing. In Chapter 9, I set out in more detail how this blueprint can be used to support the implementation of school-based interventions to reduce the workload of leaders and the emotional demands of the role. I discuss how school leadership may be redefined to meet the needs of 21st-century school, by dispersing leadership more widely. I also consider the provision of leadership time for teaching heads and principals, increased administrative support, and streamlining work processes. In Chapter 10, I suggest a range of evidence-based interventions to improve social and mental health support for leaders. I discuss the benefits of destigmatising mental ill health in schools, examine mentoring, coaching, and networking as forms of social support, and consider the need for improved leadership training.

In Chapter 11, I consider how schools can foster improved wellbeing for all stakeholders, including leaders, by creating a positive workplace culture. I suggest a range of practical approaches to improve workplace culture, by enhancing a sense of belonging and improving the quality of relationships between colleagues.

Chapters 12 and 13 focus on how headteachers and principals can more effectively manage their own stress. I begin in Chapter 12 by discussing the importance of rest and work recovery in stress management. I also consider how leaders can establish new habits to support improved rest and recovery and ensure practices become embedded into their daily lives. In Chapter 13, I discuss a wide range of self-sabotage behaviours, often rooted in deep-seated insecurities, that contribute to school leader stress and burnout. I consider how these behaviours may be addressed through self-compassion practices.

Finally, in Chapter 14, I examine what happens when leaders become overwhelmed and reach a burnout crisis. I discuss burnout recovery and the options available to individuals who feel their current role is no longer sustainable.

Throughout the book, I draw upon several large-scale studies of headteacher and principal wellbeing that have been carried out over the last ten years in Australia,[2] New Zealand,[3] Ireland,[5] Canada,[4] and the UK.[1] These studies present a current, reliable, and sometimes longitudinal overview of school leaders' experience across major education systems. They contain, in my opinion, the best quality data currently available on school leader stress and wellbeing. I also draw upon a host of smaller-scale studies from around the world to provide a wider perspective. There is extensive use of quantitative and qualitative data from my own research: my 2017 doctoral thesis, *International Schools as Emotional Arenas: Facing the Leadership Challenges*;[6] the 2020 report *School Leader Wellbeing During the COVID 19 Pandemic 2020*;[9] and the 2021 report *International School Teacher Wellbeing During the COVID 19 Pandemic 2020*,[10] as well as the many interviews I have conducted with scores of school leaders over the last seven years. It is my privilege to be able to include the words of these leaders, to help illustrate my points and bring the book to life. I am grateful for their time, trust, and candour. All necessary steps have been taken to protect their identities, but they know who they are.

This book is written with a global audience in mind. Although most of my teaching and leadership career was spent in the international school sector, my experience as a researcher and consultant extends across all sectors worldwide. My blog regularly attracts readers from over 150 countries, working in both state and independent schools, and my research involves participants from just as wide a field. There is a risk, in trying to reach such a wide audience, that my message will become overgeneralised and lack meaning or that some will feel unrepresented. This may be compounded by the fact that, although a body of research is developing globally on topics aligned to the field of school leader wellbeing, most large-scale, longitudinal studies have been carried out in a small number of Western, anglophone countries. My experience to date has shown me that the main themes emerging from this research, and covered by my own work, are universal to school leaders wherever they are located, although the fine detail may differ.

Throughout the book, I commonly use the terms "headteachers and principals" and "school leaders." This is intended to cover all senior leadership positions, including deputy and assistant headteachers, vice and associate principals, directors of learning, and other similar roles. While much of what is written also applies to those in middle leadership positions, this book is not intended to focus on middle leaders who face a set of unique demands, many of which are not discussed here.

Except for Chapter 4, which examines the impact of the COVID-19 pandemic, all the research data referred to in the book is from the pre-COVID era. I have intentionally drawn upon research prior to 2020, to reinforce the message that the issues raised are long-term problems that, while compounded by the global pandemic, were not caused by it.

A book focused on school leader stress and burnout inevitably sheds light on the negative aspects of the school leader's work experience. I feel compelled to close this introduction by highlighting the positives, as there are so many. When I reflect on my own career, I can identify many warning signs of impending burnout that I ignored in the decade before my crisis, but I also remember how much I loved my work. I have no desire to go back to it, as I am happy with where I have landed. The daily peace of mind that I now experience transcends anything I encountered in the workplace. I cannot deny, however, the joy and pride of being part of the vibrant and diverse school communities that I was privileged to serve between 2006 and 2020. I am not alone in this. In studies from Australia,[2] New Zealand,[3] and Ireland,[5] principals consistently report their work to be more varied and interesting than the average worker and feel their roles offer more opportunity for personal and professional development than is the norm. They also have higher levels of job satisfaction and experience a greater sense of meaning in their work than the general population. It is these things, as well as their sense of duty, that keep school leaders coming back to face the challenges, day after day, despite the negative impact on their health and wellbeing. What society needs are school leaders who can sustain these feelings towards their work, their energy, and their level of commitment over time. I hope this book offers a pathway towards achieving this.

Notes

1 Savill-Smith, C., 2019. *Teacher Wellbeing Index*. London: Education Support.
2 Riley, P., See, S.M., Marsh, H. and Dicke, T., 2021. *The Australian Principal Occupational Health, Safety and Wellbeing Survey 2020*. Sydney: Institute for Positive Psychology and Education, Australian Catholic University.

3 Riley, P., Rahimi, M. and Arnold, B., 2021. *The New Zealand Primary Principal Occupational Health, Safety and Wellbeing Survey 2020*. Melbourne: Research for Educational Impact (REDI), Deakin University.

4 Pollock, K. and Wang, F., 2020. *School Principals' Work and Well-Being in Ontario: What They Say and Why It Matters*. Toronto, ON: Western University.

5 Riley, P., 2015. *Irish Principals' and Deputy Principals' Occupational Health, Safety and Wellbeing Survey*. Melbourne: Research for Educational Impact (REDI), Deakin University.

6 Kelly, H., 2017. International Schools as Emotional Arenas: Facing the Leadership Challenges in a German Context. University of Birmingham, Ed.D.

7 Whitaker, K.S., 1995. Principal Burnout: Implications for Professional Development. *Journal of Personnel Evaluation in Education*, 9(3), 287–296.

8 Allison, D.G., 1997. Coping with Stress in the Principalship. *Journal of Educational Administration*, 35(1), 39–55.

9 Kelly, H., 2020. School Leader Wellbeing During the COVID 19 Pandemic 2020. Accessed online https://drhelenkelly.com/article.php?id=15

10 Kelly, H., 2021. International School Teacher Wellbeing During the COVID 19 Pandemic 2020. Accessed online https://drhelenkelly.com/article.php?id=3

Part I

What Is Causing School
Leader Stress and Burnout?

The Intensification of the School Leader's Role   1

Most school leaders are dedicated professionals who are highly committed to their work and gain great satisfaction and meaning from it. Over recent decades, however, headteachers and principals have been experienced increasing work-related stress because of the unreasonable demands placed on them. This stress is affecting physical and mental health, family life, and job performance and is causing burnout at much greater levels than is experienced by the general population. This situation is leading many headteachers and principals to consider leaving the profession. To find solutions to these issues, it is first necessary to understand how we have arrived at a point where the school leader's role has become so demanding that many individuals are becoming overwhelmed. In this chapter, I discuss the wide-ranging changes that have occurred in education over the last five decades and the growing expectations that have been placed on schools. These changes have brought about a massive shift in the work of headteachers and principals, creating an intensification of the role, manifested in long working hours and high levels of emotional and cognitive demands.

The Changing Role of Schools

The last 50 years have brought a transformation in the role that schools play in society. Universal education was originally conceived in the context of the widespread industrialisation that took place in the second half of the 19th century. This brought a need to systematise basic schooling, to equip future workers for a life spent in factories, mills, and docks. Right up until the mid-20th century, it was widely accepted that only the minority could

DOI: 10.4324/9781003198475-3

achieve a high-level education and that everyone else would be put to work in these essential industries, where jobs were plentiful.

The world was changing, however, and in the late 1960s, a combination of economic decline and increased international competition brought a new demand for skilled workers and professionals, to secure economic prosperity for nations. Education moved up the government agenda, as schools became the primary vehicle for improving the quality of the workforce.

Up until this point, it was commonly believed that a person's achievements were determined not by their schooling but by their family background, socioeconomic status, and ethnicity. In 1966, the findings of a highly influential, US government–funded study, the Coleman Report, reinforced this idea. It concluded that variations in school quality showed little association with educational attainment; instead, it was the social inequalities of class and race that governed which children would succeed.

Despite these findings, an urgent need to enhance the labour force created a huge push to raise educational standards by improving schools. School reformers looked to research to determine how schools could most effectively make a difference to a child's attainment, by pinpointing the philosophies, policies, and practices that would achieve this. There was a growing understanding that, if attainment was to be universally raised, schools needed to find ways to compensate for the social deficits and economic disparities that the Coleman Report had highlighted. This thinking brought a new expectation that schools could and should fix the inequality and disadvantage that was standing in the way of a better educated workforce.

In addition to new economic pressures, the second half of the 20th century was characterised by rapid social change, which affected social cohesion across the Western world. Growing divorce rates, increasing numbers of women entering the workforce, and greater employment mobility led to the breakup of the family unit and the disintegration of traditional communities. The social support that these communities had provided for generations began to erode, leading to growing social alienation. This decline in social cohesion could affect the success of any child, not only those living in poverty. It became apparent that if schools were to maximise the achievement of every student, they would need to offer the support that had previously been provided by families and neighbourhoods. The responsibility of schools for socialisation, morality, and citizenship greatly increased as they were tasked not only with improving a nation's economic success, but also with curing society's dysfunctions.

In recent decades, other factors such as increased globalisation, changing demographic patterns, growing immigration, evolving labour markets, and rapidly developing technologies have also brought an urgency to adapt education systems to meet the needs of contemporary society. This evolving landscape continues to bring new, multiple, and heightened expectations for schools and has driven profound and lasting change. Schools have been redefined not only as educational establishments, but as multi-service providers, offering pre-school, childcare, recreational services, meal provision, family support, and health care.

Decentralisation of Schools and Increased Accountability

Up to the late 1960s, schools had operated within highly centralised education systems and had little autonomy over their own operations. The need for growing school reform highlighted the inadequacies of this approach, and it became apparent that centralisation was no longer the most effective way to run schools. In many developed countries, including the UK, Canada, the United States, and Australia, power was transferred away from government and into the hands of individual schools. School-based management provided each school with greater levels of autonomy, allowing them to serve the unique needs of their community.

Decentralisation brought changes to the way that schools operated, creating new forms of governance and partnership with staff, parents, and the wider community. Governments still needed ways to exercise control over schools, however, and so complex systems of accountability were gradually introduced. These imposed obligations on schools to perform according to centrally defined standards, policies, curriculum, targets, and inspection regimes. Standardised testing became a key element of this accountability framework, allowing student achievement to be measured, monitored, reported, and benchmarked, leaving schools open to public and government scrutiny. School choice for parents was introduced and became a tool to raise standards, by increasing competition between schools. This forced schools to operate like businesses, marketing themselves to customers based on the facilities and services they offered and the results they achieved.

School choice for parents meant that student enrolment numbers could no longer be guaranteed. Standardised testing data became the metric on which a school's financial sustainability depended, forcing schools to give precedence to raising standards over other priorities. During this time, there was a proliferation of research into effective schooling, and multiple studies began to highlight the importance of teacher quality to student outcomes. This brought increasing demands from government and parents for improvements in the teaching profession. Using student achievement data as evidence of teacher effectiveness, schools began to place a greater emphasis on teacher quality, by building their capacity and managing their performance. International assessments, such as the Programme for International Student Assessment, brought new opportunities to compare the instructional practices of one education system with another. This increased demands for schools to update their approaches to learning and radicalise their pedagogy to model practices on schools in more successful countries.

The 21st-Century School Leader's Role

Wide-ranging changes in the purpose, autonomy, and accountability of schools brought a complete transformation in the role of headteachers and principals. The job of headteacher or principal was first conceptualised at the advent of mass education in the 19th century. The headteacher was a senior educator who retained teaching responsibilities but also handled non-teaching tasks, while the principal role was focused more on administration. In both models, schools operated within a highly centralised education system and the work of the school leader was limited in scope. Following the introduction of school-based management, the responsibilities placed on schools and their leaders continuously grew, and the role of the headteacher or principal evolved, becoming increasingly complex and demanding.

During the late 1990s, new research highlighting the role that school leaders play in student achievement caused the effectiveness of leadership to move up the agenda.[1] The role of the headteacher and principal became elevated as quality leadership was viewed as essential to a school's success. Governments acknowledged the role of school leaders as "one of the most . . . significant undertaken by any person in society."[2] A large body of research developed, claiming to identify the attributes and competencies associated with effective school leadership. This was responsible for an unprecedented increase in expectations around the purpose and practice of the headteacher's and principal's role and led to massive growth in their workplace demands. In 2002, a meta-analysis of studies on effective educational leadership identified no fewer than 121 desirable school leadership practices.[3] In 2001, Michael A. Copeland, director of the Prospective Principals' Programme at Stanford University, published a paper called *The Myth of the Superprincipal*, which began with this mock job advertisement:

> Position Opening: School Principal, Anytown School District. Qualifications: Wisdom of a sage, vision of a CEO, intellect of a scholar, leadership of a point guard, compassion of a counsellor, moral strength of a nun, courage of a firefighter, craft knowledge of a surgeon, political savvy of a senator, toughness of a soldier, humility

of a saint, collaborative skills of an entrepreneur, certitude of a civil rights activist, charisma of a stage performer and patience of Job. Salary lower than you might expect. Credential required. For application materials contact . . .[4]

Although the description seems outdated, it makes its point effectively. A decade later Duignan also described the wide-ranging role of the school leader:

legal expert, health and social consultant, security officer, technological innovator and top-notch resource manager . . . confidant, marriage counsellor, architect, engineer, and sanitary contractor.[5]

Since the early 2000s, governments across the world have implemented sets of professional standards for headteachers and principals, which formalise the expectations of the role. While these standards have had a positive impact on the professional culture of school leaders, they have also contributed to unrealistic expectations of what an individual leader can achieve. The 2020 Headteachers' Standards for England contain 38 competencies in ten separate domains: school culture, teaching, curriculum, behaviour, additional and special educational needs, professional development, organisational management, school improvement, working in partnership, and governance and accountability. The standards from the USA National Policy Board for Educational Administration contain 74 standards also in ten domains, and the Australian Professional Standards for Principals are published in a 26-page document outlining sets of leadership profiles and how they should be used.

It is clear from these standards that the school leader is no longer just an educator with managerial responsibilities, or an administrative bureaucrat. Their role is now complex and multifaceted. The 21st-century school leader is a forward-looking strategic thinker, working closely with the governing body to provide direction for the school community. They are an instructional leader, responsible for securing and sustaining effective teaching and learning to meet the needs of every child. They are a community leader, who must foster a sense of belonging, through trusting relationships, and develop, empower, and motivate others. They are also an organisational leader, ensuring prudent financial management, maintaining a positive public profile, and building connections with the wider community. They manage the health, safety, security, and maintenance of the school environment and ensure the smooth day-to-day running of the school. They remain accountable, in accordance with statutory requirements, to government, the governing body, staff, parents, and the local community. To fulfil this role effectively, school leaders need a wide range of practical, organisational, communication, and social and emotional skills.

While many welcome the greater autonomy, elevated status, and increased levels of professionalism that the transformation of the role has brought, most leaders feel that the job has become too demanding. In a 2013 study of principals in the United States, three-quarters said their work was now too complex. This was a view shared by principals regardless of demographic characteristics. In 2002, the Organisation for Economic Co-operation and Development (OECD) reported that there was growing concern among member states around the demands being made of school leaders. They highlighted how, while the expectations for school leadership have transformed in recent decades, in most schools the leadership structures have remained the same and may be no longer fit for purpose. Twenty years on, the situation is no less concerning. As the world and the pace of educational reform move rapidly, the headteacher or principal operates in an increasingly challenging and unpredictable environment. The growing scope of the role has become too large and complex for one person to have the necessary expertise in the range of disciplines required. Consequently, increasing numbers of school leaders are becoming overwhelmed by their role.

Chapter Summary

- Over the last 50 years, the role of schools has changed significantly. Governments now look to schools to provide a highly educated workforce by maximising the potential of each individual student.
- Schools are also expected to address society's dysfunctions by tackling inequality and improving social cohesion. To achieve this, schools have become multi-service providers, playing a key role in their communities.
- Educational research is constantly identifying new factors that make schools more effective, and schools are under relentless pressure to improve.
- As part of this process, schools have been handed greater autonomy in their management and operation. With this autonomy has also come increased accountability to government.
- The role of the headteacher or principal has completely transformed from an administrative manager or lead teacher to one of a CEO, responsible for all aspects of school operations.

- The quality of leadership has been identified as a crucial factor in school success. This has led to the proliferation of competencies and standards that govern expectations around the school leader's role.
- All these factors have led to an intensification of the role of headteacher or principal, which has increased the volume and complexity of their work.
- Expectations around what an individual school leader can achieve may have moved beyond what is reasonable.

Notes

1   Maden, M., 2001. *Success against the Odds: Five Years on*. London: Routledge Falmer.
2   Australian Institute for Teaching and School Leadership, 2014. *Australian Professional Standard for Principals and the Leadership Profile*. Melbourne: AITSL.
3   Leithwood, K., Jantzi, D. and Steinbach, R., 2002. *Leadership Practices for Accountable Schools*. Dordrecht: Springer.
4   Copland, M.A., 2001. The Myth of the Superprincipal. *Phi Delta Kappan*, 82(7), 528–533.
5   Duignan, P., 2012. *Educational Leadership: Together Creating Ethical Learning Environments*. New York, NY: Cambridge University Press.

The Emotional Demands of the School Leader's Role

2

In the previous two chapters, I examined the stresses encountered by school leaders in the course of their work and the impact on their health, personal, and professional lives. I also outlined the changes that have occurred in schools, in recent decades, that have led to an intensification of the headteacher's and principal's role and created an environment in which many feel overburdened. A growing body of research has identified the workplace stressors that leaders regularly encounter and has found some of these stressors to be more closely associated with burnout than others. It is not surprising that a heavy workload is among them, but what may be less expected is the impact of the emotional demands on leaders.

Researchers have described schools as "powerhouses of emotion"[1] and school leaders as "psychological containers for others' emotions."[2] Studies from multiple contexts confirm that school leaders find their work emotionally demanding. Ninety-seven percent of international school leaders say that leading their schools is emotionally challenging work,[3] while 90% of Ontario principals report that their work is emotionally draining.[4] Large-scale studies from Australia,[5] New Zealand,[6] and Ireland[7] show that the emotional demands of school principals' work are considerably higher than those experienced by the general workforce. The complexity and intensity of these experiences means that leaders are confronted daily with a range of emotional demands that need to be managed.

These emotional demands come from many sources but, while students are at the heart of the school leader's role, it is relationships with adults that are the most demanding. Adult relationships, particularly those with teachers and parents, have been identified as the single most significant stressor associated with school leader burnout.[8] In this chapter, I examine

DOI: 10.4324/9781003198475-4

these adult relationships in more detail, drawing from the research, including my own interviews with leaders. I use school leaders' own words to shine a light on the demands that interactions with adults bring to their work. While not as closely associated with leader burnout, I also discuss student-related issues, including poor student mental health and special educational needs provision, as these are areas of increasing concern, placing growing emotional demands on headteachers and principals.

Relationships With Teaching Staff

In my 2017 research, three-quarters of international school leaders said working with teachers was emotionally challenging.[3] Research shows that teachers are difficult to manage, possibly more so than professionals in non-educational settings.[9] Teachers invest their sense of *self* in their work, merging their personal and professional identities, which leaves them highly sensitive to attempts to control or influence their practice.[10] New school initiatives will often be perceived not only as a judgment on their competence but as a threat to their inherent values and beliefs, which can give rise to strong emotional reactions, often directed at leaders or colleagues.

> Teachers can be really hard work and very emotional. Most have gone from school to university back to school and have not lived in the real world. I think that if people from other businesses came into schools they would be absolutely amazed.
>
> (International School Principal, Dubai)

School leader's relationships with teachers can be complex, but several key areas emerge as flashpoints for conflict: managing teacher performance and underperformance, disciplinary issues, implementing and leading change, interpersonal conflict among staff, and staff mental health issues.

Longitudinal studies from Australia have consistently identified managing poorly performing staff as a major stressor for participants over the last decade.[5] Eighty-six percent of Ontario principals find issues around teacher performance to be draining, while over three-quarters are stressed by the level of support teachers need.[4] In my 2017 research, many participants spoke of the challenges they faced in managing staff underperformance.[3]

> It was terrible. She had no skills, she was creative, but she could not plan or teach. The kids did not even know how to use a ruler. I told her

> I would co-teach with her, which I really did not have the time for, and I ended up having to plan and teach half of her lessons.
>
> (International School Principal, Germany)

Supporting underperforming staff can be particularly demanding in countries where employees have a high level of employment protection. Two-thirds of Ontario principals said they had difficulty terminating underperforming teachers,[4] while leaders in my 2017 study spoke of the challenges of working within the strict confines of German employment law. Participants described mentoring and coaching teachers to improve their practice over many months or years, with no option for dismissal, and the emotional toll this took on everyone involved.

> My guy is still not out. It's very draining. I am building up evidence that he is not meeting the standards, but the works council are involved. They are combing over the finest details of observations and conversations trying to catch me out.
>
> (International School Principal, Germany)

Dealing with staff disciplinary issues can also be emotionally challenging for leaders. Interview participants have experienced a wide range of matters including safeguarding issues, assault on a colleague, falsification of reporting data, and failure to attend work due to drunkenness.

> During my first term as a head, I had a guy who just didn't show up for work two or three times. It took me a while to figure out it was because he was too drunk to come in. I had no idea how to handle it. I was out of my depth really and found it very stressful.
>
> (International School Headteacher, Thailand)

Managing teachers' underperformance or disciplinary matters runs contrary to the caring aspect of a leader's role as an educator. Being tough does not come naturally to many, who came into education to support and nurture others. This can lead to a dissonance between a leader's values and what the role requires, which can be very draining.

> I was supporting an older teacher, who was very weak in the classroom. It was hard being honest with him as he got upset every time I raised concerns. I tried to be respectful and compassionate, but it really took a toll on us both. I did not go into this to break people, but it is my job to do what is best for students.
>
> (Deputy Headteacher, UK)

Conflict with teachers over change initiatives is also emotionally demanding for leaders. Eighty-five percent of Ontario principals report staff resistance to change as draining,[4] while principals in both Australia[5] and New Zealand[6] identify educational reform as one of their greatest sources of stress. Unpleasant conflict about change between leaders and staff can have a significant impact on some leaders.

> I've been verbally attacked in staff meetings, in a very aggressive way. They think they can say anything and not have to take account of my feelings. Some staff expect that this person, the principal, should get everything right and can be extremely, volatile, and unforgiving. It has taken an emotional toll, feeling judged, being under a microscope, being torn apart.
>
> (International School Principal, Germany)

Addressing conflict between staff members can present leaders with considerable challenges, especially when it gives rise to confrontation. Issues may emanate from personality factors, conflicting values or approaches around learning, attitudes to change, or poor performance. Principals in Australia,[5] New Zealand,[6] and Ireland[7] all identify interpersonal conflicts between staff as a major stressor. Conflicts may be exacerbated by poor staff mental health, which is an increasing concern in schools, with a third of UK educators experiencing mental health issues.[11] Principals in Australia,[5] New Zealand,[6] Ireland,[7] and Canada[4] all identify managing staff mental health as a major source of stress. Ontario principals estimate they spend 4.4 hours out of an average 57-hour working week on staff wellbeing issues.[4] While conflict with colleagues is a common manifestation of poor mental health, other issues may include teachers failing to cope in the classroom, absenteeism, disengagement from work, or workaholism.

> I have a teacher who's an emotional minefield and can flare up unpredictably. She's great with the kids but horrible with colleagues. I've tried to support her as I can see she's struggling with her mental health but it's hard and very time consuming.
>
> (Principal, Australia)

Relationships With Parents

Studies from Australia,[5] New Zealand,[6] and Ireland[7] over the past decade have consistently identified parent-related issues as a major stressor. Eighty-two percent of international school leaders find working with parents emotionally challenging, more than any other stakeholder group.[3] Thirty-nine percent of Ontario principals say that meetings with parents is the single most draining situation they encounter.[4] Principals estimate that they spend 5.3 hours each week dealing with parent issues – around 10% of the hours they work.[4]

The greater involvement of parents in the management of schools has emphasised the need for collaboration but also provides increased opportunities for conflict between school leaders and parents, particularly in the independent sector where parents can be very demanding. The current culture of complaints, driven by an increasing consumer mentality, is identified by principals in Australia,[5] Ireland,[7] and Canada[4] as a major source of stress. Ontario principals also cite growing mental health issues among parents as significantly affecting them.

Issues with parents often involve complaints or conflict relating to their individual child. In interviews with leaders over the past seven years, many shared stories of meeting with unreasonable and sometimes aggressive parents about their child's relationships with peers, academic performance, behaviour management, or special educational needs.

> The boy was on the autism spectrum and struggled to integrate. On one occasion, he smashed things in the classroom and kicked the TA and we had to remove the rest of the class for safety. When the father arrived to take the boy home, he started shouting, saying it was our fault. The teacher was in tears and I had to call security.
>
> (International School Principal, Dubai)

Although conflict relating to individual students is common, there are often wider issues, related to school policy, curriculum, safety, security, or school transport. These situations can be most challenging when they come from a group of parents making complaints or pushing an agenda.

> During my three years I've been surprised how brutal the parents can be. There have been occasions where groups have ganged up on me. After one meeting about an important curriculum change, some parents were really, really, angry. Emotion came up pretty quickly and aggressively.
>
> (Headteacher, UK)

Parent interactions can be more emotionally draining when leaders are forced to make decisions that conflict with their values. The role of headteacher or principal sometimes involves acting against the interests of an individual student for the benefit of the majority. At times like this, there may be a clash between the caring role of the educator and the managerial role of the leader, which can place leaders under considerable strain.

> Telling a parent that their child needs to find another school, is one of the hardest things you do as a principal. You naturally want to do your best for every single one of them and it breaks my heart when we cannot meet their needs. Seeing the anxiety on the parents' faces, knowing their child is being rejected but also the fear of what will happen to them is terrible.
>
> (International School Principal, Hong Kong)

There is evidence to show an increase in the incidence of harassment, threats, and violence directed towards school leaders by parents in recent years. In 2019, a third of Australian leaders[5] and fifth of New Zealand principals[6] had received threats from parents. Almost half of Canadian principals have experienced harassment or threats of violence at work, with around two-thirds of this abuse coming from families of students.[4] Nine percent of Australian principals[5] and 5% of New Zealand leaders[6] also report that they have physically assaulted by parents at some point in their career.

Relationships With Supervisors

Studies show that a leader's relationships with their supervisors can be emotionally demanding and are closely associated with burnout. This includes relationships with more senior colleagues, members of the board of governors/trustees/directors, superintendents, and other local government representatives. In my 2017 research, over two-thirds of international school leaders said they found working with local government officials to be emotionally challenging, while 42% said the same of governors/trustees/directors.[3] Almost three-quarters of Ontario principals say that pressure from superintendents or school boards puts them in draining situations.[4] Australian principals have consistently identified the expectations of employers as one of their top five stressors over the last decade,[5] while half of UK senior leaders say unreasonable demands from supervisors are a major cause of stress.[11]

Pressure from supervisors to succeed, combined with insufficient autonomy to do the job well, is a common complaint from leaders. While this often comes in the form of local government control, it can also manifest in micromanagement by direct supervisors. In some schools, relationships with the board of governors/trustees/directors can be a significant source of stress for leaders and have been cited as the single most common reason for international school heads to resign their post.[12] In addition to board micromanagement, issues include conflicting agendas among board members, poor board cohesion, and lack of honesty and transparency.

Lack of support from supervisors is another issue commonly raised by leaders. This can take many forms, including failure to back a leader's decisions or undermining their authority. The challenges of working alongside incompetent, underqualified, or unprofessional supervisors can also bring considerable strain, as leaders struggle to fill the gaps left by another's ineptitude. Conflicts with supervisors can lead to frustration and anxiety at best but also feelings of resentment, fear, and mistrust. In a large-scale UK study,[11] a third of senior leaders identified lack of trust from above as being a trigger for poor mental health symptoms, and half of those considering leaving the profession cite trust issues as a reason for wanting to leave.

> I found out in the meeting that the board had hid crucial information from SLT. My trust in them and how this situation would make me appear to colleagues and parents caused everything to wobble. I felt sick in the stomach, an overwhelming sense of being thrown under the bus that leaves you feeling nauseous.
>
> (International School Principal, Germany)

When relationships with supervisors break down, leaders can be left feeling undervalued or drained of confidence. Three-quarters of Ontario principals say lack of recognition makes them feel drained,[4] while over half of UK senior leaders thinking of leaving the profession cite not feeling valued as a reason for wanting to leave.[11] Sadly, issues of bullying by supervisors are not uncommon. Fourteen percent of Ontario principals said they have been bullied by a superintendent, while 4.4% reported being threatened.[4]

> The board chair and I had a very difficult relationship. He would interfere in any decision, to the point of bullying. There were several incidents involving him undermining my authority and making inappropriate comments in meetings. In my last two years my confidence could not have been more broken, and I left the role in a diminished state.
>
> (Former Headteacher, UK)

Relationships With Senior Colleagues

While relationships with peers can be supportive, they can also be a source of stress for leaders. In my 2017 research, three-quarters of participants said they found working with other senior leaders to be emotionally challenging.[3] Themes raised by leaders in interview include personality issues, incompetence, disagreements over key decisions, and feeling undermined or disrespected. Feeling undermined by colleagues can lead to issues of trust and leave leaders feeling unsupported and vulnerable.

> The head and primary principal kept making important decisions without me. While I was furious on the one hand, I was also very hurt. The situation was eating away at me and I found it hard to keep a lid on my emotions in meetings. On a couple of occasions there were raised voices and it got really unpleasant.
>
> (International School Principal, Thailand)

Student-Related Issues

While the emotional demands of adult relationships in school form the closest associations with leader burnout, student-related issues are increasingly challenging for leaders. Principals in Australia,[5] New Zealand,[6] and Ireland[7] all identify student-related issues as one of their major causes of stress. Issues often relate to supporting vulnerable students, who may have mental ill health, special educational needs, or safeguarding concerns. Schools have always played a key role in supporting vulnerable children, but in recent decades, their statutory and contractual obligations have expanded. Policies such as the UK's Every Child Matters and No Child Left Behind in the United States have increased schools' accountability around provision for children with special educational needs or from disadvantaged backgrounds. Responsibilities around child protection have also grown, placing increasing expectations on schools to play a role in safeguarding students from abuse and exploitation. This increase in statutory obligations has come at the same time as funding cuts in the education sector, and in external agencies supporting schools. This has limited the resources available to headteachers and principals to meet their duties in supporting vulnerable students.

Issues around the support of vulnerable students have been identified by school leaders as some of their greatest stressors. Australian principals cite student mental health concerns as their third-highest source of stress,[5] while 80% of leaders in Canada report poor student mental health to be among the most draining situations they encounter.[4] Ninety percent of Ontario principals say that lack of support for students' special educational needs leaves them feeling drained, while two-thirds say that social issues in the community which affect students, such as poverty, drugs, and gang culture, give rise to draining situations.[4]

The Youth Mental Health Crisis

While the COVID-19 pandemic has had a severe impact on the mental health of young people, substantial evidence points to the existence of a youth mental health crisis long before this. The WHO estimates that 10%–20% of adolescents worldwide will experience a mental illness at some time.[13] In the UK, the National Health Service (NHS) have reported that 13% of 5- to 19-year-olds have a diagnosable mental health condition, with suicide being the most common cause of death for both boys and girls.[14] Half of UK teachers say they have taught a student experiencing suicidal thoughts or self-harming. Of teachers who have been teaching for more than five years, 94% say they have seen an increase in pupils presenting with mental health problems.[15]

A similar picture has emerged in Australia, New Zealand, Canada, and the United States. In a recent report from Australia, one in seven children aged 4–17 were assessed as having mental health disorders in the previous 12 months – a total of 560,000 individuals.[16] In Canada, it is estimated that one in five youth in Ontario has a mental health issue,[17] while in New Zealand, mental illness rates for young people have more than doubled in the last 20 years.[18] In the United States, 22% of American youth are thought to have a diagnosable mental illness with "serious impairment" at some point before age 18.[19]

Given the amount of time that children spend at school, mental health problems are likely to affect their school life, compromising their emotional state, attitudes, behaviour, and capacity to learn. When one considers that an average class of 30 is likely to have four or five students with mental health problems, this can place schools under considerable strain as they struggle to meet every student's needs. Student mental health issues can seriously affect both teacher and leader stress levels and create a significant amount of work for leaders. Ontario principals report spending 10.2 hours per week managing student behaviour – more than any other task – while 6.8 hours are spent on student wellbeing. Almost two-thirds of leaders said they would like to spend less time on these areas.[4] In the UK, over a third of headteachers who had experienced poor mental health symptoms identified managing poor student behaviour as a contributing factor, while a third of leaders reported this as a major reason for considering leaving the profession.[11]

> Just in one grade 5 class we have a girl who has been self-harming, two boys with serious behaviour problems and another boy whose mother committed suicide and needs a lot of emotional support. None of

these students are getting professional help. It's extremely demanding trying to look after everyone's needs and support the teacher and the parents. Some weeks I seem to spend hours managing all of the fallout.

(Principal, Canada)

The youth mental health crisis is bringing with it an increase in offensive behaviour by students towards teachers and school leaders. Forty percent of Australian principals[5] and a third of leaders from New Zealand[6] experienced physical violence at the hands of a student in 2019, while 37% and 23%, respectively, were subjected to threats of violence. Over half of Ontario principals report having been physically assaulted by a student at some time during their career, while a similar proportion say they have been threatened and a quarter report being harassed.[4]

Supporting Special Educational Needs

In recent decades, a push to secure equal learning opportunities for all has led to increasing numbers of students with special educational needs being integrated into mainstream schools. As governments have sought to make education more inclusive, the number of children requiring special education has also grown. In the UK, the percentage of students with an Education, Health and Care Plan (EHC) increased by 30% between 2017 and 2021.[20] In the United States, the number of children with learning disabilities has grown from 6.5 million to 7.3 million over the past decade. In Canada, 17% of elementary students and 27% of secondary students currently qualify for special education services, nearly double the number qualifying in 2000.[21] Special educational needs provision has become an important part of the headteacher's and principal's role. In Canada, principals estimate they spend seven hours per week on special education out of a 57-hour working week, second only to student discipline and attendance.

Research shows that schools are struggling to manage the increased demand for special education and are receiving insufficient support from external agencies. In the UK, Ofsted reports that schools are facing significant delays in obtaining support from local authorities, with some pupils waiting up to five years for their EHC to be approved.[22]

There is also a global shortage of appropriately qualified special education teachers. In 2020, the US Office of Special Education Programs identified a substantial shortage, with the number of special education educators falling 17% in the previous decade. They report that special education teachers leave the profession at twice the rate of other colleagues, citing stressful working conditions, poor pay, and insufficient support as reasons for leaving.[23]

In 2018, the OECD identified a special education skills gap among teachers. Fewer than half of Australian teachers in the study said they felt prepared to teach students with special needs when they complete their teacher training.[24] In California, only one in three special education teachers were found to have appropriate teaching credentials, with many first-year special education teachers having completed no specialist training.[25] Meeting students' needs with inadequate resources is a constant pressure for teachers and leaders. In Canada, three-quarters of Ontario principals cite poor teacher expertise in special education as being a major stressor.[4]

> There are 40 children on the SEND register, and we only have one qualified SEND teacher, who is also the SENDCO, and one TA with little experience. The SENDCO is under resourced and overwhelmed by her workload. Consequently, many children go undiagnosed, and once diagnosed, they receive only one 40-minute intervention a week, which is just a gesture rather than something meaningful.
>
> (Senior Leader, UK)

School Leader Abuse

Being at the centre of a community can render headteachers and principals vulnerable to mistreatment as they become a focal point for the anxiety and discontent of others. As already highlighted, school leaders are experiencing increasing incidents of abuse in the course of their work. In 2019, 70% of Australian principals reported having been subjected to two or more types of offensive behaviour in the previous 12 months. Leaders report bullying, gossip, slander, threats of violence or actual physical violence at much higher rates than the general workforce.[5] This is supported by findings from Canada, where only 3% of Ontario principals say they have not experienced work-related abuse. The most common types of abuse include passive-aggressive behaviour, gossip, slander, harassment, or threats. Two-thirds of Ontario principals also report having been physically assaulted in the course of their work, with one in six having to seek medical attention due to the injuries sustained.[4] Data from all major studies indicates that the general level of abuse towards school leaders is increasing year on year and giving cause for serious concern. In Australia, half of principals were subjected to violence in 2020, an 80% increase since 2011 when the study began.[5] This compares to only 3% of the general population who have experienced work-related violence.[5]

Studies indicate that workplace abuse is correlated with an increase in poor mental health among victims, including sleep disorders, depression, anxiety, post-traumatic stress disorder, and psychological distress.[26] There is a little research on the impact of abuse on school leaders, but the UK teachers' union National Association of Schoolmasters and Union of Women Teachers (NASUWT) reports that the abuse of teachers can seriously affect a victim's self-esteem, confidence in the classroom, and job performance. Teachers report experiencing increased depression, anxiety, low self-esteem, fear, and suicidal feelings following abuse. Harassment or abuse that occurs outside of the school environment exacerbates fear and anxiety and can lead to some individuals being too afraid to leave their homes.[27]

The Impact of Emotional Demands on Leader Wellbeing

The school leader's role brings them into regular contact with adults and children who are experiencing high levels of emotion. This can give rise to a range of emotional responses in leaders themselves, which can negatively affect their wellbeing and make them more vulnerable to burnout. There are several processes by which this can happen.

Firstly, the emotional demands of the role can cause a leader to engage in rumination, where their thoughts are directed, in a repetitive manner, to issues that have arisen during the working day.[28] Research has highlighted the importance of employees psychologically detaching from work to recover from the demands of their job. Work-related rumination has been found to raise cortisol levels, affect sleep, increase exhaustion, and cause dramatic decreases in psychological wellbeing over time. [29] School leaders commonly describe their inability to switch off from thinking about school at the end of the working day. This places them in a position where they are unable to find respite from the challenges of their role and potentially puts their health at risk.

The emotional demands of school leadership can also affect leaders through a psychological process called compassion stress injury (CSI). CSI is a new conceptualisation of what in the past was called compassion fatigue, secondary trauma, or vicarious trauma. It is a condition experienced by individuals working in caring professions who experience emotional and physical exhaustion from being exposed to the suffering of others. Research shows that over time, this exposure can lead to a diminished ability to empathise or feel compassion for others.[29] While CSI in school leaders has yet to be investigated, there is a growing body of research to suggest that CSI symptoms are prevalent among teachers and represent a predictable risk to their psychological wellbeing. Teachers have been shown to experience a range of impacts attributed to exposure to others' suffering, including disturbed emotions, feelings of powerlessness, and intrusive thoughts and imagery.[30]

Emotional interactions with stakeholders may have a greater impact on the wellbeing of school leaders when there is a dissonance between a leader's values and certain aspects of their role. Burnout research shows that an incompatibility between an individual's values and workplace practices are a common contributor to burnout.[31] In school leaders, this can be precipitated by "carer/manager tension,"[32] where school leaders, rooted in a profession focused on caring, are expected to make tough decisions that negatively affect others. This can put leaders in situations that lie in opposition to the values of caring that they hold dear and may, over time, contribute to emotional exhaustion and burnout.[33]

The emotional demands experienced by headteachers and principals can also affect their wellbeing through a process known as emotional labour. The term "emotional labour" was coined in 1983 by sociologist Arlie Hochschild to describe the constant suppression of an employee's true feelings, or the display of fake emotions, for the benefit of the organisation. In her research with the service sector, Hochschild identified how workers are expected to manipulate their actual emotions or the appearance of feelings, to create a positive experience for a client or customer.[33]

Studies have identified how those in caring professions, including school leaders, engage in emotional labour.[34] For example, a leader may suppress their feelings of anger or fear, to maintain a professional face when confronted by an aggressive parent or hide their anxiety when dealing with an injured child. They may fake anger when disciplining a student or express fake excitement with staff to convey enthusiasm around a new initiative. It is also common for a leader to hide their feelings to demonstrate strong leadership. This emanates from the commonly held belief that good leaders keep their emotions in check, to show they are in control and objective. It encourages headteachers and principals to wear a leadership mask, to suppress their vulnerabilities and conform to expectations around how a leader behaves. Beatty describes this as a paradox in school leadership, where a contradiction lies between the complex emotions that the work evokes and the expectation that leaders should remain clinical in their dealings with others.[35] A longitudinal study of Australian principals, over the last decade, has consistently found their demands for hiding emotions to be significantly higher than the general population.[5]

> How is it where we are always obsessing about the emotional well-being of children that we as leaders are expected to set aside our own emotion? Should leaders not show that they are human and able to empathise with any degree of human distress or discomfort? This

environment has left me feeling mentally fatigued, emotionally burnt out, and scared of "letting slip" that I actually feel.

(Assistant Headteacher, UK)

Research shows that engaging in emotional labour causes individuals to become disconnected from their true emotions. Over time, this can be psychologically harmful, may lead to emotional exhaustion, and may make an individual more vulnerable to burnout.[35] Studies indicate that emotional labour can have a significant impact on school leaders' wellbeing. A recent study of Australian principals found hiding emotions to be a strong predictor of emotional exhaustion and burnout in leaders.[36]

School Leader Loneliness

There is plenty of evidence to show that the emotional demands of the workplace can be mitigated by supportive relationships.[36] Yet headteacher and principal loneliness is a commonly recurring theme in the literature on school leadership. Forty-two percent of Ontario principals say they experience loneliness at work because they have few colleagues with whom they can share their concerns, and a similar number say they feel socially excluded by colleagues.[4] Studies from Australia show that school principals receive less social support from colleagues than employees generally.[5]

School leader loneliness does not come from physical isolation, as the average day of a headteacher or principal is filled with meetings and conversations. These interactions often fail to provide the deep human connection that individuals need to maximise their wellbeing, however. The nature of the role can make it hard for leaders to connect on a personal level with staff or parents and, particularly in small schools, headteachers and principals may lack peers with whom they can form bonds based on empathy, mutual support, and trust. There may also be a cultural aspect to leader isolation, with some cultures being more open to close social relationships between senior leaders and staff. There are many ways in which social isolation can affect a school leader and improving social support is a key strategy to enhance leader wellbeing. In later chapters, I discuss how this may be addressed in more detail.

In the past two years, since becoming a head, I have found it more stressful as there is no one else to go to. . . . There are very few people you can talk to as a head. You cannot be friends with the staff. . . . You have to be comfortable in your own company. It is an oxymoron as it is such a sociable job but you have to like being alone too.

(International School Principal, Germany)

Chapter Summary

- Headteachers and principals experience significant emotional demands in their role.
- The emotional demands of adult relationships are among leaders' most serious stressors and are closely linked to the incidence of leader burnout.
- Interactions and conflict with teachers can be highly demanding for leaders. These interactions may involve addressing staff underperformance, disciplinary issues, leading change, conflict among staff, and managing staff mental ill health.
- Relationships with parents are also highly challenging. Issues may arise with individual parents or with groups of parents. These issues may directly involve student learning and welfare, or wider matters related to school policy.
- Relationships with supervisors and senior colleagues can also be emotionally demanding for leaders.
- Student-related issues are on the increase in schools. The global youth mental health crisis and growth in the number of students with special educational needs are having a significant impact on schools and bringing additional burdens for leaders.
- Emotional demands affect leaders' wellbeing through a variety of processes, including rumination, compassion stress injury, and emotional labour.
- Issues may be more emotionally demanding for leaders when there is a dissonance between their values and the requirements of the role.
- School leader loneliness can exacerbate the impact on leaders of the emotional demands of the role.
- School leader abuse is increasing and is of serious concern in many Western countries.

Notes

1 Harris, B.M., 2007. *Supporting the Emotional Work of School Leaders*, p. 23. London: SAGE.

2 Gronn, P., 2003. *The New Work of Educational Leaders: Changing Leadership Practice in an Era of School Reform*, p. 58. Thousand Oaks, CA: SAGE.

3 Kelly, H., 2017. International Schools as Emotional Arenas: Facing the Leadership Challenges in a German Context. University of Birmingham, Ed.D.

4 Pollock, K. and Wang, F., 2020. *School Principals' Work and Well-Being in Ontario:*

What They Say and Why It Matters. Toronto, ON: Western University.

5 Riley, P., See, S.M., Marsh, H. and Dicke, T., 2021. *The Australian Principal Occupational Health, Safety and Wellbeing Survey 2020.* Sydney: Institute for Positive Psychology and Education, Australian Catholic University.

6 Riley, P., Rahimi, M. and Arnold, B., 2021. *The New Zealand Primary Principal Occupational Health, Safety and Wellbeing Survey 2020.* Melbourne: Research for Educational Impact (REDI), Deakin University.

7 Riley, P., 2015. *Irish Principals' and Deputy Principals' Occupational Health, Safety and Wellbeing Survey.* Melbourne: Research for Educational Impact (REDI), Deakin University.

8 Friedman, I.A., 2002. Burnout in School Principals: Role Related Antecedents. *Social Psychology of Education,* 5(3), 229–251.

9 Nias, J., 1989. Teaching and the Self. In M.L. Holly and C.S. McLoughlin, eds. *Perspectives on Teachers Professional Development,* pp. 155–171. London: Falmer Press.

10 Day, C., Kington, A., Stobart, G. and Sammons, P., 2006. The Personal and Professional Selves of Teachers: Stable and Unstable Identities. *British Educational Research Journal,* 32(4), 601–616.

11 Savill-Smith, C., 2019. *Teacher Wellbeing Index.* London: Education Support.

12 Benson, J., 2011. An Investigation of Chief Administrator Turnover in International Schools. *Journal of Research in International Education,* 10(1), 87–103.

13 World Health Organization. Global Health Estimates. Accessed online www.who.int/data/global-health-estimates.

14 National Health Service, 2018. *Mental Health of Children and Young People in England, 2017.* London: NHS Digital.

15 Young Minds, 2018. *A New Era for Young People's Mental Health.* London: Young Minds.

16 Lawrence, D., Johnson, S., Hafekost, J., Boterhoven De Haan, K., Sawyer, M., Ainley, J. and Zubrick, S.R., 2015. *The Mental Health of Children and Adolescents. Report on the Second Australian Child and Adolescent Survey of Mental Health and Wellbeing.* Canberra: Department of Health.

17 Patten, S., 2019. The Ontario Child Health Study. *The Canadian Journal of Psychiatry,* 64(4), 225–226.

18 Menzies, R., Gluckman, P. and Poulton, R., 2020. *Youth Mental Health in Aotearoa New Zealand.* Auckland: The University of Auckland.

19 Child Mind Institute, 2019. *Children's Mental Health Report.* New York, NY: Child Mind Institute.

20 Office of National Statistics, 2021. *Special Educational Needs in England.* London: ONS.

21 People for Education, 2018. *The New Basics for Public Education.* Toronto, ON: People for Education.

22 Ofsted, 2021. *Supporting SEND*. London: UK Department for Education.

23 Snyder, T.D., de Brey, C. and Dillow, S.A., 2019. *Digest of Education Statistics 2018*. Washington, DC: Institute of Education Sciences, U.S. Department of Education.

24 OECD, 2018. *Teaching and Learning International Survey*. Paris: OECD.

25 Ondrasek, N., Carver-Thomas, D., Scott, C. and Darling-Hammond, L., 2020. *California's Special Education Teacher Shortage*. Palo Alto, CA: Policy Analysis for California Education.

26 Gunnarsdottir, H.K., Sveinsdottir, H., Bernburg, J.G., Fridriksdottir, H. and Tomasson, K., 2006. Lifestyle, Harassment at Work and Self-assessed Health of Female Flight Attendants, Nurses, and Teachers. *Work*, 27(2), 165–172.

27 NASUWT. Accessed online www.nasuwt.org.uk/advice/health-safety/social-media-and-online-abuse-of-teachers.html.

28 Cropley, M. and Millward, L.J., 2009. How Do Individuals 'Switch-off' from Work during Leisure? A Qualitative Description of the Unwinding Process in High and Low Ruminators. *Leisure Studies*, 28, 333–347.

29 Russell, M. and Cowan, J., 2018. The Making of Compassion Stress Injury: A Review of Historical and Etiological Models Toward a De-Stigmatizing Neurobehavioral Conceptualization. *Challenges*, 9(1), 7.

30 Briggs, R., 2021. "What About Me?" Teachers' Psychological Wellbeing and How It Can Be Supported When Teaching Pupils Experiencing Vulnerabilities and/or Trauma. University of Bristol, Ed.D.

31 Maslach, C. and Leiter, M.P., 2016. Understanding the Burnout Experience: Recent Research and Its Implications for Psychiatry. *World Psychiatry*, 15(2), 103–111.

32 Crozier-Durham, M., 2007. Work/Life Balance: Personal and Organisational Strategies of School Leaders. Victoria University, M.Ed.

33 Hochschild, A.R., 2012. *The Managed Heart: Commercialization of Human Feeling*. Berkeley, CA: University of California Press.

34 Maxwell, A. and Riley, P., 2017. Emotional Demands, Emotional Labour and Occupational Outcomes in School Principals Modelling the Relationships. *Educational Management, Administration & Leadership*, 45(3), 484–502.

35 Beatty, B., 2000. The Emotions of Educational Leadership: Breaking the Silence. *International Journal of Leadership in Education*, 3(4), 331–357.

36 Wood, S., Stride, C., Threapleton, K., Wearn, E., Nolan, F., Osborn, D., Paul, M. and Johnson, S., 2011. Demands, Control, Supportive Relationships and Well-being amongst British Mental Health Workers. *Social Psychiatry Psychiatric Epidemiology*, 46(10), 1055–1068.

Workload Demands and Other Stressors

3

In Chapter 2, I examined the emotional demands of the school leader's role and discussed how the strain of adult relationships and student-related issues can increase stress and contribute to burnout. The sheer quantity of work that leaders undertake is also a significant source of stress and has a close association with burnout. In this chapter, I examine the workload demands placed on leaders, the long hours, pace and intensity of their work, and their poor work-life balance. I discuss the impact these factors may have on their health, life satisfaction, and job performance. I also consider a range of other major stressors identified by leaders, including lack of resources and accountability.

In longitudinal studies from Australia[1] and New Zealand,[2] principals have been asked to rate 19 potential sources of stress on a scale of 1 to 10. The "sheer quantity of the work" has consistently rated as the number one stressor for leaders over the past decade. Using the Copenhagen Psychosocial Questionnaire II (COPSOQ II) to compare school principals' work demands to the average worker, studies consistently find the perceived quantitative demands of school leaders' work to be much higher than those of the general population.

Working Hours

Data from the United States on changing principal workloads shows that between the 1960s and late 2000s, the average hours worked by a principal increased 23%.[3] The working hours of headteachers and principals are not only higher than they used to be but are also considerably longer than the average full-time worker. Across all OECD countries, the average

DOI: 10.4324/9781003198475-5

full-time employee works 37 hours per week.[4] Data from Australia, New Zealand, the UK, and Canada shows that school leaders work significantly longer hours. Australian principals report working an average of 55.2 hours a week during the school term, with almost three-quarters working over 50 hours. They also work an average of 21.4 hours a week during the school holidays.[1] A similar study of New Zealand principals found that in every year since the survey began in 2016, over half of all participants reported working more than 50 hours a week, while over a quarter worked in excess of 60 hours.[2] A 2019 study of UK senior leaders reported that, while only 3% of headteachers were contracted to work over 50 hours, 68% did so, with a third working more than 60 hours and 11% over 70 hours.[5]

Despite the long hours they put in, many leaders find they are unable to keep on top of their work. Nearly three-quarters of Ontario leaders report not having enough time to complete their work tasks, while more than half say they often feel overwhelmed by their workload.[6] A study from New South Wales found that, while participants acknowledge the need to work beyond standard hours, most consider their workload to be unreasonable, with three-quarters finding it either difficult or impossible to achieve and sustain.[7]

> My workload sometimes feels inhumane. Leaders like myself per-
> form multiple roles, are given a heavy teaching load and expected
> to work 14 hour days. This workload has left me feeling burnt out.
> I come home on Friday evening so exhausted that I have nothing left
> in me. All I want to do is sleep and hope that come Monday I will feel
> refreshed, but I never do.
>
> (Senior Leader, UK)

It is not only the long hours that leaders find overwhelming and unsustainable but the wide range of activities that their roles involve and the unpredictability of their days. In a UK study carried out by the National College for School Leadership, almost two-thirds of heads described undertaking large numbers of tasks each day, often simultaneously, with multitasking seen as the norm. Half of participants said there was no such thing as a typical day, but instead their work involved responding to unexpected challenges, sometimes critical and needing immediate attention. This requires considerable flexibility and the reorganisation of priorities as the day unfolds, which leads to days being highly fragmented and work schedules going completely off track.[8] Principals in New South Wales, Australia, report undertaking an average of 45 activities during the school day. Their day involves multiple interruptions, making it difficult to complete activities that require sustained attention, with those tasks being continued in the evenings or at weekends.[7] Ninety-three percent of Ontario principals also say they find their work unpredictable.[6]

> I go in with a full calendar for the day but it's a very rare day that it all goes to plan. We can have a bad accident on the playground, a member of staff in tears, or an angry parent on the phone. Yesterday the fire alarm went off and I went from a meeting with caterers to being responsible for evacuating nearly 2000 people from the building.
>
> (Headteacher, UK)

The sheer volume of tasks to be completed during each day necessitates school leaders to work at a much more rapid pace than the average worker. In studies from Australia,[1] New Zealand,[2] and Ireland,[9] principals report their work pace as considerably higher than the general population. Australian longitudinal data shows work pace increasing year on year since 2011.[1] In an Ontario study, over half of principals found the pace of their work to be too fast, with many describing it as "unrelenting," while two-thirds reported getting behind with their work.[6]

> One day last week, I had thirteen meetings, starting at 7am and finishing at 5pm. I was literally running to get to meetings. I had no time to catch my breath, go to the toilet, drink water, or bring the adrenaline levels down. I was pumped all day and that really takes its toll.
>
> (International School Principal, Hong Kong)

The relentless workload means that many leaders do not have time to take breaks to recover during the school day or take time off when they are sick. Three-quarters of Ontario principals report being unable to take a break during the day or take sick leave.[6] Over half of UK senior leaders report feeling compelled to go into work when they are ill (presenteeism). Those who work the longest hours feel the most compelled to go in and those with the highest levels of presenteeism report the most stress. Forty-one percent believe that having time off work will have a negative effect on students, and a similar number worry it will affect team morale.[5]

> I have not had a day off work in the five years that I've been head. I drag myself in no matter how wretched I am. I just feel the governors expect it and as a woman I worry about how they will view me if I take sick leave. I don't want to be thought of as weak or not up to the job.
>
> (Assistant Headteacher, UK)

Most school leaders also feel pressure to always be available, both during and outside school hours. Ninety-two percent of Ontario principals say their work requires them to always be on call.[6] While advances in technology bring indisputable benefits, they have also brought further workload demands for leaders. The advent of technologies like email, electronic messaging, and social media has created a situation where it is easier for leaders to be constantly on call, blurring the lines between home and school.

The increased accessibility of leaders outside of normal working hours has affected their ability to switch off, and the volume of communication leaves most struggling to manage their inboxes. Studies from Australia found that 20 years ago, principals rarely used email to communicate with multiple groups of stakeholders[10] and did not feel the need to check their email daily,[11] while only half reported receiving more than 20 emails per week.[12] By contrast, studies from Ontario, conducted in 2019, found that principals receive over 100 emails a day[13] and spend 10.5 hours per week dealing with email in an average 57-hour working week.[6] The number of hours spent emailing was thought to be excessive by most leaders, and nearly three-quarters said the volume of daily emails was "highly draining."[12] The rise of instant messaging platforms like WhatsApp and Facebook Messenger has led to another significant increase in work-related communications. Ontario principals report spending 2.2 hours a week texting and 1.7 hours on social media.[6]

> I wake up at 5am and answer school emails and messages before I get up and during breakfast. In the evening, I receive and answer messages even when I am eating and watching TV with my family. I switch off the notifications after 8pm so the dinging stops but the messages don't stop.
>
> (Principal, Canada)

The Impact of Working Long Hours

The long hours that school leaders work is directly linked to their levels of stress. Data from the UK shows that a headteacher's stress rises incrementally with increases in working hours. Of those working 41–50 hours per week, 22% report not feeling stressed by their work, but as working hours increase to 51–60 hours, the percentage who are not stressed falls to 15% and then to 6% among those working 61–70 hours.[5] Long working hours may also be directly responsible for the poor health some leaders experience. Studies from the UK report that leaders working long hours are more likely to suffer a mental health issue than those who work under 40 hours a week, while those working over 60 hours report the most mental health concerns. Of those who have experienced work-related symptoms linked to poor mental wellbeing, three-quarters feel that excessive workload is a contributory factor.[5]

This link between workload and poor health is backed by medical research. A recent paper containing a meta-analysis of 46 studies, involving 800,000 participants, found that working long hours increases the likelihood of serious health problems, including heart disease, heart attack, stroke, high blood pressure, type 2 diabetes, anxiety disorders, and depression.[14] A study from the US Department of Health found that working more than 40 hours per week is associated with increased alcohol and tobacco consumption and unhealthy weight gain, while working over ten hours a day leads to a 60% increased risk of cardiovascular disease. The study also found a strong correlation between long working hours and poor sleep, with an increase in the number of hours worked being proportional to a reduction in the number of hours slept.[15] Insomnia has been shown to increase the risk of anxiety by almost a third and depression by over two-thirds. Less than seven hours sleep per night is associated with an increased risk of death and correlates with a range of serious threats to health.[16]

There is also evidence to show that productivity and performance may be affected by long working hours. A study from Stanford University found that productivity per hour declines significantly when a person works more than 50 hours a week. After 55 hours, productivity drops so sharply as to make further working hours pointless.[17] A meta-analysis of research by the UK Institute for Employment Studies found that long working hours, especially when combined with sleep disruption, cause a significant deterioration in task performance, increasing errors and reducing the pace of work. The same review found an association between long working hours and poor staff motivation, increased absence, and employee turnover.[18]

Work-Life Balance

How employees balance their time inside and outside of work is an important aspect of a healthy work environment that helps reduce stress and prevent burnout. The long hours that school leaders work, and their high level of commitment to their role, makes it difficult for many to maintain a proper balance. Principals in Australia,[1] New Zealand,[2] and Ireland[9] all identify the inability to get away from school or the school community as a major stressor. Poor work-life balance negatively affects personal relationships and home life. A study from the United States found a third of employees working more than 60 hours per week experienced relationship problems, three times as many as those working 40 hours.[19] Studies from

Australia,[1] New Zealand,[2] and Ireland[9] show principals to have double the level of "work-family conflict" of the average employee, often having neither the mental or physical energy nor the time to spend with their families.

Poor work-life balance also affects health and wellbeing. A 2014 study of employees across seven cultures showed that work-life balance was negatively related to anxiety and depression.[20] Studies have found a strong correlation between poor work-life balance among school leaders and high stress levels. Three-quarters of UK senior leaders who had suffered symptoms of poor mental health blamed lack of work-life balance, describing an inability to switch off and relax as a major contributor.[5] Poor work-life balance is also affecting the school leader recruitment and retention crisis. Eighty-one percent of UK leaders who had considered leaving the profession in the previous two years identified poor work-life balance as a major reason for considering leaving.[5]

> I did not have a personal life for years and this year, since I took the new role, I realise how much of a personal life I did not have because I have it back. I now have time in the evening and have had to remember what people do with this time.
>
> (Former Headteacher, UK)

Other Workload Factors

Long working hours and work pace are not the only workload-related factors contributing to headteacher and principal stress. Leaders consistently report that their days are filled with tasks which they feel take them away from the core work of the school leader. Principals in Australia,[1] New Zealand,[2] and Ireland[9] all identify lack of time to focus on teaching and learning as their second biggest stressor, after the volume of work. In Canada, Ontario principals spend an average of 14 hours per week on managerial matters, such as administrative directives, internal school management, school board committees, and building maintenance, all matters which leaders feel they would like to spend less time on. Three-quarters of principals say they would like to spend more time on curriculum and instructional leadership, while a similar number want to spend more time on classroom walkthroughs and teacher evaluation.[6]

While workload, together with the emotional demands of the leader's role, are the most likely factors to precipitate burnout, research has found that cognitive demands are also a factor contributing to overload. Studies from Australia,[1] New Zealand,[2] and Ireland[9] found demands on the cognitive abilities of school leaders to be significantly higher than average employees. Likewise, principals in all three countries report cognitive stress to be around 50% higher than the norm. Research from Ontario shows that a third of principals feel their cognitive wellbeing is affected by work pressures, having a range of impacts on their cognitive functioning. Forty-one percent admit to being unfocused or disorganised at work, while a similar number find they are forgetful. A third report that they are absent-minded or have delayed memory retrieval, while a quarter are indecisive.[6] Similar results were found in the UK, where nearly half of leaders said they had difficulty concentrating, and over a third experienced forgetfulness.[5]

> By the end of the semester, I have complete brain fog and it is hard to think properly as I have so much information in my head and so much to think about. It feels like my brain is bursting. I find that on some days I forget basic things and struggle to hold a conversation.
>
> (Principal, Australia)

Other Major Stressors

In addition to emotional demands and workload pressures, school leaders identify a range of other stressors that affect them in the course of their work. Issues related to resources and the financial management of the school present as significant stressors for many. Leaders in Australia,[1] New Zealand,[2] and Ireland[9] all identify lack of resources, financial management, and declining enrolment as major causes of work-related stress. Only a third of principals in Ontario say they have the resources they need to do their job and identify this as a major stressor.[6] In the UK, half of senior leaders cite lack of resources as a reason for considering leaving the profession.[5]

> I was promised a non-teaching role but have ended up with a 30% time-table because the head says she cannot afford it. I am juggling DSL and pastoral care for the whole school with having to plan and teach in two different year groups. I'm just not sure how long I can go on like this.
>
> (Assistant Headteacher, UK)

Issues relating to the recruitment and retention of teaching staff is a major theme that emerges from the research. Principals in Australia,[1] New Zealand,[2] and Ireland[9] identify teacher shortages as a significant source of stress. In Canada, two-thirds of principals report that high levels of teacher turnover affects their work negatively, 92% have problems finding qualified supply teachers, and a similar number have difficulty recruiting the right teaching staff.[6]

Accountability and statutory obligations are also identified by leaders as major causes of stress. Ontario principals highlight the implementation of new government policies, designed to reduce risk and litigation, as a significant cause of anxiety.[6] UK leaders identify unnecessary paperwork and data-gathering, associated with their statutory obligations, to be major stressors. They also report other accountability-related issues, such as target-setting and school inspection, as major concerns. Nearly two-thirds of UK senior leaders considering leaving the profession identify the target-driven culture as a major reason for wanting to leave.[5]

> I sometimes feel that most of the targets are not only unrealistic but completely meaningless. They don't improve children's learning. They just put pupils, staff and headteachers under unbelievable pressure.
>
> (Headteacher, UK)

Vice Principal and Deputy Head Stressors

While the issues discussed in this chapter relate to all senior leaders, and much of the research cited involves leaders at multiple levels, those who play supporting roles in senior leadership teams encounter a unique set of stressors that headteachers and principals do not experience. Deputy and assistant headteachers and vice, deputy, and assistant principals have been described as "the forgotten leaders,"[21] as their specific experience is so under-researched. It is, however, crucial to understand the stressors and pressures that these roles involve, as they play a key part in school effectiveness and make up an increasingly large proportion of the school leadership profession. As the size of the school population, and the demands of school leadership, have increased, supporting leadership roles have proliferated. In the United States, between 1990 and 2016, the number of assistant principals grew from 44,000 to 81,000,[22] while in England, the number of assistant headteacher roles increased by 7,000 between 2010 and 2016.[23]

A small number of key studies show that those in supporting leadership roles are reporting issues of work intensification and experiencing considerable strain and overload.[24] This manifests in issues already discussed, such as an inability to manage competing aspects of their role, insufficient time to complete work, work pace, unpredictable days, and pressure to work long hours or always be on call.[25] In addition to these issues, however, supporting leaders also report stressors that are specific to their role. These include lack of autonomy and an unclear work portfolio,[26] as their tasks and responsibilities are commonly assigned by the headteacher or principal, who is "the gatekeeper of leadership functions."[27]

Supporting leaders also experience a lack of alignment between the actual role they perform and their ideal role. They are normally tasked with ensuring that the school functions effectively and are often involved in day-to-day administrative functions, rather than real leadership. This is contrary to their ideal role, which would involve a greater focus on strategic and instructional leadership.[28]

The supporting leader spans the organisational boundary between the headteacher or principal and staff.[28] While this can be a privileged and important position, it also has potential to create issues for the leader, especially for those new to senior leadership. The transition from teacher to senior leader can create tension between the individual's former identity as a teacher and their new identity.[26] This can create a blurring of boundaries between personal and professional relationships and create significant stress. The role that supporting leaders play in supervising the daily work of teaching staff can also give rise to contradictions between a leader's collegial role and their supervisory role. This role conflict can affect staff-leader relations and become a major stressor.[29]

The relationship between a supporting leader and their headteacher or principal can also bring challenges. Forty-five percent of Ontario vice and assistant principals report finding the relationship with their principal emotionally demanding. Issues are most likely to arise from a clash of values or vision between the headteacher or principal and the supporting leader, with the latter expected to comply with the former's approach.[24] Finally, supporting leaders commonly feel undervalued or unacknowledged in their role. Seventy percent of Ontario vice and assistant principals report experiencing a lack of recognition for their work or the importance of their role.[25]

Chapter Summary

- The intensification of the school leader's role in recent decades has led to rising workload demands, including longer working hours, faster work pace, and increasingly complex work.
- Most leaders are unable to find time for breaks or take days off, even when they are ill. Technological changes have also increased the availability of leaders outside school hours, making it harder for them to escape from work.
- Headteachers and principals are struggling to achieve a proper work-life balance.
- Long working hours and poor work-life balance are associated with increased stress in school leaders and work-family conflict. They are also

associated with a wide range of mental and physical ill-health outcomes in the general population, as well as reduced job performance.
- Headteachers and principals are involved in an excessive amount of administrative and managerial work, which takes them away from teaching and learning and is a significant cause of stress. The cognitive demands of the work are also a major stressor.
- Other stressors, such as lack of resources and increased accountability, are also having an impact on leaders' stress levels.
- Supporting leaders, such as deputy or assistant headteachers and vice, deputy, and assistant principals have a unique set of stressors not experienced by those working in the headteacher and principal role.
- The excessive workload demands and other stressors are influencing leaders' decisions to leave the profession.
- Heavy workloads and poor work-life balance, combined with the emotional demands of the role, are increasing leaders' vulnerability to burnout.

Notes

1 Riley, P., See, S.M., Marsh, H. and Dicke, T., 2021. *The Australian Principal Occupational Health, Safety and Wellbeing Survey 2020.* Sydney: Institute for Positive Psychology and Education, Australian Catholic University.
2 Riley, P., Rahimi, M. and Arnold, B., 2021. *The New Zealand Primary Principal Occupational Health, Safety and Wellbeing Survey 2020.* Melbourne: Research for Educational Impact (REDI), Deakin University.
3 Oplatka, I., 2017. Principal Workload: Components, Determinants and Coping Strategies in an Era of Standardization and Accountability. *Journal of Educational Administration,* 55(5), 552–568.
4 OECD, 2020. *Employment and Labour Market Statistics: Hours Worked.* Paris: OECD.
5 Savill-Smith, C., 2019. *Teacher Wellbeing Index.* London: Education Support.
6 Pollock, K. and Wang, F., 2020. *School Principals' Work and Well-Being in Ontario: What They Say and Why It Matters.* Toronto, ON: Western University.
7 Deloitte, 2017. *The Principal Workload and Time Use Study.* Sydney: New South Wales Government.
8 National College for School Leadership, 2007. *A Life in the Day of a Headteacher: A Study in Practice and Wellbeing.* Nottingham: NCSL.
9 Riley, P., 2015. *Irish Principals' and Deputy Principals' Occupational Health, Safety and Wellbeing Survey.* Melbourne: Research for Educational Impact (REDI), Deakin University.
10 Anderson, R.E. and Dexter, S.L., 2000. *School Technology Leadership: Incidence and Impact.* Los Angeles, CA: The University of California.

11 Gurr, D., 2000. The Impact of Information and Communication Technology on the Work of School Principals. *Leading & Managing*, 6(1), 60–73.

12 Schiller, J., 2003. Working with ICT: Perceptions of Australian Principals. *Journal of Educational Administration*, 41(2), 171–185.

13 Pollock, K. and Hauseman, D.C., 2019. The Use of E-mail and Principals' Work: A Double-Edged Sword. *Leadership and Policy in Schools*, 18(3), 382–393.

14 Wong, K., Chan, A.H.S. and Ngan, S.C., 2019. The Effect of Long Working Hours and Overtime on Occupational Health: A Meta-analysis of Evidence from 1998 to 2018. *International Journal of Environmental Research and Public Health*, 16(12), 2102.

15 Caruso, C.C., Hitchcock, E.M., Dick, R.B., Russo, J. and Schmit, J.M., 2004. *Overtime and Extended Work Shifts: Recent Findings on Illnesses, Injuries, and Health Behaviours*. Washington, DC: Centers for Disease Control and Prevention.

16 Chattu, V.K., Manzar, M.D., Kumary, S., Burman, D., Spence, D.W. and Pandi-Perumal, S.R., 2018. The Global Problem of Insufficient Sleep and Its Serious Public Health Implications. *Healthcare*, 7(1), 1.

17 Pencavel, J., 2014. *The Productivity of Working Hours* (IZA Discussion Papers 8129). Washington, DC: Institute of Labour Economics (IZA).

18 Kodz, J., Davis, S., Lain, D., Strebler, M., Rick, J., Bates, P., Cummings, J. and Meager, N., 2003. *Working Long Hours: A Review of the Evidence*. London: Department of Trade and Industry.

19 Unger, D., Sonnentag, S., Niessen, C. and Kuonath, A., 2015. The Longer Your Work Hours, the Worse Your Relationship? The Role of Selective Optimization with Compensation in the Associations of Working Time with Relationship Satisfaction and Self-disclosure in Dual-career Couples. *Human Relations*, 68(12), 1889–1912.

20 Jarrod, M., Haar, Russo, M., Suñe, A. and Ollier-Malaterre, A., 2004. Outcomes of Work – Life Balance on Job Satisfaction, Life Satisfaction and Mental Health: A Study across Seven Cultures. *Journal of Vocational Behaviour*, 85(3), 361–373.

21 Cranston, N., Tromans, C. and Reugebrink, M.A.J., 2004. Forgotten Leaders: What Do We Know about the Deputy Principalship in Secondary Schools? *International Journal of Leadership in Education*, 7(3), 225–242.

22 Goldring, E., Rubin, M. and Herrmann, M., 2021. *The Role of Assistant Principals: Evidence and Insights for Advancing School Leadership*. New York, NY: Wallace Foundation.

23 Department for Education, 2018. *School Leadership in England 2010–2016*. London: DfE.

24 Mitchell, C., Armstrong, D. and Hands, C., 2017. Oh, Is That My Job? Role Vulnerability in the Vice-principalship. *International Studies in Educational Administration*, 45(1), 3–18.

25 Pollock, K., Wang, F. and Hauseman, D.C., 2017. *The Changing Nature of Vice*

Principals' Work. Final Report for the Ontario Principals' Council. Toronto, ON: OPC.

26 Armstrong, D.E., 2012. Connecting Personal Change and Organizational Passage in the Transition from Teacher to Vice Principal. *Journal of School Leadership*, 22(3), 398–424.

27 Harris, A., Muijs, D. and Crawford, M., 2003. *Deputy and Assistant Heads: Building Leadership Potential.* Nottingham: National College for School Leadership.

28 Ho, J., Shaari, I. and Kang, T., 2021. Vice-principals as Leaders: Role Ambiguity and Role Conflicts Faced by Vice-principals in Singapore. *Educational Management Administration & Leadership*, April 2021.

29 Marshall, C., Mitchell, B., Gross, R. and Scott, D., 1992. The Assistant Principalship: A Career Position or a Stepping-stone to the Principalship? *NASSP Bulletin*, 76(540), 80–88.

Leading Through a Crisis   **4**

In the previous four chapters, I described the growing expectations placed on schools and the emotional and workload demands made of their leaders. These factors have been instrumental in increasing headteacher and principal stress and, as a result, an unprecedented number of school leaders are at risk of burning out. In this chapter I consider what happens when schools encounter a crisis. How do leaders, already experiencing unprecedented stress, lead their communities through an emergency and manage the additional burden this brings? I begin by considering the kinds of crises that schools may encounter and the impact that a crisis can have on schools and their leaders. I then discuss the COVID-19 pandemic and examine how this crisis has affected school leaders globally. I draw upon a growing body of research published while the situation is still ongoing, including my own 2020 study.

The COVID-19 global pandemic is the most large-scale crisis experienced by schools in living memory, but school crises are not uncommon and can take many forms. They arise from events which take place on-site or within the school community but may also involve events or situations that occur locally, nationally, or globally and affect a school. Since tragedy struck Dunblane Primary School in Scotland and Columbine High School in the United States in the late 1990s, acts of violence in schools have become more widespread but are still, thankfully, rare. A crisis is more likely to involve the death of an individual member of the school community, missing students, suicide attempts, accidents, hate crimes, natural disasters, fire, civil unrest, war, terrorism, and a range of other incidents. A crisis has the potential to harm physical and mental health, disrupt learning, and threaten safety.

DOI: 10.4324/9781003198475-6

It can lead to psychological trauma, which can be devastating for groups of students, staff, parents, or the whole community. This trauma is something from which some individuals may never recover. Unfortunately, a crisis can happen at any time, in any school, usually without warning. It is likely to bring sudden and drastic change which can overwhelm the community and affect its coping abilities.

Over the last two decades, education systems and schools around the world have sought to improve safety and security to minimise the risk of a crisis occurring. They have also put in place crisis prevention and response mechanisms to allow them to effectively address the community's needs should a crisis occur. Despite this, a crisis brings with it unprecedented demands for school leaders, where they are involved in high-stakes decision-making that may have a long-term effect on members of their community.

> What school leaders, teachers, psychologists and other supporters do in responding to critical incidents and how they do it is of vital import-ance in minimising the extent of the immediate and long-term debili-tating effects of shock, grief and trauma.[1]

Crisis leadership involves addressing practical concerns and problem-solving, while at the same time attending to the emotional needs of those directly and indirectly affected. The most immediate concern is to address the needs of those directly affected and support the most vulnerable. Leaders bear a heavy weight of responsibility for ensuring that students are supported during this time, as with appropriate community support 80%–90% of those experiencing traumatic reactions to an emergency situation will go on to recover within a year.[2] For those who do not recover, however, there may be serious consequences for the child's future, with some facing long-term behavioural and social changes and school-related problems, including drop-out and loss of educational attainment.[2]

It is important to acknowledge that while school leaders are man-aging the needs of others, they will also be experiencing their own indi-vidual response to the crisis.[3] They may be personally affected or suffer a retriggering of a previous traumatic event. They may also feel a sense of responsibility for what has gone wrong. At the very least, they are likely to experience an emotional impact as the leader of a community in crisis. Research shows that teachers and school leaders are often not prepared for the effects that a school crisis will have on their personal and professional lives or their overall wellbeing.[2]

In over 20 years working as an international school teacher and principal, I experienced many crises that affected my school communities. In 2001,

I arrived in Kuwait only a week before 9/11 and experienced the shared anxiety of expatriates living through a major crisis connected to the region where we lived. At first, school was cancelled, and we were afraid to leave the apartment building. Over the next 18 months, as the political situation escalated, we experienced growing uncertainty over our safety and the security of the country. Gas masks went on sale in supermarkets, colleagues talked about creating safe rooms, we participated in air raid drills with our students. We eventually curtailed normal daily activities, like going to the beach club or shopping during busy times. Finally, in February 2003, we decided to leave Kuwait and watched from the safety of our new home in the UK as friends fled the country on the final flights to leave before the second Gulf War began in March.

In 2006, a military coup took place only a week after our arrival in Bangkok. There were tanks on the corner of our street and school was closed for several days, as the city locked down. By this time, I was in senior leadership, and while everyone else stayed home, the senior leadership team (SLT) went in to school to access phone lists and contact parents to advise them of the current situation and offer reassurance. This was my first taste of the responsibility we bear as leaders during a crisis. In the following days, months, and years, as Thailand experienced ongoing bouts of political unrest, we put emergency learning plans together, communicated with stakeholders, assuaged people's fears, and helped them to make sense of what was happening. We did all of this without support from the authorities, with no training and with little crisis leadership experience.

In 2009, I had my first experience of a pandemic as H1N1, better known as swine flu, swept through Thailand. Decisions on whether to keep the school open, or to close to prevent the spread, were left to individual schools, and we felt pressure from equal numbers of parents on each side of the argument. We decided to stay open but came under increasing attack from anxious parents and staff who saw our decision as negligent. This was not helped by the fact the some of our competitor schools decided to close. There was no culture of collaboration or consultation among Bangkok schools back then. Student and staff numbers dwindled further each day, as individuals came down with the virus. We had to put classes together and bring in supply teachers to keep learning going, as well as provide work for students recovering at home.

The years 2010–12 were particularly bad for crises in Bangkok and unforeseen events at school. In April 2010, volcanic ash from Iceland brought air traffic to a standstill and prevented teachers returning to school after the Easter break. I was stuck in the UK and had to manage a severe staff shortage from long distance. The situation soon resolved but by June, civil protest in the city reached new heights. The protesting crowds came closer to school each day, then suddenly things escalated, and Bangkok unexpectedly went into lockdown. Staff, students, and their families were trapped in their homes, some without adequate provisions, many fearful and anxious.

In October 2011, unprecedented flooding hit central Thailand, leaving 224 people dead and thousands homeless. The school closed for three weeks, and we were advised to leave the city. There were shortages, including a lack of bottled water, and queues formed outside 7-11 shops each day waiting for deliveries. We were all in a heightened state of alert, but fortunately the school buildings did not flood, although many members of our community were not as lucky in their homes. The options for distance learning were not as sophisticated a decade ago, and it was hard to deliver an effective programme during shutdowns. This forced us to agree to extend the school day for the rest of the 2011–12 school year to provide "make-up time" for student learning, which was unpopular with many staff and created conflict with the leadership team.

Just as things began to quiet down in December 2012, I was in London, about to leave my hotel for a job interview, when I received a call informing me that the primary school building was on fire. Within an hour I could view video footage on YouTube of our lovely, new facility burning and local firefighters attending to put out the flames. Fortunately, no-one was hurt, but it had occurred during the lunch break, and we had not practised a fire drill outside of normal class time. The area where we would normally gather was too close to the site of the fire to be deemed safe, and the leadership team and staff had to think on their feet to ensure everyone was safe and accounted for.

I wish I could say that my experience of crisis ended there but, very sadly, in Berlin in 2015 a young member of our school community met a violent death. Supporting her parent through this experience – as a friend, colleague, and member of the crisis response team – is something that will stay with me for the rest of my life.

After moving to Hong Kong in 2016, I was once again thrown into the middle of ongoing political unrest, which began at the start of the 2019–20 school year. Protests flared up unpredictably all over the city, some violent, and some targeted at passers-by. Police dispersing crowds with tear gas became an almost daily occurrence, making the whole city feel unsafe. There was a high level of anxiety among the school community, especially among those new to Hong Kong. The political context of the protests also brought challenges for the school. There were fears that students from some groups would be singled out or marginalised and concerns that older students and staff would get involved in the protests. Little did we know as we grappled with decisions about whether to keep the school open, and how to transport students into school safely, that the COVID-19 pandemic was just around the corner.

When speaking to interviewees about their experiences of crisis leadership, the overwhelming message is how privileged leaders feel to support their communities through the most challenging of times. Leaders also talk, however, of the personal toll that this takes on them.

> This is no doubt one of the most rewarding and stressful situations that I have ever experienced personally or professionally. The complexities and the emotions involved. People looking to you to have the answers, day after day. The exhaustion, the sense of responsibility, the fear of getting it wrong and the deep, deep concern for people's welfare. Just wanting to get it right but knowing your personal resources are wearing thin.
>
> (International School Principal, Germany)

The COVID-19 Pandemic

COVID-19 was declared a global pandemic on 11 March 2020. Around the world, nations responded to keep the population safe and prevent healthcare systems becoming overwhelmed. As a result, schools in 188 countries were closed, heavily disrupting learning and work for more than 1.7 billion young people, their families, and educators. School leaders and their staff were suddenly involved in an unexpected transition to distance learning and implemented an unplanned transformation of pedagogy. In many places, they also took on responsibility to provide for the basic needs of their communities. This brought significant stress and placed leaders and their staff under considerable strain.

In the early summer of 2020, while hundreds of millions of employees continued to work from home, face-to-face learning returned. Schools represented the largest, multigenerational community gatherings taking place at the time. Facilitating a safe return to school, implementing government guidance, and dealing with the anxieties and fears of stakeholders brought a monumental set of new challenges for leaders.

As the crisis wore on, many became overwhelmed by the relentless and complex nature of the work and the unpredictability of a situation for which there was no playbook. Leading through a period of such intense and consistent turmoil began to take its toll on the wellbeing of leaders.

> Reassuring everyone about being safe and supporting the emotional needs of staff and parents when I don't feel safe myself. I'm a headteacher not a health care or health and safety expert. It's just exhausting and so worrying – what if I get this wrong. Big responsibility! If a member of staff dies, I'm not sure if I'd ever sleep again.
>
> (Headteacher, UK)

Studies carried out between mid-2020 and mid-2021 raised awareness of growing and continuing headteacher and principal stress and were widely discussed in the media. In the UK, 89% of headteachers reported feeling stressed.[4] Seventy-eight percent of Irish principals reported feeling drained at the end of the day by the constant challenges of the pandemic,[5] while 57% of principals in Ontario said their stress levels were not manageable.[6]

In October 2020, I carried out a worldwide survey to explore headteachers' and principals' experiences of leading through the pandemic. The results were published in 2020 in the report *School Leader Wellbeing During the COVID 19 Pandemic 2020*.[7] Data was collected from 721 participants, working in 36 countries, across state, independent, and international school sectors. Ninety percent of participants said their work-related stress levels had increased during the pandemic, while nearly three-quarters rated their current stress levels as "extremely high" or "very high." Two-thirds described stressful events or situations happening daily or more frequently.

The report shines a light onto the stressors leaders experienced between January and October 2020. During this period, responses to the pandemic and its effects varied considerably, and the contexts in which participants operated were very diverse. The findings show, however, that despite these differences, the experiences of school leaders during this time were broadly similar.

Main Stressors During the Pandemic

Ninety-one percent of participants said their workload had increased since the start of the pandemic, while 90% reported their work to be more emotionally challenging than usual. Eighty-four percent of leaders said they were supporting the emotional needs of others more than usual, with parents and teaching staff representing the neediest groups. Addressing parental anxieties about the safe return to school and supporting distressed parents, who were juggling working from home with supporting home learning, were common stressors. Leaders also spoke of the challenge of supporting educators, describing staff as "distressed," "overwhelmed," "burnt out," and "drained." Two-thirds of leaders found their work with students to be more challenging than usual, while around half said the same about supervisors and senior colleagues.

Several themes emerged from the study around the demands experienced by leaders. The most significant was confusing and shifting guidance from government. Leaders referred to unworkable and ever-changing plans presented by government departments, involving little consultation or opportunity for feedback from schools. Complying with unrealistic government expectations while balancing the needs of the school community proved particularly challenging for leaders globally.

> The fact that the district's plan is horrible and unsustainable. The fact that I have to do double the work because they couldn't create a plan that actually works.
>
> (Principal, United States)

Poor and untimely communication from government was also an issue. This was confirmed by a later 2021 UK-based study where over two-thirds of participants said lack of timely resources from government was the biggest challenge.[8] Leaders in my own study described how new guidance often came last minute and led to increased confusion, while interpreting, translating, and implementing guidance brought considerable stress.

> It's been very very frustrating with mixed messages from the government. It feels like I'm planning for something unknown, blindfolded with one hand tied behind my back! It's all about communicating and their information streams are severely lacking.
>
> (Headteacher, UK)

The relentless need for daily logistical problem-solving was also cited as a major stressor for leaders. In the early months, many headteachers and principals were involved in serving the urgent needs of their communities, coordinating access to food, housing, and internet.

Managing the competing needs of different stakeholder groups was another theme to emerge from the study. Major challenges included the need to deliver effective distance or blended learning, in complex contexts, with few resources. Participants described balancing the expectations of parents with what overextended staff could realistically offer. The amount of live, online instruction available, preparation of senior students for pending examinations, and making adequate online provision for early years students were common areas of parental concern. Leaders also described managing the expectations of boards of governors, who often lacked a real understanding of the pressures that teaching staff were under.

> Parents and governors expect the same number of contact hours online, but teachers have extremely heavy schedules and are stressed and exhausted. Students are disengaged and hard to reach but parents still expect school to be responsible for implementing a full programme.
>
> (International School Principal, Switzerland)

When schools returned to face-to-face learning, new challenges were presented, as leaders took on responsibility for the health and safety of their communities. Forty-two percent of UK leaders found worrying about the safety of the community to be their biggest stressor during this period.[9] Leaders became responsible for a wide range of health and safety measures, including screening arrivals on campus, implementing social distancing, rigorous cleaning regimes, and administering lateral flow testing and contact tracing. As schools remained open, escalating numbers of COVID-19 cases created daily management issues, including staff shortages and large numbers of absent students to service.

> Every day I'm in fear of what will happen if we have someone get seriously sick or die. I feel a tremendous weight of responsibility for keeping everyone safe, like I need to be a COVID expert, whereas in reality I'm just a human being with a family who loves working with children and teachers.
>
> (Principal, Canada)

Finally, dealing with anger and aggression from others emerged as a major issue. Many leaders spoke about anger being directed at them by staff, parents, and the media. One described feeling like a "punchbag for everyone's anxieties." Another referred to the "constant vitriol spouted in the direction of schools," and how disheartening this was. Sadly, many reported a concerning level of hostility from some parents towards teachers and leaders.

> The worst thing has been the judgement, critique and sometimes threatening behaviour that our teachers have been subjected to from frustrated, and often desperate families.
>
> (Principal, United States)

The words of one headteacher summed up the experience of hundreds:

> Everyone . . . I mean, EVERYONE is angry . . . all.the.time.
>
> (Headteacher, UK)

Support for School Leaders During the Pandemic

Many school leaders reported receiving low levels of support during the crisis. In a 2020 study of New Jersey principals, most participants said they received little support from within school and reported suppressing their stress and anxiety to remain positive for students, staff, and parents.[9] In my own study, only a third of participants said they received enough practical support in school, and fewer than a third reported receiving sufficient emotional support. When asked what kind of support they wanted, over half of leaders said they needed more support from the government, while a third wanted support from staff. Thirty-one percent said they would like to receive professional coaching or counselling, and a similar number wanted opportunities to connect with other leaders for peer support.

Most felt their training had not prepared them for the logistical and emotional demands of the crisis. Forty-two percent expressed a desire to take part in crisis leadership training, while a similar number wanted professional development focused on supporting the emotional needs of others. A third also requested training on supporting their own emotional needs, while more than half said they needed more time to attend to their own needs.[8]

Impact of the Pandemic on School Leader Wellbeing

Leading through the chaos of such an unprecedented crisis has had a noticeable impact on the health, personal lives, and professional effectiveness of headteachers and principals. In my own study, over two-thirds of participants reported experiencing declining health due to work-related stress, while only 16% felt they were getting enough sleep. Half admitted to falling back on passive coping strategies like alcohol, food, spending, and drug use. Two-thirds of leaders reported a negative impact on their personal life, and nearly half said that stress had affected their ability to do their job well. More than two-thirds said that at some time during 2020 they had felt close to breaking point.

> The effect of the stress is overwhelming. I feel like I am barely surviving, barely able to function, but I just keep going. To be honest it is completely crushing me.
>
> (Headteacher, UK)

The annual Australian Principal Occupational Health, Safety and Wellbeing Survey, which was carried out in late 2020, reported significantly higher results for burnout, sleeping troubles, stress, depressive symptoms, and somatic stress than previous years. Longitudinal data showed the risk of burnout and somatic stress as the highest recorded since the study began in 2011. In 2020, 33% of participants received a red flag email from the study's organisers, informing them that their wellbeing was a cause for concern, a 5% increase on the previous year.[10]

A UK study, which compared pre-pandemic data to findings from the spring of 2021, showed that leaders' ability to switch off and relax had dropped from 43% pre-pandemic to only 7%.[9] The UK Teacher Wellbeing Index 2020 reported noticeable increases in the number of senior leaders reporting mental and physical health symptoms, including insomnia, irritability, mood swings, overeating and recurring headaches, compared to previous years.[5]

> I've been diagnosed as clinically depressed and suffering with insomnia since the pandemic started. The anti-depressants make my sleep worse and I haven't had a good night's sleep in months. I just have a complete inability to relax. My brain just won't switch off. I'm a mess really.
>
> (Principal, United States)

Lessons to Learn

It is clear there are serious lessons to learn from the pandemic, and there are long-term effects. There is a growing body of evidence that exacerbated stress levels, caused by the crisis, have influenced headteachers' and principals' intentions to leave the profession. Nearly half of participants in an August 2020 survey by the US National Association of Secondary School Principals (NASSP) said they may resign their post because of poor working conditions and concerns brought on during the COVID-19 pandemic. The NASSP study reports that this figure was split between principals who said COVID-19 had accelerated their plans to resign and those who said the pandemic was the first time they had considered leaving.[11] Likewise, in a 2020 survey conducted by the UK National Association of Head Teachers, almost half of heads said they were likely to leave their jobs prematurely, once they had steered their schools through the current crisis. More than two-thirds reported they were less or much less satisfied in their role than the previous year.[12]

Governments around the world, and those responsible for managing schools, must take time to reflect upon the significant impact of a crisis of this magnitude and take steps to improve crisis leadership before the next major crisis hits – as it certainly will.

Chapter Summary

- Schools can be exposed to a crisis at any time and without warning.
- Any crisis is likely to bring additional pressure to bear on headteachers and principals, who are already under considerable strain. This is likely to have an impact on leaders' stress levels.

- There is clear and mounting evidence that the COVID-19 pandemic significantly exacerbated headteacher and principal stress and increased the incidence of burnout.
- Research shows there are universal themes around the major stressors brought about by the pandemic.
- These major stressors include poor and shifting guidance from government; the relentless need for daily, logistical problem-solving; balancing competing demands from different stakeholder groups; fears around health and safety of the community; and dealing with anger and aggression targeted at teachers and school leaders.
- Research also shows that many school leaders felt unsupported during the pandemic, both by governments and those within the school community.
- The pandemic has had a significant impact on the health and wellbeing of headteachers and principals.
- The fallout from the pandemic has led to increasing numbers of school leaders considering leaving the profession. These intentions are largely due to, or exacerbated by, issues that have emerged during the crisis. This is likely to have a significant impact on the global headteacher and principal recruitment and retention crisis.

Notes

1 Whitla, M., (ed.), 2003. *Crises Management and the School Community*. Sydney: Acer Press.
2 Currie, S. and Hayes, B., 2021. *Psychological Support for Schools Following a Crisis or Disaster: The Journey of Recovery*. London: The British Psychological Society.
3 Greenway, C., 2005. Trauma in Schools: Understanding Staff Reactions through the Application of Psychoanalytic Concepts and Systemic Metaphors. *Educational Psychology in Practice*, 21(3), 235–243.
4 Savill-Smith, C., 2019. *Teacher Wellbeing Index*. London: Education Support.
5 Fahy, A., Murphy, C., Fu, N. and Nguyen, T., 2020. *Irish Primary School Leadership During COVID-19. Principals' Study Report 2020*. Dublin: Trinity College Dublin.
6 People for Education, 2021. *Ontario Principals Challenges and Wellbeing: Annual Ontario School Survey 2021*. Toronto, ON: People for Education.
7 Kelly, H., 2020. School Leader Wellbeing During the COVID 19 Pandemic 2020. Accessed online https://drhelenkelly.com/2020/12/13/school-leader-wellbeing-during-the-covid-19-pandemic-the-2020-report/.
8 Greany, T., Thomson, P. and Martindale, N., 2021. *Leading in Lockdown*. Nottingham: University of Nottingham.

9 Reid, D.B., 2022. Suppressing and Sharing: How School Principals Manage Stress and Anxiety During COVID-19. *School Leadership & Management*, 42(1), 62–78.

10 Riley, P., See, S.M., Marsh, H. and Dicke, T., 2021. *The Australian Principal Occupational Health, Safety and Wellbeing Survey 2020.* Sydney: Institute for Positive Psychology and Education, Australian Catholic University.

11 United States National Association of Secondary School Principals. NASSP Survey Signals a Looming Mass Exodus of Principals from Schools. Accessed online www.nassp.org/news/nassp-survey-signals-a-looming-mass-exodus-of-principals-from-schools/.

12 National Association of Head Teachers, 2020. *Fixing the Leadership Crisis: Time for a Change.* London: NAHT.

The Challenges of Leading an International School

5

While in the course of my work, I connect with thousands of school leaders around the world, in all sectors, my background is as an international school principal, and I still feel strong ties to the international school community. Fifteen years of leadership in this sector has helped me to understand the very specific challenges that international schools and their leaders face. The experience of leading an international school is very intense, and the responsibilities placed on leaders often go well beyond what leaders experience in a domestic setting. This, coupled with the reduced personal and professional support available, may render international school leaders particularly vulnerable to stress and burnout. In this chapter, I draw upon research and use leaders' own words to highlight their challenges.

What Are International Schools?

While there are thousands of schools around the world calling themselves international schools, the term *international school* is difficult to define and the schools using it vary considerably. Historically, international schools were founded to service the needs of internationally mobile (IM) families and were run on a not-for-profit basis. These schools are now in a minority as new, privately owned institutions have come to dominate the market. Run on a for-profit basis, most schools now operate, at least in part, to serve wealthy local families looking for an English language education and to gain access to overseas universities. Over the last decade, there has been a huge increase in the number of schools owned by conglomerates often linked to elite private schools in the UK. The

DOI: 10.4324/9781003198475-7

market has also seen growth in international bilingual schools offering a dual language environment and an international curriculum within a national educational context.

The demographic of an international school's student population will vary depending on the type of school and the location. In terms of phase, size, and gender, schools may include children from ages 3–18 or focus on one phase only, be co-educational or single sex, and range from 20 to 5,000 students. Many offer a national curriculum and set of standards designed to meet the needs of a specific expatriate population, such as British international schools, which will also attract local families. Others offer an international curriculum, like the International Baccalaureate, that emphasises principles of international-mindedness and the appreciation of global issues, which have wide market appeal. What they have in common is that they are fee-paying, employ both expatriate and local staff, and comprise culturally diverse stakeholders. In many countries, international schools operate outside of the governmental framework that regulates and supports institutions in the local school sector. They are, however, often authorised by an accreditation agency, which provides formal recognition of their international school status and attests to the quality of their programme.

Leadership Challenges

While leading an international school can be incredibly rewarding, it is also highly demanding. In my 2017 study, 97% of participants said they found leading an international school to be emotionally challenging work.[1] Many leaders are attracted to the role for the opportunities it brings to see the world and experience new cultures. This means that most leaders are themselves IM, working and living away from their home countries. While some headteachers and principals remain in the same school for two decades or more, this is not the norm. Research from 2011 found that the average tenure of an international school headteacher or principal was only 3.7 years,[2] and there is no evidence to suggest that this has changed over the last decade. Individual leaders are likely to lead several international schools during their career, often in different countries and sometimes on different continents. Each international school operates in a unique context, with a distinct cultural environment, legal framework, and mix of languages. The leadership conditions and skills needed will vary considerably from one place to another, and what constitutes effective leadership in one school may not always translate to another. This can be challenging for leaders as they move from one job to another.

> When I moved to Europe, I thought it would be easy, but I just felt lost. I struggled to master the language and the workplace culture was so different to what I was used to in Asia. It took over a year for me to find my feet.
>
> (International School Principal, Germany)

Operating outside of the regulatory and support framework, provided for schools within the local education system, also poses a challenge for leaders. The strict operational parameters and high levels of accountability that are the norm in a leader's home country are often absent. While leaders may enjoy higher levels of autonomy, they are also often left without an advisory network or any kind of safety net.

> There is no network to look to for support. You have to create your own network. There is no infrastructure for dealing with problems outside the school and so you have to create all of this inside the school and deal with things you would not have to deal with ordinarily.
>
> (International School Principal, Thailand)

Many international school communities are made up, in part, of highly mobile families and teaching staff. Schools are placed in a perpetual state of transition as individuals move in and out of the school. This transition may have a significant impact on some individuals, and many experience culture shock as they adjust to their new environment. Moving to an international school often involves significant life changes for IM adults and children. While many students and their parents adjust well, others can experience difficulties.[8] The transient nature of international schools also affects the rest of the community, who are affected by the constant change of personal and professional dynamics.

When new families and staff first arrive in a country, the school plays a central role in providing for their needs. For many, that does not change with time, and the school community becomes the focal point of their lives. The headteacher or principal becomes the leader of their community, responsible for the care and support of students, parents, and staff. Consequently, headteachers and principals may find themselves taking on roles and responsibilities that would not be considered reasonable in other contexts.

> I think many people would be shocked if they knew more about the things I do as an international school head. The responsibility I take and the involvement I have in the lives of members of the community, staff, parents, goes well beyond anything I have experienced in the past.
>
> (International School Principal, Hong Kong)

An international school community is composed of a rich cultural mix of stakeholders. The opportunity to work alongside such a diverse community is a major attraction for leaders, enriching their personal and professional lives. Cultural diversity can bring challenges, however, as groups and individuals bring different values and expectations into school, which may be potential sources of misunderstanding and disagreement. This can be compounded by the fact that educational policies, theories, values, and practices are often transported from cultures very different to those where they are implemented.[3] A lack of coherent ethos between leaders, staff, students, and parents can generate mistrust, frustration, and discontent. This can lead to conflict among stakeholders that may bring significant challenges for leaders. In my 2017 study, over two-thirds of leaders said that working with people from other cultures was emotionally challenging.[1]

The challenges of working with a highly transient, culturally diverse community can affect a school leader's professional relationships. These relationships can be highly demanding and a source of considerable stress for leaders.

Relationships With Teachers

As discussed in earlier chapters, relationships with teachers are closely associated with school leader burnout.[4] In my 2017 research, three-quarters of international school leaders said working with teachers was emotionally challenging.[1] The challenges of leading and managing teaching staff, described in Chapter 2, are all evident in international schools, but the context also brings unique demands. As most expat staff live away from their extended social networks, they look to school for support in a whole range of personal matters. The headteacher or principal plays a key role in providing this support. This changes the relationship between individual staff members and their school leaders, as leaders become more involved in supporting teachers' personal needs.[5] Helping staff through life's challenges and personal crises becomes a regular part of the school leader's role.

Participants in interviews have described supporting staff through a range of situations, including serious accidents, mental and physical illness, relationship breakdown, miscarriage, and the death of loved ones.

> I was the first person she told about the miscarriage. She was devastated. I was glad that I am older and have so much life experience to draw upon, so I could find the right words to comfort her. It is much harder when they do not have that network of support. Mom is not there, and no aunties, so they really look to you.
>
> (International School Principal, Dubai)

This heightened responsibility towards staff means leaders are expected to always be available should a situation arise where a member of staff may need personal support. This can sometimes lead to demands being made of leaders, which would be unthinkable in a different context.

> It was the half term break and I had been out for a few drinks. In the taxi on the way home, I noticed several missed calls from a member of staff. She was in a panic about a colleague who had injured herself overseas and needed an ambulance to collect her from the airport within the hour. I was expected to sober up and figure out how to make this happen.
> (International School Principal, Hong Kong)

The transient nature of international schools can also make it difficult for leaders to build positive relationships with staff. The high turnover of teachers and leaders often means that neither remain at the school long enough to build a sense of trust.[6] Turnover also creates challenges in establishing consistent expectations around staff conduct and the delivery of instruction. Developing a common understanding and language around learning can affect a leader's relationships as they try to establish systems to improve classroom practice. This can also affect a leader's ability to be an effective agent of change.[7]

> It is one of the most exhausting things I have ever done. It is like herding cats. Everyone comes from different backgrounds and has their own idea of what learning should look like. We don't even use the same words to describe things. Most of them just nod and smile and then shut their door and carry on like before. They think I will leave and they can wait me out.
> (International School Principal, Thailand)

Cultural differences can create discord or conflict between staff and leaders, as individuals bring their cultural norms and expectations into school. This can involve issues such as work ethic, leadership styles, teaching practices, student behaviour management, and teacher performance evaluation.

Cultural differences can also give rise to professional conflict between colleagues. This often involves incompatible approaches to collaboration, learning, or classroom management and can lead to disharmony and sometimes confrontation.

> The board brought me in to drive learning forward but the work ethic is very different. Pushing staff to give a bit more, created massive problems for me. The works council and I came to blows. They felt

my ethos was not in line with the school's. It was a battle of wills. It caused me a lot of stress.

(International School Principal, Germany)

Relationships With Parents

In my 2017 study, more than two-thirds of international school leaders found relationships with parents to be emotionally challenging.[1] The international school setting provides a range of highly demanding parent-related matters for leaders to navigate. The central role that schools play in the lives of IM families changes the dynamic between school and parents. Parents, especially non-working mothers, commonly called "trailing spouses," are much more involved in the daily life of the school than would be expected elsewhere.

You have these highly professional women who have moved to a new country with their husband's job. They have no community, so the school is the centre of their world, and they are overly involved. They can be a great help but can also cause a lot of problems.

(International School Principal, Switzerland)

Like teachers, parents are isolated from friends and extended family and seek support from school when problems arise in their personal lives. Leaders can find themselves not only supporting parents through a difficult transition, but counselling them through marital difficulties, financial problems, illness, and death in the family.

In my second year, a young father died of a stroke. The mother had no-one else, so I ended up supporting her through the whole process of identifying the body, the post-mortem, sending the body home to the UK as well as helping her to come to terms with what happened and being there for her boys.

(International School Headteacher, Dubai)

As with teachers, the transient nature of the community can make it hard for leaders to build trust with parents. This can place relationships under strain and lead to tension that may sometimes flare up into confrontation. The challenges of living in a strange country, away from family and friends, can also cause some parents to be highly emotional. Particularly during the transition period, it is common for parents to experience, guilt, worry, or fear about their child's wellbeing and bring these emotions into school.[8] This can lead to conflict between parents and staff, or parents and leaders.

The mother was having a terrible transition, she was very unhappy and there was a lot of anxiety about her child who had learning needs, which she would not accept. She would come into school very emotional and confront the teacher or the EA and I would then have to intervene. It turned quite unpleasant on a few occasions, and she wouldn't be reasoned with.

(International School Principal, Germany)

Cultural differences between parents and teachers, parents and leaders, or among different groups of parents can also be problematic. Educators and parents may have different understandings of what constitutes good learning, classroom management, or playground behaviour, based upon their upbringing and cultural values. This can be a source of discontent among parents and can create conflict with teachers, which leaders are expected to resolve. Groups of parents from different cultural backgrounds may also come into conflict with each other as they seek to push agendas about how the school should operate, based upon their cultural values and expectations.

Relationships With the Board of Governors

International schools usually operate, to some extent, outside of the governmental framework established for local schools in their country. This provides school leaders with high levels of autonomy, which many feel is a major benefit. It also elevates the role of the board of governors as, with reduced government oversight, they have greater responsibility for policy-making and accountability. In these circumstances, the relationship between the board and the school leader is crucial to the success of the school. This dynamic intensifies the nature of the relationship and can create potential for conflict.[9]

While many boards are highly professional, competent, and supportive, international schools also have a reputation for incompetent and unscrupulous boards. Appointed boards, of the kind that are common in for-profit schools, often lack transparency and stakeholder voice, which can lead to issues of trust. They may also pursue financial profit at the expense of student learning or staff and student wellbeing. Not-for-profit schools tend to favour elected boards, which usually involve parents, at least in part. While transparency and community involvement are likely to be high, parent boards may bring a range of challenges for leaders. Parent-governors often lack skills in key areas, like finance and strategic planning; they are also associated with high board turnover, which brings lack of stability and consistency. It is also common for parent governors to pursue an individual agenda, rather than take a whole school perspective. Both appointed and elected boards commonly lack board training. This means they often fail to understand the limitations and responsibilities of their role, have insufficient expertise in educational matters, and have a poor understanding of how schools operate.

In my 2017 research, 42% of leaders said they found relationships with the board of governors to be emotionally challenging.[1] While leaders consider their relationships with staff and parents to be much more challenging than those with governors,[1] relationships with the board have been found to be the most common reason for international school leaders to leave their post.[2] Board-related issues that most commonly give rise to a leader resigning or being dismissed include board micromanagement, differences with the board, and poor board behaviour.[1,2] Micromanagement can arise when boards fail to understand or disregard the limitations of their role. This can cause them to interfere with the day-to-day running of the school and other operational matters that are within the purview of the headteacher or principal. This can be exacerbated by differing cultural expectations around the role of a board of governors.

> A group of local parents have the ear of the chair who is also the owner. For wealthy parents in this culture, influence is everything. He will call me at any time of the day or night to interfere in things. He's used to getting his own way and he can get unpleasant. He's very intimidating. I've tried to explain diplomatically that this is not his role but he really doesn't care and I have to tread carefully or I could be out of a job.
>
> (International School Headteacher, Malaysia)

International schools are complex organisations, and there are many issues over which differences between the headteacher or principal and the board can arise. These can range from matters relating to students, curriculum, or classroom practice, over which the board should have no influence, to differences over fundamental issues, such as the school's mission, vision, and strategic direction.

> Their priorities just do not line up with those of the SMT and school community. They want an elite private school focused 100% on academics and admission to top universities. We have a vision and mission, which is not built around that, but they won't accept it. They are dinosaurs and it is a constant battle that is incredibly wearing.
>
> (International School Principal, Hong Kong)

In my interviews with school leaders over the last seven years, many wanted to share stories of poor board behaviour and the impact this had on them. When headteachers and principals arrive at their new school, they are often totally dependent on the board of governors, especially the board chair, for personal and professional support. Boards often fail to understand the isolating nature of the international school leader's role and overlook appropriate transition measures to address this. The quality of support provided in these early weeks sets the tone for the ongoing relationship between the board and the headteacher or principal.

> No-one is looking out for the head of school. The board doesn't treat them like a human being and care for them. It would be nice for the chair to take me out for lunch occasionally, or take my wife and I out for dinner, or even just to ask how I am, to have a personal connection and feel like they give a damn, but the truth is they don't. We are just an expendable commodity.
>
> (International School Headteacher, Thailand)

Student-Related Issues

The presence of what are known as third-culture kids (TCKs)[10] creates a unique environment in many international schools and a provides a distinct set of challenges for international school leaders. TCKs are children of IM families, who find themselves frequently moving countries and changing schools. This can have a serious impact on some students, as they experience loss of friends and family and adjust to a completely new lifestyle.[11] TCKs commonly lack a stable network of relationships and may have difficulty in establishing anything other than superficial friendships, which can leave them feeling lonely and can affect their sense of identity and belonging.[8] Exposure to new cultures, all presenting different sets of norms and values, can often leave TCKs feeling culturally confused or adrift.[12] Problems may also arise with a student's learning as they move between schools, sometimes changing curriculum or interrupting learning partway through the academic year.

> Most Third Culture Kids go through more grief experiences by the time they are twenty than mono-cultural individuals do in a lifetime.[11]

While many TCKs learn to adapt quickly, others will need a high level of support. Some may present with social, emotional, or learning difficulties that have gone unnoticed or unaddressed in previous schools. This can bring significant challenges for teachers, counselling staff, and leaders.

Addressing such issues with parents can be challenging, as parents may bring their own feelings of anxiety, guilt, and fear for their child's wellbeing into the equation.

Where there is a limited framework of governmental support for international schools, leaders can find themselves taking responsibility for student-related matters that would ordinarily be outside of their purview. A level of involvement in child safeguarding, which would be unthinkable elsewhere, can give rise to highly stressful situations for leaders. It is not uncommon for schools to receive minimal support from local authorities and external agencies in protecting the welfare of expatriate children. Overly harsh or lax approaches to addressing suspected abuse also create challenges for leaders when deciding how to address matters in the best interests of the child. These issues can produce some of the most stressful situations that school leaders encounter, as the stakes are so high. In interviews, leaders shared stories of receiving calls at home from school counsellors worried for the immediate safety of a child, having to address parents directly about abuse allegations, and taking responsibility for securing a child's safety when no other options were available.

> We had to remove a child from the family home as they were being abused. The authorities would not intervene and so we had to smuggle the child out of the house in the middle of the night and put them on a flight to the USA. It just seemed crazy that we had to get involved in such a thing. My wife and I had many sleepless nights.
>
> (International School Headteacher)

Leader Isolation and Lack of Support

Leader loneliness can be more prevalent in international schools where individuals are living away from their home countries and isolated from normal support systems. International school teachers look to colleagues to form the basis of their social support network, but this is not usually possible for senior leaders, who often lack in-school peers they can confide in. The need to keep a professional distance from teaching staff and parents can leave leaders out on a limb socially. While becoming too close to staff or parents can backfire on leaders, the alternative can be very isolating.

> I have been burned a couple of times with relationships with parents and it has created awkward situations that I have had to extricate myself from. I also avoid going out with staff. No-one wants to be

approached by a glassy-eyed teacher who has had a few too many and wants to tell you some home truths. I would rather be on my own.

(International School Primary Principal, Germany)

The demands of the leadership role, especially during a leader's transition period, also leave little opportunity for making friends outside of school. Those who arrive without a family to support them can be the most vulnerable. For some, this can go well beyond professional loneliness.

Being a principal is the loneliest job in the world. It is so hard to make friends. I have not had anyone in my apartment for two years. I have a massive DVD collection and I play a lot of patience. I think of myself as a lone wolf but really I am very lonely.

(International School Principal, Dubai)

While the international school leader plays a key role in supporting the transition of others, their own transition and that of their family is often overlooked. Headteachers and principals may receive minimal support from school with transition and are usually expected to hit the ground running. It is common for little thought to be given to supporting the transition of their spouse, who may find it hard to settle and make friends in the community, especially if they do not have school-aged children. It is also not unusual for international schools to have rules preventing the headteacher's or principal's spouse from working in the school. Consequently, spouses may struggle to find their place in the community or build their own support network. This is especially the case where there is a language barrier.

We have been here less than a year and my wife has not settled but she is not working and is home with a child and emotionally struggling. Getting to grips with this job means I am not there much and she feels I am not supporting her at home. It is putting our marriage under terrible strain and I don't want to lose them but I don't know how I can find more time to be there just now.

(International School Headteacher, Switzerland)

The COVID-19 Pandemic

The COVID-19 pandemic hit international schools hard, as in addition to the challenges facing schools generally, they experienced a range of unique impacts. My 2020[13] and 2021[14] reports into the challenges of teaching and leading through the crisis highlighted the issues facing international schools in the period January to October 2020. Teachers and leaders reported the common pandemic stressors, discussed in Chapter 4, such as struggling to implement online learning, constant change and uncertainty, the blurring of home and work boundaries, and the unrealistic demands of parents. They also spoke of issues specific to the international school context.

When the crisis emerged in Asia in January 2020, international schools experienced an exodus of staff, students, and their families, many of whom returned to their home countries or sought refuge in COVID-free locations. During the early months, the daily business of school, including online learning, took place across multiple time zones. This brought unprecedented challenges for leaders as they tried to ensure that staff and students remained engaged and that everyone's needs were met. Many teachers and leaders were left overwhelmed and exhausted by the demands of delivering a continuous programme of learning during this time.

> Some teachers were working from home in Hong Kong, but others were in places like Thailand, with poor internet connections, or in the US or Europe, trying to manage the time difference and sometimes live streaming lessons through the night. Our students were literally all over the world. We did not even know where many of them were.
> (International School Principal, Hong Kong)

Later in 2020, as countries came out of lockdown and schools began to return to face-to-face learning, international school communities were still spread around the globe, with some members reluctant or unable to return to their host countries. Thousands of teachers working in China were unable to return, due to government restrictions, and continued to deliver learning online. Many experienced pay cuts and some had their contracts terminated, which created genuine hardship. Reductions in student enrolment and demands for fee refunds by parents had a financial impact on schools, and some were forced to make changes to teachers' terms and conditions to reflect the ongoing situation.

> Trying to get staff back into China when the borders are closed has been highly challenging and made worse by board members being unsympathetic to the stresses of those not in the country. Staff have had their salary halved for almost 8 months as a punishment for not being back in the country despite doing their job online. This has created real hardship and anxiety that I am having to help them manage. Despite my appeals the board will not be moved.
> (International School Headteacher, China)

Restrictions on gathering and working from home caused social isolation for many international school staff. This was felt most by those who were new to the host country and had not yet had an opportunity to build social networks.

> I am new to my school and feel like nobody, beyond a few colleagues, care that I'm here and struggling. I would really like for some sort of effort to be made to bring me into the community. This is such an isolating experience.
>
> (International School Teacher, Thailand)

As the crisis wore on, social isolation was exacerbated by the inability to travel overseas to visit family and friends. In January 2021, 70% of international school teachers said they had been unable to travel home since the pandemic started. By January 2022, many had not returned home for more than two years, due to limited or expensive flights and quarantine regulations requiring travellers to isolate for long periods. This resulted in thousands becoming disconnected from their families and friends and caused suffering for many.

> I have two staff who have lost parents and have been unable to travel home for the funeral. One guy lost his father to COVID in the US and had to attend the funeral by Zoom, alone in his apartment, with no-one to comfort him. It has been heart breaking.
>
> (International School Principal, Switzerland)

Finally, the fear and anxiety of living through an unprecedented global crisis can be magnified for those living away from home. In January 2021, over half of international school teachers said they did not feel safe and supported in the country where they lived. Issues included social isolation and lack of support from school but also low levels of trust in government and fears of draconian government measures.

> If one of us gets COVID we will be sent to hospital and the other will be forced to go into a government quarantine centre. I am terrified about what will happen to my kids.
>
> (International School Teacher, Hong Kong)

Dealing with a very high level of staff anxiety, alongside the other demands that the pandemic has brought, has been a monumental challenge for international school leaders. Many leaders have experienced high levels of anxiety themselves but have felt it necessary to prioritise the needs of the school community above their own needs and those of their families.

> I've been at home on my own with a three-year-old, struggling with the isolation, the massive workload, the anxious staff and the constant complaining from parents. The most challenging thing has been reassuring everyone about being safe and supporting the emotional needs of staff and parents when I don't feel safe myself and I'm also going through this myself.
>
> (International School Principal, Dubai)

Chapter Summary

- International school leaders face the same demands as all headteachers and principals, but they also experience unique challenges.
- Some of these challenges arise from the independent status of international schools operating outside of local government systems. This brings high levels of autonomy and low levels of accountability but also low levels of support.
- School leaders play a key role in supporting IM staff, students, and their families through their transition to the new environment. They also provide ongoing support for those who have no support network.
- The cultural diversity of international schools can bring additional challenges for leaders as groups and individuals bring their own cultural norms and expectations into school. This can lead to misunderstanding or cultural dissonance, which can create conflict.
- These issues can affect leaders' relationships with staff, parents, and the board of governors.
- The COVID-19 pandemic was particularly challenging for international school leaders who faced a set of unique demands in addition to those commonly experienced by headteachers and principals.

Notes

1 Kelly, H., 2017. International Schools as Emotional Arenas: Facing the Leadership Challenges in a German Context. University of Birmingham, Ed.D.
2 Benson, J., 2011. An Investigation of Chief Administrator Turnover in International Schools. *Journal of Research in International Education*, 10(1), 87–103.
3 Dimmock, C. and Walker, A., 2010. *Educational Leadership: Culture and Diversity*, p. 17. London: SAGE.

4 Friedman, I.A., 2002. Burnout in School Principals: Role Related Antecedents. *Social Psychology of Education*, 5, 229–251.

5 Murakami-Ramalho, E. and Benham, M., 2010. Around the Fishing Net: Leadership Dynamics for Change in an American International school. *Educational Management Administration & Leadership*, 38(5), 625–643.

6 Gurr, D., 2015. A Model of Successful School Leadership from the International Successful School Principalship Project. *Societies*, 5(1), 1–15.

7 Gardner-McTaggart, A., 2018. International Schools: Leadership Reviewed. *Journal of Research in International Education*, 17(2), 148–163.

8 McLachlan, D.A., 2007. Global Nomads in an International School: Families in Transition. *Journal of Research in International Education*, 6(2), 233–249.

9 Stout, W., 2005. Conflict and Its Resolution in the Governance and Management of International Schools. *International Schools Journal*, 25(1).

10 Useem, J., Useem, R. and Donoghue, J., 1963. Men in the Middle of the Third Culture: The Roles of American and Non-Western People in Cross-cultural Administration. *Human Organisation*, 22(3), 169–179.

11 Pollock, D. and Van Reken, R., 2010. *Third Culture Kids: Growing Up among Worlds*. Boston, MA: Nicholas Brealey Publishing.

12 Gillies, W.D., 2001. American International Schools: Poised for the Twenty-first Century. *Education*, 122, 395–401.

13 Kelly, H., 2020. School Leader Wellbeing During the COVID 19 Pandemic 2020. Accessed online https://drhelenkelly.com/2020/12/13/school-leader-wellbeing-during-the-covid-19-pandemic-the-2020-report/.

14 Kelly, H., 2021. International School Teacher Wellbeing During the COVID 19 Pandemic 2020. Accessed online https://drhelenkelly.com/2021/04/10/full-report-on-international-school-teacher-wellbeing-during-the-covid-19-pandemic-published-today/.

More About Burnout   6

In the previous five chapters, I examined the ever-increasing work demands of headteachers and principals, and the impact this has on their stress levels, health, and personal and professional lives. The COVID-19 pandemic raised the alarm about the burnout of education professionals and prompted new discussion around the causes of burnout and its prevention. It would be a mistake, however, to think of school leader burnout as a phenomenon created by the COVID-19 crisis as there is plenty of evidence to show that this problem has been escalating for many years. While foremost burnout researchers, Maslach and Leiter, estimate that 10%–15%[1] of the working population may experience burnout, longitudinal studies carried out in Australia[2] and New Zealand,[3] over the last decade, have consistently found the incidence of principal burnout to be around 1.7 times that of the general population. In this chapter I look more closely at the phenomenon of school leader burnout, examining the causes of burnout and the burnout process.

The Causes of Burnout

While in a small number of countries burnout is a clinical diagnosis, it is generally not considered to be a medical condition. It is defined by the WHO as an occupational syndrome characterised by the three dimensions of exhaustion, feelings of detachment, negativity, or cynicism towards the workplace, and reduced professional effectiveness. According to Maslach and Leiter,[2] burnout occurs when there is a chronic imbalance between the needs of an employee and the demands of their job, in one or more of six areas – workload, control, rewards, community, fairness, and values. There

DOI: 10.4324/9781003198475-8

follows an examination of each of these six areas and their relevance to the school leader's experience.

Workload

Maslach and Leiter define workload as "job demands exceeding human limits,"[2] and their research shows workload to have a consistent association with all three dimensions of burnout. Unreasonable job demands are especially associated with exhaustion, as those who have insufficient time and support to allow them to manage their work demands are vulnerable to becoming chronically exhausted. In Chapter 3, I examined the unreasonable workload of headteachers and principals, the pace and intensity of their work, and their poor work-life balance. I drew on research from a range of sources to illustrate how many leaders find their workload difficult or impossible to achieve and sustain and are at risk of becoming physically exhausted.

> "Some days I go through the whole day with no time to take a beat or even refill my coffee cup. On days like that I can barely function by the end. I am a husk. I then have to get up and do it all over again the next day."
>
> Principal, Canada

Workload demands are not only quantitative, however, as leaders encounter significant emotional demands that many find draining, as discussed in Chapter 2. Although headteachers and principals enter the profession actively seeking emotionally engaging and rewarding work, long-term participation in such work can be damaging. Emotional interactions with stakeholders can be hard for leaders to shake off at the end of the day, and the processing of such events can encroach on an individual's home life or cause loss of sleep. This can seriously impede the recovery that should take place during evenings, weekends, and holidays.

Studies show that the impact of work that is so emotionally draining can be mitigated by a high level of social support. Failure to receive such support can exacerbate an imbalance between the emotional demands of the role and what an individual can sustain. This may render individuals more susceptible to emotional exhaustion. Emotional labour can also render a school leader more vulnerable to emotional exhaustion, as their role involves constant suppression of an individual's true feelings and frequent displays of emotions that they do not feel. Over a prolonged period, this can result in emotional dissonance, which can be psychologically harmful and contribute to burnout.

> During my first week on the job I had to inform the whole staff that the board had decided to cut their pay. Quite a few came to see me to talk about the hardship that this meant for them. It was appalling but I had to put a brave face on it and reassure everyone that things would get better.
>
> (International School Headteacher, Middle East)

The imbalance between work demands and the capacity of a leader to manage them will be greater when their personal attributes, skills and experience fail to match the requirements of the role. Role conflict of this kind has been shown to be highly emotionally exhausting as well as physically draining and has a close association with burnout.[4]

> I was a new principal and I was just finding my feet when we were plunged deep into a crisis that I felt unprepared for and I was out of my depth. Every day it was a struggle to show that I could lead the school and stay sane.
>
> (Principal, Australia)

Control

According to Maslach and Leiter, individuals need to feel that they are in control of their work.[1] This means having choices, making decisions, solving problems, and having input into the process of achieving the outcomes for which they are accountable. An employee may be more vulnerable to burnout if an imbalance occurs between the level of control they need to do a job well and the control provided. For school leaders, lack of control is a common problem. It can manifest in the unpredictability of their day, the hours they work, the resources available to them, the interactions they have with stakeholders, and the degree of autonomy granted by supervisors. Such issues are linked with all three dimensions of burnout but are most closely associated with detachment. This detachment occurs as an individual disengages from their work, the environment, and the people around them, to protect themselves from the impact of low control and high expectations.

> It is like nothing is under our control. The government are calling the shots but they are doing it badly, expecting us to keep the school open and teach students under impossible conditions but giving us no autonomy about how we go about it. Just a lot of useless guidance that we are expected to implement.
>
> (Headteacher, UK)

Reward

Burnout is also more likely to occur when an employee's job rewards, whether financial, institutional, social, or intrinsic, do not match their expectations. Individual school leaders may prioritise different rewards but generally want to be well paid and receive good benefits. They also want to feel they are doing a good job and achieving something worthwhile, and that this is acknowledged by those around them. An imbalance of rewards expected and those received is linked to both emotional exhaustion and detachment/cynicism. When leaders don't receive the recognition they think they deserve, they feel devalued, and this may cause them to become disengaged or experience negative feelings towards the workplace. Participants in a large-scale study of UK senior leaders identified "not feeling valued" as a significant factor in the development of work-related mental health symptoms and reported this as a major reason for considering leaving the profession.[5]

> I was Acting Head and the board led me to believe I would get the post but I got passed over. I was gutted as I knew I deserved it more than the person they appointed. I felt sad and dejected and completely undervalued because the board handled it so badly. It changed the way I felt about the school. It changed everything.
>
> (Assistant Headteacher, UK)

Community

Maslach and Leiter argue that a strong sense of community in the workplace can mitigate against imbalances between the job demands and employee's needs.[1] A sense of belonging to the school community, therefore, plays a key role in predicting headteacher and principal burnout. While a supportive community can help prevent burnout occurring, an imbalance between the community a leader needs and that provided can have a damaging impact on their wellbeing. A toxic school culture, chronic workplace conflict, and feelings of isolation make it less likely that leaders receive support during tough times or feel able to seek advice and comfort from others. Isolation is often a problem for school leaders, with many lacking a sense of belonging to a group within their school and unable to share an emotional bond with people they like and respect. This may be particularly so in the first years after taking up a new role, as leaders struggle to come to grips with the demands of the job and are left with insufficient time or energy to build on social and professional connections. School culture has a significant impact here. Leaders are less likely to experience a mismatch between their social needs and the support available if there is a vibrant and responsive community and a communal orientation towards students, staff, and parents.

> At home there is a great camaraderie between the leadership team and staff, that is just part of the culture. When I moved here, I was told quite clearly by staff representatives that I was not allowed to sit in the staffroom. Where else do they think I can go to sit in a comfortable chair and have a chat?
>
> (International School Principal, Germany)

Fairness

Fairness in the workplace is an indicator of mutual respect and is crucial to maintain trust, both in the organisation and among colleagues. In studies from Australia[3] and New Zealand,[4] school leaders report a higher "sense of justice" in the workplace than the general population and feel they are usually treated fairly. However, situations such as inequity in workload or pay, inappropriate handling of promotions or evaluations, unfair distribution of resources, and poor dispute resolution practices can lead to a sense of unfairness. This erodes trust and may result in detachment from the workplace, which over time can lead to feelings of cynicism towards supervisors and the school as an organisation.

> I had been trying to get the head to put some of the weaker teachers on a plan but he didn't have the guts to do what was needed. . . . Then the results went down, so he got a former Ofsted inspector in to do some work scrutinies and observations and she absolutely annihilated us. The head told me I was responsible for the results going down. I went off sick with stress for three days, I was so upset.
>
> (Assistant Headteacher, UK)

Values

A mismatch in values occurs when an individual's principles and goals are not in line with those of the organisation they work for. School leaders are often driven by a strong sense of values, which will commonly be at the heart of their relationship with their work, reflecting the ideals and motivation that brought them to education in the first place. Compatibility of values between the leader and the school often provides the leader with an opportunity to use the resources and reputation of the school to pursue their personal agenda. This results in what Maslach and Leiter call a "productive psychological contract"[1] that benefits both parties. When values are divergent, however, this places the leader under strain, which may lead to reduced energy, motivation, and accomplishment and play a central role in burnout.

> I realised that I no longer believed what I was doing was in the best interests of students. I felt we were enabling parents to push their kids too hard and prioritising academics over everything else that childhood should bring.
>
> (International School Principal, Hong Kong)

The Burnout Process

As discussed in the preface, burnout is not a single event but can be thought of as a continuum with *Engagement* at one end and *Burnout* at the other. In between are three further profiles, one or two of which may be used to describe an individual's workplace experience – *Overextended*, *Disengaged*, and *Ineffective*. These profiles may place an individual on the road to burnout if their situation does not improve.

The process of burnout for a headteacher or principal creeps up over a long period of time. A typical leader is likely to begin their leadership career at the *Engagement* end of the continuum, where they experience low levels of exhaustion and detachment and high levels of professional efficacy. Over time, imbalances occur between the individual's needs and the role's demands. As discussed in earlier chapters, for school leaders these imbalances are most likely to involve the strain of dealing with adult relationships. These relationships may affect the leader's need for community, control, fairness, or impact their values, and create an imbalance in one or more of these areas. The volume of work and emotional demands of the role, are also likely to create a workload imbalance, as the physical, mental, and emotional demands of the job become more than an individual leader can manage and sustain.

As a result, a leader will begin to feel drained and overwhelmed and struggle to recover during non-work time. They may become caught in a downward spiral where, while the job remains the same, their tolerance for the demands gradually declines, their resources become depleted, and they experience physical, mental, and emotional exhaustion. At this point an individual is likely to fit the *Overextended* profile on the burnout continuum.

The leader may respond by disconnecting from the school environment, to protect themselves from the unrelenting pressure. Their commitment to their role may diminish and they may begin to experience negative feelings towards colleagues, other stakeholders, and the school as an organisation. The leader is now both *Overextended* and *Disengaged* but not yet burnt out.

As the weeks or months progress, negativity may develop into cynicism and loss of purpose. This, together with the exhaustion they are experiencing, diminishes a leader's capacity to perform their leadership role and they eventually become *Ineffective*. When this occurs, they are experiencing all three dimensions of burnout.

As a leader moves through the continuum burnout is not inevitable. If they can recognise the signs of impending burnout and take measures to significantly reduce their stress, then burnout may be avoided. Signs that an individual is moving towards burnout are often subtle and likely to be ignored. It is, therefore, crucial that leaders and their supervisors can identify early signs and symptoms of exhaustion, detachment, and reduced work effectiveness so that steps can be taken to avoid burnout occurring.

Signs of Exhaustion

- Chronic fatigue that is not improved with normal rest
- Impaired focus or concentration
- Physical symptoms – chest pain, heart palpitations, shortness of breath, gastrointestinal problems, dizziness, more colds, and flu than usual
- Anxiety, manifesting in increased tension, worry, or edginess
- Depressive symptoms – sadness, hopelessness, guilt, or worthlessness
- Lack of self-care
- Anger or irritability with others
- Inability to relax, which may affect sleep
- Increased use of alcohol, drugs, food, spending, gambling, and other passive coping strategies

Signs of Detachment/Cynicism

- Feeling disconnected from others in the school community or the school environment
- Seeking isolation and withdrawing from the job physically and psychologically; avoiding involvement in projects; planning ways to escape work altogether
- Increased absence from work
- Negative feelings about the workplace
- Loss of enjoyment – not wanting to go to work and being eager to leave
- Disillusionment with the purpose or of value of the work or the role

Signs of Reduced Professional Efficacy

- Lack of productivity or poor performance, despite longer hours spent working
- Lack of motivation or uncharacteristic lack of enthusiasm for work
- Abnormal preoccupation with work; failing to take time out from thinking about work or working obsessively

I realise now that my own journey from *Engagement* to *Burnout* took at least eight years and possibly longer. During this period, I experienced imbalances in each of the six areas of workload, control, rewards, community, fairness, and values. Towards the end, I was experiencing imbalances in all six areas at the same time. There were many early warning signs, such as chronic fatigue, anxiety, anger, and irritability. Later, a lack of control and sense of unfairness affected my enjoyment of the work, and I began to doubt my purpose. The only way I knew to regain control was to work harder. I filled my spare time with activities that were aligned to my work-related passions, to allow me to seek the validation I craved. After eight years of moving along the burnout continuum, this was ultimately my downfall.

Chapter Summary

- Burnout is not a medical diagnosis but an occupational condition, recognised by the WHO.
- Burnout consists of three dimensions, all of which need to be present:
  o Exhaustion
  o Feelings of detachment, negativity, or cynicism towards the workplace
  o Reduced professional effectiveness
- Burnout is a continuum from *Engagement* to *Burnout*. In between are three further profiles – *Overextended*, *Disengaged*, and *Ineffective*.
- An individual can move up and down the burnout continuum, depending on their level of work-related stress and how it is managed.
- Burnout occurs when there is an imbalance between what an individual needs and what the work provides in one or more of six areas – workload, control, reward, community, fairness, and values.
- Headteachers and principals commonly experience an imbalance of workload as their quantitative workload, and the emotional demands of their role often exceed what they can reasonably manage or sustain.
- School leaders also regularly experience imbalances in control, reward, community, fairness, and values.

- These imbalances may lead to leaders becoming *Overextended, Disengaged,* or *Ineffective* and may eventually lead to burnout, when all three are present.
- The journey along to continuum from *Engagement* to *Burnout* will take many months or years.

Part I Closing

In Part I, I outlined the extent of the stress that headteachers and principals are experiencing and the causes. I looked at the changing role of schools, in recent decades, and the increasing demands placed on their leaders. I examined the emotional demands of the role and the considerable workload, which most leaders are finding unsustainable. I also discussed the impact of leading through a crisis for leaders who are already overwhelmed. Finally, I outlined how these increasing stress levels can lead to burnout if steps are not taken to reduce, manage, or mitigate stress.

In Part II, I look at the steps that can be taken to reduce, manage, or mitigate school leader stress and prevent burnout. I make recommendations for changes at governmental, organisational, and individual levels and provide a range of practical ideas and tools that schools and leaders can use to improve working conditions and support leader wellbeing.

Notes

1 Leiter, P. and Maslach, C., 2016. Latent Burnout Profiles: A New Approach to Understanding the Burnout Experience. *Burnout Research*, 3(4), 89–100.
2 Riley, P., See, S.M., Marsh, H. and Dicke, T., 2021. *The Australian Principal Occupational Health, Safety and Wellbeing Survey 2020.* Sydney: Institute for Positive Psychology and Education, Australian Catholic University.
3 Riley, P., Rahimi, M. and Arnold, B., 2021. *The New Zealand Primary Principal Occupational Health, Safety and Wellbeing Survey 2020.* Melbourne: Research for Educational Impact (REDI), Deakin University.
4 Jawahar, I.M., Stone, T.H. and Kisamore, J.L., 2007. Role Conflict and Burnout: The Direct and Moderating Effects of Political Skill and Perceived Organizational Support on Burnout Dimensions. *International Journal of Stress Management*, 14(2), 142–159.
5 Savill-Smith, C., 2019. *Teacher Wellbeing Index.* London: Education Support.

PART II

Preventing Burnout, Managing Stress, and Improving Wellbeing

What Governments Can Do

7

In Part I, I explained how the role of headteacher or principal has intensified in recent decades. This has brought increased expectations and workload, and has placed many leaders under significant pressure, resulting in high levels of stress. While the characteristics and attitudes of individual leaders may contribute to them becoming *Overextended, Disengaged*, and *Ineffective*, it is primarily organisational factors that create the situations in which leaders become overwhelmed.

The organisational systems, structures, and practices that contribute to headteacher and principal burnout are to some extent created by schools themselves but, in most contexts, they are also created by government policy. Examining what governments can do to reduce the burden placed on school leaders and alleviate their stress, is therefore, an obvious starting point for Part II of this book. In later chapters, I also discuss what schools can do to improve headteacher and principal working conditions and consider how leaders can take responsibility for managing their own stress.

In this chapter, I examine five key areas that governments can address to improve the working conditions of headteachers and principals. I begin by discussing the political context in which schools operate, where neoliberal policies place increasing expectations on schools to address the social disadvantage that causes the attainment gap. I consider how this may be addressed through a more direct government approach to tackling inequality. I then discuss the funding of schools and how they may be resourced more effectively in several key areas that affect teacher and school leader stress. Later in the chapter, I examine the negative impact on educator wellbeing of high-stakes accountability and offer solutions. I discuss the urgent need

DOI: 10.4324/9781003198475-10

for governments to review the role of headteachers and principals, to ensure the role meets the need of 21st-century schools. I also consider how policymakers can improve support and training to help leaders to manage the demands of their work more effectively. Finally, I examine the issue of school leader abuse and how this can be addressed.

Addressing Inequality and Disadvantage

Over recent decades, governments around the world have placed an increasing responsibility on schools to provide a more effective workforce, by improving the quality of education and maximising outcomes for all students. This has piled pressure upon schools to not only provide exceptional learning but to close the attainment gap between children from high-income, highly educated families and those from lower down the social strata.

Social disadvantage is complex but is primarily caused by poverty. Schools can only successfully address issues of social and economic deprivation if supported by wide-ranging government policies to reduce poverty and disadvantage. For three decades following World War II, the policy of Western governments focused on creating a fairer society. High levels of government intervention, wealth redistribution, and investment in infrastructure saw huge increases in social spending and the provision of a safety net for the most vulnerable. During this time, upward social mobility for individuals with lower educated parents increased significantly.

The OECD reports that, since 1975, social mobility has stagnated across the developed world as the inequalities of family income, education, and opportunity have made it harder for many to move up the social ladder. Despite decades of educational reform, schools find they are no longer able to level the playing field for children from disadvantaged backgrounds. Pupils from higher educated parents now have numeracy and literacy scores 20% higher than those with lower educated parents, representing more than three years of additional schooling. Only 10% of people with lower educated parents have a university education compared to 60% of those with higher educated parents. Individuals from middle-income families are now also affected by low rates of social mobility and are more likely to fall into a low-income bracket or experience poverty than 20 years ago.[1]

This has come about due to a huge shift in political and economic thinking, which has driven major changes in government policy. This new, neoliberal paradigm does not view inequality as something to be corrected, but rather as a desirable characteristic of a thriving economy, where hard work, merit, and success are rewarded. Poverty is viewed as a punishment for failure, with no account being given for the disadvantage that keeps many people poor or the advantage that allows others to succeed. This approach advocates for minimal government regulation, reduced public spending, and low taxation. It has led to a move away from the policies of wealth redistribution and has brought significant cuts in welfare spending. This has benefited the wealthy, who have flourished in recent decades, while the disadvantaged have grown in number and inequality has increased across the developed world.[2] Economists have long recognised equality as a key indicator of the success of a nation and have identified how countries become inefficient, unproductive, and unhealthy when wealth distribution is very unequal.

As the gap between rich and poor has grown, the pressures on schools to ensure all children succeed has also increased. During this time, education funding has not kept pace with the increasing demands placed on schools and in some situations has been significantly cut. This has reduced the likelihood that schools can make an impact on the lives of needy students. It has become clear that the way forward is not to find more and different ways for schools to use limited funds to overcome disadvantage but for government policy to focus on removing the barriers that prevent the disadvantaged from succeeding.

In its 2018 report *A Broken Social Elevator*, the OECD recommended a raft of measures that governments should implement to address inequality and improve social mobility across the developed world.[1] While many of these measures focus upon the education sector, they do not place responsibility on schools alone to make a difference. Instead, they set out a comprehensive approach to improve educational opportunities within the context of wider-reaching policies to address inequality directly.

OECD recommendations for improving educational opportunity include increasing access to quality pre-school services, investing more in low performing schools and schools in marginalised communities, and getting the best teachers into these schools. They also include increasing access to extracurricular learning for those from low-income families, managing school choice to avoid segregation, and a raft of proposals to address school drop-out and provide greater access to higher education.

The report emphasises how these measures will only be effective if they are implemented within a context of more holistic policies to tackle disadvantage, however. These include policies to affect wealth accumulation, such as progressive taxation systems and tackling tax avoidance. They also include increased investment in healthcare, to prevent illness affecting an individual's capacity to earn, and the provision of adequate income support for those who are sick, disabled, or unemployed. The report also recommends measures to address regional divides and spatial segregation in cities, which affect an individual's access to work, including improved transport links and quality housing.

If governments can create enabling environments that support people to fulfil their potential, then the pressure on schools to address the attainment gap would be reduced. Until that time, schools are fighting a losing battle as the measures they implement to help level-up society can have only limited impact.

Review Education Funding

While the funding of education is a complex and controversial issue, there is no doubt that recent cuts in public spending have affected schools. In the UK, the Institute of Fiscal Studies reports that there has been a 13-year real-terms freeze in education funding, representing an unprecedented period of, at best, stagnating investment in schools.[3] The National Audit Office confirms that between 2015 and 2020, the cost pressures on mainstream schools exceeded funding increases by £2.2 billion.[4] A 2021 report from the UK National Association of Head Teachers found that overall funding for schools in England was insufficient, with a quarter of headteachers predicting a deficit budget for 2021–22 and a third reporting the need to make cuts to balance their budget in the previous year.[5]

In Australia, it is estimated that by the end of the decade, public schools will be underfunded by AUS$60 million.[6] Data from the United States shows that in 2015 (the most recent year that data is available), 29 states provided less overall state funding per student than in 2008.[7] Public schools in America are collectively underfunded by about US$150 billion every year, with almost two-thirds of the nation's public schools facing a funding gap between what they receive and what they need.[8]

Funding shortfalls translate into the inadequate resourcing of schools, which studies show is a major stressor for school leaders. UK headteachers identify lack of resources as a major factor affecting wellbeing and their intentions to leave the profession.[9] Over the last decade, studies from Australia,[10] New Zealand,[11] and Ireland[12] have also consistently identified resourcing needs as a major stressor, while 90% of Ontario principals find the availability of finite resources to meet demanding constituents to be an issue for them.[13]

The lack of resources affects leaders differently in a range of contexts, but some broad trends are apparent. Three main resourcing issues place considerable strain on headteachers and principals. These are staffing provision, meeting students' mental health needs, and the funding of special educational needs.

Staffing Provision

Issues around staffing provision are a continuous source of stress for school leaders. Principals from Australia,[10] New Zealand,[11] and Ireland[12] consistently identify teacher shortages as one of their major stressors. Two-thirds of principals in Ontario say teacher turnover and lack of replacement teachers have a negative impact on their work.[13]

Teacher shortages are increasing in many developed countries. In the UK, teacher numbers fell 7% between 2015 and 2019, while one in five new teachers left the profession after only two years and 40% within five years. Exit rates have increased for every successive cohort in recent years, with growing numbers leaving to enter other non-teaching professions. This is a greater challenge for schools in disadvantaged areas, where vacancy rates are higher.[14] In Australia, there are also unprecedented teacher shortages, which are nearing crisis point in some states. In New South Wales, almost half of principals reported teacher shortages in 2020, and it is estimated there will be an overall shortfall of 2,425 teachers in the state by 2025.[15]

The cause of the teacher shortage is multidimensional and includes factors such as a growing student population, teachers leaving the profession and a significant decrease in applicants for teacher training programmes. In Australia, universities reported a fall of up to 40% in the number of applicants for initial teacher training between 2015 and 2017.[16] Shortages have also been affected in some countries by the COVID-19 pandemic. A survey carried out by Rand, in January 2021, found that one in four US teachers were likely to leave their jobs by the end of the 2020–21 school year, compared with one in six prior to the pandemic.[17] In California there was a 26% increase in the number of teachers retiring during spring 2020 compared to the previous year.[18]

Most issues affecting the teacher shortage relate back to poor working conditions for teachers. These have made the profession increasingly unattractive to incumbent and prospective teachers alike. In the United States, teacher salaries have been mostly stagnant over the past decade, with a 19% pay gap having developed between teachers and other university educated professionals.[19] Increasing levels of stress is also a key factor driving people away from teaching. Long working hours, low levels of support, insufficient resources, increasing student/teacher ratios and high-stakes accountability are all contributing to an insufficient supply of educators.

To address this, and to create a more stable workforce, governments need to take serious steps to improve the working conditions of teachers, retain the teachers they have and make the profession more attractive to young people. Improving salary and compensation packages is a key part of this, but financial incentives alone are not sufficient to make a real impact. In the UK, recent incentives to encourage teachers into disadvantaged schools have gone largely untapped.[20] Improving working conditions by reducing contact hours; providing access to better resources, including mental health and special education support for students; and reducing class sizes are likely to have a much greater impact. These factors can have a tangible effect on teacher stress, make teaching a more sustainable long-term career and help restore interest in joining the profession. Other factors that governments need to address include rolling back the target-driven culture and improving the quality of teacher training and professional development to provide teachers with the skills they need to cope with the demands of the modern-day classroom.

Meeting Students' Mental Health Needs

In Chapter 2, I discussed the youth mental health crisis and the impact this is having on both teachers and school leaders. Australian principals cite student mental health concerns as their third highest source of stress,[10] while 80% of leaders in Ontario report poor student mental health to be among the most draining situations they encounter.[13] Headteachers and principals are spending a significant number of hours each week managing student behaviour, and behaviour-related issues are closely associated with leaders' intentions to leave the profession.

These issues are exacerbated by the lack of funding to support students' mental health needs.

A 2018 UK report found that over two-thirds of schools faced funding challenges in providing mental health support for pupils. Thirty-nine percent of schools offered no counselling services, while more than half had no specific staffing in place to support student mental health. Where mental health support was available, most schools were able to offer a total of only five hours or less per week. Only 4% of schools said they experienced no barriers to mental health provision.[21]

In Canada, sufficient funding to support students' mental health needs is also a serious concern. A 2017 report found that schools in Ontario had inadequate access to guidance counsellors, educational assistants, psychologists, and other mental health professionals. Only 14% of elementary schools had guidance counsellors, the majority of whom were part-time, working an average of only 1.5 days per week, while only 40% of secondary schools had regularly scheduled access to a psychologist.[22]

Since the onset of the pandemic, increases to mental health funding for schools has made headlines as governments seek to address pandemic-related youth mental health issues. In some countries, the sums involved have drawn criticism from local government and mental health charities. Organisations have expressed concern that ad hoc provision will go nowhere near to addressing years of chronic underfunding or clear the massive backlog of cases waiting to be assessed. There is also scepticism that this flurry of high-profile funding may provide only temporary respite, rather than the long-term, systematic financial support needed to make a real difference.

To make meaningful impact on youth mental health and decrease the pressure on schools, governments need to develop a holistic, multi-agency approach to prevention, support, and treatment. In schools, provision needs to focus on a three-tier approach that begins with mental health promotion for all students. This should focus on social and emotional learning, and mental health literacy programmes, to raise awareness around and destigmatise mental ill health. A second tier of provision needs to be focused on prevention and intervention for students identified as being at risk, with an emphasis on skill-based interventions to help students to cope. A third tier should provide school-based specialised interventions, delivered by mental health professionals, for those diagnosed with mental health conditions.

To facilitate this, governments need to make funding available for the training of school staff and the provision of specialist support. This should include mental health awareness training for all school employees and the inclusion of similar content in initial teacher training programmes. It should also include the training of at least one designated mental health lead in every school, and more in larger schools, as well as the provision of a sufficient number of social emotional counsellors. Finally, all schools should have access to qualified mental health professionals, including mental health nurses and psychologists, who can deliver targeted provision.

In addition to these school-based measures, governments need to improve youth mental health support services in the community. This should include investment in community-based early help and prevention services, where young people can access mental health support without the need for a referral, and families can access information and support. Links between schools and external agencies should also be strengthened. Finally, governments need to review and address the causes of increasing mental ill health among children and young people, with a particular focus on the impact of poverty on the mental health of the young.

Funding of Special Educational Needs

In Chapter 2, I highlighted the increasing demand for special educational needs provision in mainstream schools across the developed world. A lack of appropriate resources to meet students' special educational needs is a growing concern for headteachers and principals and is a significant source of stress. In Ontario, leaders identify lack of special education support and resources as the single most draining thing about their work. Over 80% report lack of special education support for teachers, and a scarcity of teachers with special education expertise, as major issues affecting their work.[13]

A 2020 UK parliamentary report concluded that many children with special educational needs and disabilities were being failed by the system. The report found many schools were struggling to meet students' needs and identified significant, unexplained disparities in the quality of provision. It highlighted the lack of additional local authority funding for mainstream schools and identified the expectation that mainstream schools cover the first £6,000 of extra support costs for each pupil as a major issue.[23]

In the United States, special education provision has also been chronically underfunded for decades. Despite a mandate that federal government meet 40% of special educational needs costs, support has never reached this level and currently stands below 15%. Notwithstanding this shortfall, federal laws require schools to maintain funding levels for special education services, requiring districts to use general funds to support special educational needs, leaving shortfalls elsewhere.[24]

As outlined in Chapter 2, the global shortage of special education teachers also affects provision and brings significant stresses for school leaders. Shortfalls are mainly caused by high turnover rates of staff in what is a high-burnout profession. Heavy workloads, low pay, lack of support, and professional isolation all contribute to specialist teachers leaving the profession at much higher rates than other teachers.[25] Significant numbers of mainstream teachers report feeling inadequately prepared to support students' special educational needs,[26] and many governments lack a coherent plan to include sufficient preparation as part of initial teacher training or post-qualification professional development programmes.

In recent years, many governments have carried out large-scale reviews of special education provision, and additional funding has been made available. As with mental health support, the sums involved are viewed by many as insufficient to overcome the impact of chronic, long-term underfunding coupled with increasing demand for services.

To make real progress in this area, central governments need to implement cohesive, long-term plans to provide and fund good-quality universal services for children and young people with special educational needs, across education, health, and wider children's services. This includes adequate funding for special education programmes and services in schools and the streamlining of such funding to make it less complex. Governments need to allocate sufficient finance to train more specialist teachers and direct funds to improve working conditions, to keep special needs educators in the profession. There is also a growing need to train all new mainstream teachers to be competent and confident in the delivery of special education provision and ensure that all teachers have regular, compulsory training that combines theory with experience in inclusive settings. Finally, research shows that not only is the number of students with special educational needs growing but an increasingly disproportionate number of these students are from disadvantaged backgrounds.[27] Governments need to commission research to enable them to understand what is causing the huge increase in students presenting at school with special educational needs and tackle the root causes of the trend.

Address the High-Stakes Accountability Culture

Since the introduction of school-based management in the 1960s, state schools have become increasingly accountable to government through top-down accountability mechanisms based around the close monitoring of student, teacher, and school performance data. Education policy is underpinned by the idea that this practice can contribute directly to improvements in academic outcomes for students and ensure that society receives the maximum benefit from publicly funded education.

This accountability places schools under considerable pressure and increases teacher and leader stress. A 2012 study from the United States found being constantly accountable was one of the top five stressors for teachers,[28] while the annual UK Teacher Wellbeing Index has consistently found the target-driven culture to be a major factor influencing teachers' and leaders' decisions to leave the profession.[9]

Studies highlight several ways in which accountability affects teachers' and leaders' stress. Uncertainty around the results of accountability measures leads to high levels of anxiety for many educators[29] and can damage the atmosphere of the workplace as the contagion of emotions causes stress to spread among colleagues.[30] This may lead to increased workplace conflict and reduced morale. For headteachers and principals, the pressure of accountability may change the way they lead and cause them to pass pressure down the chain or engage in micromanagement to maintain control. This can affect relationships with staff and negatively affect the workplace culture.[31]

Data-driven accountability also affects teachers' autonomy in the classroom. The maximisation of student outcomes across a small range of subjects erodes the time and resources available for non-tested subjects and

forces teachers to teach to the test.[32] Schools may become focused dispro-
portionally on students who are close to the accountability threshold, which
may lead to lack of support for students with special educational needs or
lost opportunities to provide deeper learning for the most able.[33] High-stakes
accountability also allows less time to focus on the needs of the whole child
and provide students with a well-rounded education. These factors may
cause some teachers and leaders to lose touch with their purpose as an educator and become disenchanted with the work. Accountability measures
are also associated with excessive paperwork and administration, which
increases workloads for teachers and leaders.

These factors mean that accountability can contribute significantly to
teacher and school leader stress and burnout. It may also affect job performance, engagement, motivation, and job satisfaction, and may also have
negative consequences for teacher and leader retention.[34] While accountability measures can bring short-term improvements to student outcomes,
governments need to be aware that these approaches may prove to be
counterproductive in the longer term, as the effectiveness and supply of
teachers and school leaders are negatively affected. The higher the stakes
are for schools, the more these unintended effects of accountability are
likely to occur.

To address this, governments should consider alternative accountability
frameworks, that would remove the current high-stakes measures, or combine them with other forms of data and feedback that are less hierarchical. A multi-pronged approach that includes process-oriented measures and
horizontal structures could be highly beneficial, reducing stress and providing a richer picture of a school's performance.

Process-oriented measures allow schools to be evaluated from multiple
angles, using a much wider range of standards and criteria. This can involve
not only quantitative measures but also qualitative data, narratives, reports,
observations, and self-assessment. Such approaches have the potential to
significantly decrease teacher and school leader stress and reignite their
passion for their work. They could also benefit students, by reducing the
negative consequences of test-based accountability. Horizontal accountability provides opportunities for a wide range of stakeholders to have
input, including experts, critical friends, parents, students, partner schools,
and the local community. This approach provides an opportunity to
capture factors that are hard to quantify. It makes schools accountable
to multiple stakeholders and provides a more collaborative approach, as
teachers, leaders, and the school and wider community work together to
ensure schools are held accountable for providing the best, well-rounded
education.

Review the School Leaders' Role

As discussed in Chapter 1, the headteachers' and principals' role has expanded significantly in recent decades, becoming more complex, wide-ranging, and challenging. To reduce school leader stress and minimise the risk of burnout, governments should review the headteacher and principal role, in consultation with school leaders, to enable them to understand the challenges that they face in the daily running of their schools. Governments need to consider how school leadership may be reconceptualised and updated to reflect the work of the 21st-century school. They should also examine how more support may be provided for leaders to help them to manage their work demands more effectively.

The current model of school leadership is based on the traditional, hierarchical model of sole headship or principalship. There are, however, many ways in which the power and responsibility of school leadership can be dispersed beyond the sole headteacher or principal. Governments should consider whether moving away from sole leadership, and increasing leadership capacity in schools, might provide leadership structures more able to meet the demands faced by schools.

In many education systems, the structure of school leadership is decided at school level by those responsible for school governance. In others, it is the responsibility of local or central government to determine leadership structures. In all systems, government should invest more in research to determine the most effective models of school leadership, for a wide range of different contexts, and be open to and encouraging of alternative leadership structures in schools. They should also provide more information for schools on the benefits, drawbacks, and practicalities of implementing alternative approaches to leadership and include this information in school governance training programmes. In Chapter 8, I examine in more detail how schools might expand leadership capacity and disperse leadership beyond the headteacher or principal.

Provide Support for School Leaders

Governments have a key role to play in providing support for school leaders, to enable them to cope with the daily demands of their role. In the wake and aftermath of the pandemic, many governments have allocated funds to support school leader mental health and wellbeing. In most, however, the amounts involved are small and initiatives ad hoc, rather than part of a more comprehensive strategy to address the wellbeing of leaders.

In Australia, a small number of states, including Victoria and Queensland, have developed comprehensive principal health and wellbeing strategies. This is in direct response to issues identified by the Australian Principal Occupational Health, Safety and Wellbeing Survey, which has made clear recommendations to government to reduce principal stress and burnout. Victoria's Principal Health and Wellbeing Strategy 2018–22 was developed in collaboration with the authors of the survey and representatives from the profession. Over the initial four-year period, $51 million was invested with a goal of extending and expanding initiatives into ongoing services for principals. These initiatives include a principal mentor programme, which connects principals with an experienced retired principal mentor. They also include a raft of measures to support leaders' health, such as voluntary, free, and confidential health checks and access to wider health and wellbeing services, including psychological support and physical therapy. The strategy also offers practical support for leaders, in the form of a hotline and intervention team to support with complex matters, expert advice in human resources and workforce matters, and a school policy templates portal. A similar strategy, implemented recently by Queensland, has included wellbeing coaching for principals, training in stress management, the development of peer support networks and improved induction training and resources for new leaders.

An independent evaluation of the Victoria initiatives has found them to be working effectively to promote and address the mental and physical health of principals. These findings are consistent with the results of the most recent Australian Principal Occupational Health, Safety and Wellbeing Survey, which shows Victoria to be the only state to report reduced levels of stress and burnout and improved health for leaders.[35]

Governments elsewhere can learn from the early successes of Victoria. They should seek to develop comprehensive strategies and allocate appropriate levels of funding to support meaningful initiatives to support school leader wellbeing.

Improve Training and Professional Development

It is widely acknowledged that the training of school leaders often fails to prepare them for the breadth and complexity of their role. In many countries there is no systematic pre-service training and preparation for headteachers and principals and what is available is often of poor quality. A report by the Wallace Foundation highlights how training has failed to keep pace with the evolving role of principals, affecting their capacity to manage the cognitive and emotional demands of the work.[36] The

Australian Principal Occupational Health, Safety and Wellbeing Survey also identifies inadequate training in the emotional aspects of the role as being a major concern.[10] They recommend governments provide initial and in-service training for leaders in managing the emotional demands of the job. This should include training in debriefing self and others, as occurs in other emotionally demanding professions, such as psychology and social work. They also recommend a focus on building and maintaining positive relationships, developing effective communication skills, and dealing with workplace conflict.

Principal and headteacher training also fails to provide leaders with tools to manage their mental health and wellbeing and support that of others. In 2020, 85% of UK headteachers said they felt their training had not prepared them to manage their own mental health, while three-quarters felt unprepared to support the wellbeing of students and staff.[9] Crisis leadership is another area where training is severely lacking. In my 2020 study on school leadership during the pandemic, 42% of leaders said they received no crisis leadership training prior to 2020. Governments should mandate that training in these vital areas be included in headteacher and principal preparation courses and be made compulsory for all new leaders.

Many leaders find there are obstacles preventing them from receiving professional development training, including lack of time and funds. This is an area that can easily be addressed by government, through the provision and ring-fencing of funds specifically allocated for headteacher and principal training. In North Carolina, for example, the Principal Fellows programme supports a master's degree and yearlong internship under the supervision of a veteran principal, the cost of which is paid back in service and may be offered in exchange for a commitment to serve in a high-poverty or rural school. Compulsory study-leave for leaders involved in longer-term programmes, such as master's degrees and doctorates, should also be considered.

Tackle School Leader Abuse

In Chapter 2, I discussed the offensive behaviour that school leaders are subjected to by students, staff, parents, supervisors, and members of the general community. Leaders are subjected to slander, gossip, and bullying, with the growth of social media bringing an increase in this kind of abuse. Headteachers and principals are also victims of violence and threats of violence, mostly at the hands of students and parents. In some countries there is a general cultural of disrespect towards the teaching profession that is encouraged by elements of the media. This has grown during the pandemic, with teachers feeling they have been misunderstood and presented as villains, while headteachers and principals have borne the brunt of parents' anger and frustration around pandemic-related issues. This kind of abuse and antipathy towards the teaching profession can have a significant impact on the stress levels of teachers and school leaders.

Governments need to take offensive behaviour towards educators more seriously, rather than just accepting that abuse comes with the work. The Australian Principal Occupational Health, Safety and Wellbeing Survey recommends that governments establish an independent authority to investigate adult-on-adult bullying, threats of violence, and actual violence towards school principals. This investigation would establish which types of leaders are most at risk and what can be done to protect them.[10]

Most developed countries already have comprehensive legislation in place around the prevention and treatment of workplace abuse. At the very least, local authorities should work with schools to raise awareness of this legislation and support them in fulfilling their statutory duties. This would include guidance and resources to enable schools to carry out their own risk assessments and develop policies, protocols, and practices around the prevention of abuse. Governments should also ensure that teachers and school leaders are provided with regular training on how to manage abusive situations. This should include raising awareness of rights, guidance on responding to and reporting abuse, and providing support for victims. Schools also need guidance and resources on how to work with their communities to reduce offensive behaviour and online harassment. Finally, the provision of appropriate funding and measures to support students' mental health and special educational needs, discussed earlier in the chapter, would lead to a reduction in the abuse of teachers and leaders by students.

Chapter Summary

- Governments can play a huge role in decreasing school leader stress and preventing the burnout of headteachers and principals.
- Government policies that focus on addressing inequality and disadvantage would alleviate the pressure on schools to reduce the attainment gap.
- Cuts in education spending are affecting the resourcing of schools, placing leaders under considerable pressure. Governments need to take steps to address the teacher shortage, develop comprehensive approaches to support the mental health needs of children and young people, and improve funding to meet students' special educational needs.
- High-stakes accountability brings major stressors for leaders and their staff. Governments should consider moving away from product-based,

top-down accountability and explore a range of broader measures, including process-oriented and horizontal approaches.
- The school leader's role has changed beyond recognition in recent decades and the sole leadership model no longer fits the demands of the work. Governments need to commission research into more effective leadership models and provide schools with information and support to transform leadership to meet the needs of modern-day schools.
- Governments can play a key role in supporting the wellbeing of headteachers and principals. Governments should develop comprehensive, strategic frameworks to improve the wellbeing of leaders, coupled with appropriate levels of funding. Strategies such as those being implemented in Victoria, Australia, can act as a model for governments elsewhere.
- Headteacher and principal training has long been considered inadequate to prepare leaders for the demands of the role. Governments need to ensure that all leaders are provided with comprehensive preparation and ongoing professional development to help them develop the skills they need to carry out their work effectively. This includes training around the emotional aspects of the work, relationship building, supporting the wellbeing of self and others, and crisis leadership.
- School leader abuse is a growing problem around the world. Governments need to take this issue more seriously, investigate the causes and extent of abuse, and takes steps to address it. They should start by ensuring that schools are supported to implement existing legislation around the treatment and prevention of workplace abuse.

Notes

1 Organisation for Economic Co-operation and Development (OECD), 2018. *The Broken Social Elevator?: How to Promote Social Mobility*. OECD.
2 Thévenot, C., 2017. Inequality in OECD Countries. *Scandinavian Journal of Public Health*, 45(18_suppl), 9–16.
3 Institute for Fiscal Studies (IFS), 2021. *Annual Report on Education Spending in England*. London: IFS.
4 National Audit Office (NAO), 2021. *School Funding in England*. London: NA.
5 National Association of Head Teachers (NAHT), 2021. *A Failure to Invest: The State of School Funding in 2021*. London: NAHT.
6 Cobbold, T., 2021. Private Schools Brawl to Get Their Snouts Deeper in the Funding Trough. *SOS Australia*. Accessed online https://saveourschools.com.au/funding/private-schools-brawl-to-get-their-snouts-deeper-in-the-funding-trough/#more-4966.

7 Leachman, M., Masterson, K. and Figueroa, E., 2017. *A Punishing Decade for School Funding*. Washington, DC: Center on Budget and Policy Priorities.

8 The Century Foundation, 2021. Closing America's Funding Gaps. Accessed online https://tcf.org/content/report/closing-americas-education-funding/.

9 Savill-Smith, C., 2019. *Teacher Wellbeing Index*. London: Education Support.

10 Riley, P., See, S.M., Marsh, H. and Dicke, T., 2021. *The Australian Principal Occupational Health, Safety and Wellbeing Survey 2020*. Sydney: Institute for Positive Psychology and Education, Australian Catholic University.

11 Riley, P., Rahimi, M. and Arnold, B., 2021. *The New Zealand Primary Principal Occupational Health, Safety and Wellbeing Survey 2020*. Melbourne: Research for Educational Impact (REDI), Deakin University.

12 Riley, P., 2015. *Irish Principals' and Deputy Principals' Occupational Health, Safety and Wellbeing Survey*. Melbourne: Research for Educational Impact (REDI), Deakin University.

13 Pollock, K. and Wang, F., 2020. *School Principals' Work and Well-Being in Ontario: What They Say and Why It Matters*. Toronto, ON: Western University.

14 Sibieta, L., 2020. *Teacher Shortages in England*. London: Education Policy Institute.

15 Baker, J., 2021. Public School Teacher Shortage Raises Fears They Will 'Run Out of Teachers.' *Sydney Morning Herald*, 7 October. Accessed online www.smh.com.au/national/nsw/public-school-teacher-shortage-raises-fears-they-will-run-out-of-teachers-20211003-p58wtq.html.

16 Australian Institute for Teaching and School Leadership (AITSL), 2019. *Initial Teacher Education Data Report*. Sydney: AITSL.

17 Steiner, E. and Woo, A., 2021. *State of the US Teacher Survey*. Washington, DC: Rand Corporation.

18 California State Teachers' Retirement System, 2021. Understanding the Increase in Teacher Retirements. Accessed online www.calstrs.com.

19 Alegretto, S. and Mischel, L., 2020. *Teacher Pay Penalty Dips But Persists in 2019*. Washington, DC: Economic Policy Institute.

20 Allen, A. and MacInerney, L., 2019. *The Recruitment Gap*. London: Sutton Trust.

21 Brown, R., 2018. *Mental Health and Wellbeing Provision in Schools*. London: Department for Education.

22 People for Education, 2017. *Competing Priorities (Annual Report on Ontario's Publicly Funded Schools 2017)*. Toronto, ON: People for Education.

23 Long, R., Roberts, N. and Danechi, S., 2020. *Special Educational Needs: Support in England*. London: House of Commons Library.

24 Dragoo, K., 2019. *The Individuals with Disabilities Education Act (IDEA) Funding: A Primer*. Washington, DC: Congressional Research Service.

25 National Coalition of Personnel Shortages in Special Education and Related Services. Accessed online https://specialedshortages.org/about-the-shortage/.

26 Warnes, E., Done, E. and Knowler, H., 2022. Mainstream Teachers' Concerns about Inclusive Education for Children with Special Educational Needs and

Disability in England under Pre-pandemic Condition. *Journal of Research in Special Educational Needs*, 22(1), 31–43.

27 Shaw, B., Bernardes, E., Trethewey, A. and Menzies, L., 2016. *Special Educational Needs and Their Links to Poverty*. London: Joseph Rowntree Foundation.

28 Richards, J., 2012. Teacher Stress and Coping Strategies: A National Snapshot. *The Educational Forum*, 76(3), 299–316.

29 Grupe, D. and Nitschke, J., 2013. Uncertainty and Anticipation in Anxiety. An Integrated Neurobiological and Psychological Perspective. *Nature Reviews Neuroscience*, 14(7), 488–501.

30 Hatfield, E., Bensman, L., Thornton, P. and Rapson, R., 2014. New Perspectives on Emotional Contagion: A Review of Classic and Recent Research on Facial Mimicry and Contagion. *Interpersonal: An International Journal on Personal Relationships*, 8, 159–179.

31 Jerrim, J. and Sims, S., 2022. School Accountability and Teacher Stress: International Evidence from the OECD TALIS Study. *Ed Educational Assessment, Evaluation and Accountability*, 34, 5–32.

32 Donnelly, L.A. and Sadler, T.D., 2009. High School Science Teachers' Views of Standards and Accountability. *Science Education*, 93, 1050–1075.

33 Jones, B.D. and Egley, R.J., 2004. Voices from the Frontlines: Teachers' Perceptions of High-stakes Testing. *Education Policy Analysis Archives*, 12(39).

34 Lynch, S., 2016. *Engaging Teachers: NFER Analysis of Teacher Retention*. London: National Foundation for Educational Research.

35 See, S.-M., Kidson, P., Marsh, H. and Dicke, T., 2022. *The Australian Principal Occupational Health, Safety and Wellbeing Survey 2021*. Sydney: Institute for Positive Psychology and Education, Australian Catholic University.

36 The Wallace Foundation, 2015. *Building Principal Pipelines*. New York, NY: The Wallace Foundation.

What Schools Can Do   8

A Strategic Approach to Prevent School Leader Burnout

In the previous chapter I discussed comprehensive steps that governments can take to address headteacher and principal stress and reduce the risk of burnout. The key changes needed to redress the deep-seated flaws endemic in our education systems will take years, if not decades, to make an impact. Schools can make a meaningful difference to the working conditions of their leaders much more quickly. While some schools understand the importance of staff wellbeing to the success of their organisation and wish to make lasting improvement, many are looking for a quick fix that involves the adoption of piecemeal actions, which have no long-term effects. Worthwhile change can only come about using strategic approaches to headteacher and principal wellbeing, driven or supported by governance and leadership.

In this chapter, I set out a strategic approach to improve leader wellbeing called the School Leader Wellbeing Framework. This framework is a blueprint for schools to improve the working conditions of their leadership teams. It can be used by any school, in any context, to make a real and lasting difference to the mental health and wellbeing of school leaders. The framework will allow schools to reduce leader stress and help mitigate the risk of burnout. While the context of this book is headteacher and principal wellbeing, the framework can be modified to be used with all staff. Improvements to the wellbeing of school leaders will be most effective if they come within the context of a strategy to maximise wellbeing for all staff. The information contained in this chapter can also be used by individual school leaders to help them advocate to supervisors for improvement in their working conditions.

The School Leader Wellbeing Framework is built around a six-stage process. It begins with preparing the ground, identifying needs, and setting goals. It then moves on to designing and implementing interventions to

DOI: 10.4324/9781003198475-11

improve working conditions and evaluating progress. The six stages are as follows.

1   Laying Foundations
2   Educating Stakeholders
3   Gaining Insights
4   Setting Goals
5   Planning and Implementing Interventions
6   Evaluating Interventions and Tracking Progress

Laying Foundations

To establish a successful strategic approach to improve school leader wellbeing, it is important that the process is effectively led and managed. In all but the smallest schools, a steering group or committee should be formed that comprises representatives from multiple stakeholder groups. This sends a message to the whole community that school leader wellbeing is a priority for the school and allows for a range of perspectives. Ideally, a school will already have a Staff Wellbeing Team in place that should include leader wellbeing as part of its remit. If not then a group may be formed to guide work on improving leader wellbeing. This group should include representatives from governance, the leadership team, and human resources staff. Where possible, it should also include parent and staff representatives. At the start, the culture of the school and the levels of trust and comfort may not allow for this. Where this is the case, schools can move towards greater community involvement as awareness around the importance of leader wellbeing grows.

The steering group should have a clearly defined purpose and terms of reference to guide members. Roles within the group should be allocated, and regular meeting time should be determined preferably during the school day. The group, its membership, and its purpose should be shared with the whole school community, to clarify and raise the profile of its work.

Educating Stakeholders

The next element of the framework focuses on educating the school community around the importance of school leader wellbeing, to ensure that all stakeholder groups understand and support the need for improvement. This involves drawing on research that highlights the key role that headteachers and principals play in the success of schools and the link between their wellbeing and job performance. It also involves raising awareness around the value to the school of retaining leaders and the connection between leader wellbeing and retention.

There is a substantial body of evidence to suggest that the quality of school leadership is key to a school's success. Leadership plays a significant role in student engagement, academic outcomes,[1] staff motivation and commitment, and effective school organisation.[2]

> As far as we are aware, there is not a single documented case of a school successfully turning around its pupil achievement trajectory in the absence of talented leadership. One explanation for this is that leadership serves as a catalyst for unleashing the potential capacities that already exist in the organisation.[2]

Numerous studies also highlight the impact of employee health on job performance, in a range of contexts. Workers with good health have more energy,[3] superior concentration skills, make better decisions, complete tasks more effectively,[4] demonstrate greater levels of resilience, and are more reliable.[5]

School leadership is a high-pressure job which involves daily complex problem-solving, working at a fast pace and with high levels of unpredictability. It also requires nuanced people leadership skills and emotional intelligence. To carry out this work effectively, schools need their leaders to be in peak condition. Work-related stress is associated with coping less well with workplace pressure, uncertainty, and change.[6] Stressed workers are also more likely to engage in incivility towards colleagues[7] or get involved in workplace bullying.[8] In a recent UK study, 40% of senior leaders said that their job performance had suffered because of work-related stress or mental ill health.[9]

Stress and ill health also affect an employee's rates of absenteeism. In the UK in 2019–20, stress, depression, or anxiety accounted for 55% of all working days lost due to work-related ill health and were the biggest causes of long-term absence from work.[10] A fifth of UK headteachers said they have taken time off work in the past year because of work-related ill-health problems.[12] This kind of absenteeism comes at great cost to schools, both financially and organisationally.

A growing body of research into the incidence and effects of presenteeism shows how attending work when ill can affect an organisation at least as much as absenteeism. A study by Unilever found the impact of employees attending work when highly stressed, or suffering from depression, anxiety, or a sleep disorder, accounted for three times as much lost productivity as absence from work.[11] The high levels of commitment that school leaders feel towards their work means they are more likely to go in to work when they are highly stressed or experiencing physical or mental ill health. This is confirmed by a recent UK study, which found that 87% of headteachers feel compelled to go into work when they are unwell.[12]

Work-related stress has been linked to poor employee retention across a wide range of professions.[12] In 2021, two-thirds of UK senior leaders said they had considered leaving the profession in the previous two years due to concerns about their health and wellbeing.[12] Studies indicate that unplanned headteacher or principal turnover is one of the most common sources of a school's failure to improve, negatively affecting a range of school improvement initiatives. The effects of school leader turnover most notably include losses in student achievement and increased teacher turnover, with teachers more likely to leave a school that has recently lost its headteacher or principal.[13] These impacts have been shown to continue for the first three years of a new leader's tenure, and the effects become compounded if a school loses multiple heads or principals in succession.[14]

Schools need to make their communities aware of these facts and facilitate conversations about the importance of headteacher and principal wellbeing to the school's success. The aim is to move towards a culture where school leader stress is seen as an occupational risk that needs to be addressed in the same way as other health and safety hazards. This helps remove the stigma that leaders feel when they experience work-related stress, encouraging them to seek support before stress becomes unmanageable. Most importantly, it places responsibility on the school, as employer, to reduce headteacher and principal stress and treat leader wellbeing as an investment.

Most schools find it hard to justify the expense of initiatives to improve school leader wellbeing, but the big picture reasons to do so are compelling. Once stakeholders are educated to understand the benefits that healthy headteachers and principals can bring to their school, it is much easier for them to see leader wellbeing as an investment. Those doubting the return on investment of employee wellbeing initiatives can look to studies from outside the field of education. These show how companies promoting best practice in employee health and wellbeing have outperformed the stock market by around 2%–3% per year over a 25-year period and are 3.5 times more likely to be creative and innovative than other companies.[15] A large-scale review by Deloitte of 125 reports about workplace mental health interventions found that, on average, for every £1 spent on supporting employees' mental health, employers get £5 back on their investment in increased productivity, reduced absenteeism and presenteeism, and improved staff retention.[16]

There is also evidence to show that a focus on employee wellbeing is likely to enhance a company's brand in the employment market. Research from the UK has found that workers increasingly need to feel happy with the work-life balance offered by companies before they accept a job offer.

Companies that have a corporate wellbeing strategy have a better chance of attracting top candidates and retaining staff, rather than losing them to competitors.[17] For schools, which trade upon being friendly and caring, a focus upon employee health and wellbeing gives depth to these claims and provides a way to stand out in a competitive marketplace.

Educating stakeholders not only involves informing the school community about the value of leader wellbeing but also raises awareness of the importance of self-care for leaders. The headteacher's and principal's role involves supporting the needs of others, and in doing so, leaders often lose sight of the need to care for themselves. Many leaders think they do not have time for self-care or feel that they should not need it. There may be a stigma attached to the necessity to take care of oneself, as this can sometimes be seen as a sign of weakness. Deepening understanding around the potential effects of stress and burnout on leaders, and the consequences for schools, provides an opportunity for leaders and their communities to view self-care as an investment in sustained leadership.

Overcoming the stigma associated with self-care and the habit of prioritising the needs of others can be challenging. While some headteachers and principals are prepared to take the bold step of setting new parameters to ensure that self-care is possible, most need support with this. It is essential that governance and leadership teams shift thinking around headteacher and principal self-care so that it is viewed as a key leadership attribute and an essential part of leadership development.

Gaining Insights

Gaining Insights is the third part of the School Leader Wellbeing Framework. This involves drawing on leaders' perceptions and experiences to get to the heart of what is affecting their stress and wellbeing, as well as reviewing policies and practices. An insight-driven strategy is much more effective than taking a generalised approach, as it allows for the specific issues of a school and its leaders to be addressed with targeted interventions.

There are five main ways to gain insights into school leader health and wellbeing. These are administering a tailored school leader wellbeing survey, carrying out regular wellbeing check-ins with leaders, conducting focus groups, analysing human resources data, and reviewing school policies.

School Leader Wellbeing Survey

The most efficient format for gathering headteacher and principal insights is a school leader wellbeing survey. Staff wellbeing surveys have grown in popularity in recent years and many schools conduct annual surveys or more regular pulse surveys. It is important that schools also use a survey tailored to the needs of leaders as issues affecting leaders may be different to those of other employees. This provides headteachers and principals with the opportunity to reflect on their individual experience, the organisational culture, and the school's policies and practices and how these affect their health and wellbeing. A survey will identify the key issues and also provide benchmarking data.

This book includes School Leader Wellbeing Insights, a survey designed for schools to gain an understanding of their leaders' needs. This is an instrument specifically tailored to identify leaders' needs and draws on research about the causes of school leader stress and burnout. It is built around the six areas of work associated with burnout, discussed in Chapter 6. School Leader Wellbeing Insights is divided into three sections: School Leader Experiences, School Culture, and Mental Health Awareness and Support.

The first section is designed to gain insights into a participant's daily work experience. Excessive workload demands can be a major source of stress for leaders and are a major contributor to burnout. The survey enables schools to understand the extent of a leader's workload, their perceptions of its manageability, and their work-life balance. It also identifies issues with role clarity and job-person fit. Where there is a mismatch between how a leader perceives their role and how others define it, there is potential for stress and exhaustion to develop. Likewise, an imbalance between the requirements of the role and the capacity of a leader to carry it out can contribute significantly to stress and burnout.

Lack of control over work is another area closely associated with stress and burnout. If the level of autonomy needed to do the job, or expected by a leader, differs from that provided, then an individual will be more vulnerable to burnout. The survey explores the level of autonomy granted to leaders by supervisors, as well as control over working hours and the predictability of a leader's day.

Issues around rewards and fairness can also create stress for leaders and leave them vulnerable to burnout. This section of the survey explores leaders' perceptions around remuneration, evaluation procedures, professional learning, and career development. Other aspects of rewards and fairness are considered in the School Culture section.

The second section of the survey is designed to gain insights into the culture of the school as an organisation and as a workplace. It focuses on understanding imbalances in the areas of community, values, and rewards. School culture is determined by its community's shared beliefs, expectations, language, customs, habits, and attitudes. It determines how its leaders, staff, students, parents, and other stakeholders, think, feel, and behave.

Relationships with colleagues have been identified as the single factor most associated with school leader burnout. A positive workplace culture plays a key role in fostering strong collegial relationships, respectful interactions, trust and a sense of belonging. Lack of community and leader isolation may be highly damaging to an individual, while a positive workplace culture not only builds community but can mitigate against imbalances in other areas of work life.

The emphasis that a school places on shared values also supports a leader's wellbeing. Values are key drivers for many leaders and a mismatch between their values and those of the school as an organisation, the school community, or the leadership team can place a leader under considerable strain. A positive workplace culture will enhance a leader's sense of purpose and allow them to feel valued and appreciated. This internal and external validation are important rewards for any school leader and can contribute significantly to their wellbeing.

The final section of School Leader Wellbeing Insights focuses upon school-based mental health support for headteachers and principals. It addresses mental health awareness and assesses the extent to which mental health is on the agenda of a school. A 2020 study, which surveyed over 4,000 office workers globally, found that while over two-thirds of employers believe they provide good access to health and wellness support, only a quarter of employees agree. It is, therefore, essential that schools gain insights on leaders' perspectives.[18] This section finishes with six questions designed to assess the current vulnerability to burnout of participants, adapted from the Maslach Burnout Inventory.[19]

There are important factors to consider before conducting any employee wellbeing survey. It is essential to develop a plan before the survey is administered, which should address the following questions.

- Who will oversee the administration of the survey?
- Who will take part in the survey?
- How frequently will the survey be conducted and at what time(s) of the year?
- How will data be collected?
- How will participants be guaranteed anonymity or confidentiality?
- How will data be analysed, collated, and presented and by whom?
- How will the results be shared, and who will they be shared with?
- How will the school follow up on and respond to the results of the survey? What will be the time frame for this?
- How will the school track the progress of interventions implemented following the survey?

School Leader Wellbeing Insights is primarily intended for senior leadership teams. It is important that the survey is, where possible, a collaborative process supported by the whole SLT. To create support for the survey, it is essential that all SLT members understand the purpose of the survey, how it will be conducted, how and when they will receive feedback on the results, and what steps will be taken to act on the findings. This will ensure higher participation rates and increase the chances that participants will answer questions honestly.

Ideally, the administration of the survey will be overseen by a neutral party, such as the human resources (HR) department or an independent consultant. Where schools do not have an HR team or another neutral party to take charge of the process, a member of the SLT or governance team can be appointed as administrator.

The level of confidentiality of the survey is a key issue for consideration. The survey can be visible, where the administrator can see each participant's name. It can be confidential, where names are not visible but other identifiers may be known, such as the section of the school where a participant works. It may also be anonymous, where all participant identifiers are completely unknown by the administrator. Schools should expect this to be an issue with participants as, even where there is a high level of trust and openness, individuals may feel that the survey has potential to expose them. In an environment where there is mistrust, leaders may be fearful that their responses will render them vulnerable to reprisals. It is better to guarantee participants anonymity if there is to be a high level of honest engagement.

There are three main ways to guarantee anonymity to participants. The first is through the use of an external third-party consultant. While there are many other advantages of using a consultant, this is not something all schools can afford. In a culture of very low trust, however, some may feel that even this approach can be open to abuse. Using a consultant with a solid reputation in the industry should help allay these fears. Anonymity can also be secured with the use of technology. For example, if access to the survey is provided via a link placed on a web page or sent via an instant messaging group, rather than through email, then users cannot be identified when they access the survey. Finally, anonymity can be ensured using a paper survey, which can be printed by the user from a common link or can be collected from a common pile. Paper-based surveys bring additional work in collecting and analysing data, however, which may be problematic when there are many participants.

Clearly, schools with very small SLTs will struggle to ensure anonymity of participants. This is something that should be discussed openly by the leadership team before embarking on the survey. In low trust environments, a survey may have limited success in gaining real insights from small teams. Ways around this might involve including middle leaders in the survey to widen the pool of participants and make anonymity easier to secure. Focusing on building trust and openness, to allow leaders to be honest about their challenges, is the ideal way forward, but this can take time.

Regular Check-Ins

In addition to a wellbeing survey, regular check-ins with leaders can provide useful, informal insights into their wellbeing. These may include conversations around wellbeing that take place during appraisal, mentoring or coaching meetings, or regular leadership meetings. It is important to preserve the confidentiality of issues discussed in such meetings and share the content of discussions only with a leader's consent.

Focus Groups

Focus groups are particularly useful in schools that have large leadership teams, or in groups of schools, although they can also be used in smaller schools. They can enable a school to obtain rich, qualitative data, in a short space of time, using open-ended questions. They are an effective way to gather information on leader wellbeing or receive feedback on a particular wellbeing-related topic. They can also be used to generate and develop ideas among a group of leaders.

There are several considerations for planning a focus group. Firstly, it is crucial to establish a safe environment for participants to speak freely. This involves establishing ground rules and ensuring they are adhered to. If it is a one-off session, then a group agreement should be discussed at the start of the session, while for a regular forum, terms of reference will need to be put in place. Agreements or terms should include clear guidance and commitments around confidentiality and establish an understanding of how the data gleaned from the sessions will be used.

Focus group participants can be invited to attend or may volunteer, but they must feel comfortable with each other. Focus groups usually work best with between six and ten participants per group, but they can be smaller, while groups larger than ten are not recommended. Sessions are usually moderated by a facilitator and attended by a note-taker, or the session can be audio- or video-recorded, with the participants' consent.

Using Human Resources Data

Valuable insights may be obtained from a review of human resources data. This may include absenteeism rates, use of employer-provided healthcare, rate of leader turnover, and exit interview records. This data should always be treated with inviolable confidentiality, which may only be achieved by anonymising information. Where this is not possible, or in schools with small leadership teams, the use of such data may be inadvisable.

Policy Review

A review of relevant school policies can provide clarity about what kind of support is already in place for leaders and what is missing. Policies reviewed should include those that cover leader health and wellbeing provision, appraisal, disciplinary matters, and recruitment and retention. Policies covering sickness absence and leave entitlements, opportunities for flexible working, professional development, and measures to ensure equality, diversity, and inclusion should also be reviewed. The review should include leaders' contracts of employment, job descriptions, and any other documents pertaining to duties and working conditions.

Setting Goals

Once insights have been gained, the real work begins. Setting Goals is about identifying and establishing priorities to improve leader wellbeing. This involves agreeing the type of interventions that may be needed and the process by which they will be designed and delivered. The types of interventions that schools may decide to implement are discussed in later chapters. Setting effective goals depends upon having a solid understanding of school leaders' needs. Priorities should flow naturally from the data gathered during Gaining Insights. Data should be analysed and priorities determined in collaboration or consultation with the SLT. In schools with large leadership teams, or in groups of schools, it may be necessary to develop a communication strategy to ensure all leaders can become involved.

High-level priorities should be included in the school's strategic plan. Goals and tasks should be clearly defined, taking account of the school's organisational systems and structures and the resources available. Specific tasks should be assigned to members of the steering committee, the leadership and governance teams, or to relevant others, such as human resources or finance staff.

Planning and Implementing Interventions

Once goals are set, the next stage involves designing and implementing interventions. The detail of design and delivery will depend on the nature of the interventions, the size and structure of the school, and the time and budget available. Some schools will prefer to design and deliver interventions in-house, sometimes with the support of a specialist consultant, while others may use external providers for at least some of their interventions. If the leadership team is large, it is important that a communication plan ensures leaders know what interventions are available to them and how to get involved, to ensure high participation rates. In Chapters 9, 10, and 11, I discuss interventions that schools might consider.

Evaluating Interventions and Tracking Progress

Evaluation is an essential step in helping schools understand the impact or value of an intervention. Evaluation needs to be considered during Setting Goals and Planning and Implementing Interventions to ensure that evaluation methods are built into each intervention and that baseline data is gathered to enable before and after comparisons.

To evaluate an intervention, it is first necessary to determine exactly what the intervention consists of, how it is meant to work, and the anticipated effects.

Evaluation will most commonly focus on the impact of an intervention, but it can also assess the intervention process with a view to improving design or delivery. A wide range of metrics can be used to evaluate effects, including leader awareness of the intervention, levels of participation and satisfaction, and changes brought about by the intervention. Changes can be measured in a variety of ways, including subjective wellbeing measures, health outcomes, behaviour changes, rates of absenteeism and retention, and healthcare costs.

There is a variety of tools available to help schools measure the impact of employee wellbeing interventions. These include follow-up surveys, informal check-ins and focus groups, regular analysis of HR data, and monitoring of policy changes. There are also simple instruments specifically designed to measure wellbeing across a population, such as Maslach's Burnout Inventory,[19] the Warwick-Edinburgh Mental Wellbeing Scale,[20] and the Perceived Stress Scale.[21] All of these tools require a baseline to be established prior to the intervention being carried out.

In the corporate world, return on investment (ROI) is considered the gold standard for evaluating the impact of workplace wellbeing interventions. This is a financial metric that calculates the amount of money gained, or costs avoided, relative to the amount spent on an intervention. ROI is calculated by dividing the money gained, or costs avoided, by the cost invested in the intervention. The result is expressed as a percentage or a ratio (e.g., an ROI of 5:1 means that the employer saves £5 for every £1 spent). ROI may not be a feasible way to evaluate interventions for many schools, as they may lack resources to collect and analyse quantitative data. It may also be impossible to quantify the impact of many wellbeing interventions in monetary terms. However, for very large schools or groups of schools, ROI may be a useful metric for the evaluation of some wellbeing interventions.

Chapter Summary

- Schools need to take a strategic, long-term approach to improve school leader wellbeing.
- The School Leader Wellbeing Framework provides a strategic approach to drive improvements in school leader wellbeing and consists of six stages.
- The first stage, Laying Foundations, involves establishing agreed working practices for the leadership and management of the process.
- The second stage, Educating Stakeholders, focuses on informing school communities about the importance of school leader wellbeing to the success of the school. It encourages stakeholders to view the wellbeing of its leaders as an investment and inspires leaders to think of self-care as a core leadership attribute.
- Stage three, Gaining Insights, involves gathering data about the current state of leader wellbeing and the support already available to leaders. This can be done using School Leader Wellbeing Insights, a survey tailored to the needs of school leaders. Survey data is supplemented using data collected from formal and informal check-ins and focus groups through an analysis of human resources data and a review of school policies.
- The fourth stage, Setting Goals, involves using the insights gained during stage three to agree priorities and establish goals to improve leader wellbeing.
- Stage five, Planning and Implementing Interventions, focuses on the design and delivery of a range of wellbeing interventions. These are discussed further in the next three chapters.
- The final stage, Evaluating Interventions and Tracking Progress, involves using a range of tools and metrics to assess the effectiveness of interventions and track progress towards goals set.

Table 8.1 School Leader Wellbeing Insights

Part 1. School Leader Experiences					
I have control over the hours I work and how I spend my working day	Strongly disagree	Disagree	Neither disagree nor agree	Agree	Strongly agree
I have a high level of autonomy over my work, and I feel I am trusted to carry out my job effectively	Strongly disagree	Disagree	Neither disagree nor agree	Agree	Strongly agree
I feel that I am fairly remunerated for my work	Strongly disagree	Disagree	Neither disagree nor agree	Agree	Strongly agree
In an average week, I spend the following number of hours in school:	Less than 40	40–45	46–50	51–55	More than 55
In an average week, I spend the following number of hours working at home:	None	Less than 5	6–10	11–15	More than 15
I feel I have a reasonable workload that is manageable	Strongly disagree	Disagree	Neither disagree nor agree	Agree	Strongly agree
I feel that workload is distributed fairly within the leadership team	Strongly disagree	Disagree	Neither disagree nor agree	Agree	Strongly agree
I have a written contract or employment agreement, which clearly states the terms and conditions of my job	Strongly disagree	Disagree	Neither disagree nor agree	Agree	Strongly agree
I have a job description that accurately reflects my role and responsibilities	Strongly disagree	Disagree	Neither disagree nor agree	Agree	Strongly agree
I have sufficient time to perform my leadership duties well	Strongly disagree	Disagree	Neither disagree nor agree	Agree	Strongly agree

	Strongly disagree	Disagree	Neither disagree nor agree	Agree	Strongly agree
I find my work emotionally draining	Strongly disagree	Disagree	Neither disagree nor agree	Agree	Strongly agree
I feel able to manage the emotional demands of my work	Strongly disagree	Disagree	Neither disagree nor agree	Agree	Strongly agree
I have the skills and experience I need to do my job effectively	Strongly disagree	Disagree	Neither disagree nor agree	Agree	Strongly agree
I have the support I need to do my job effectively	Strongly disagree	Disagree	Neither disagree nor agree	Agree	Strongly agree
My workload is regularly reviewed, and I receive support and advice on how to manage my workload	Strongly disagree	Disagree	Neither disagree nor agree	Agree	Strongly agree
I feel I have a reasonable work-life balance	Strongly disagree	Disagree	Neither disagree nor agree	Agree	Strongly agree
What steps could the school take to make your workload more manageable?					
What steps could the school take to improve your work-life balance?					
I feel the appraisal system works well and my performance is evaluated fairly	Strongly disagree	Disagree	Neither disagree nor agree	Agree	Strongly agree
The school supports my professional development and career aspirations, and I am able to access the right learning and development opportunities when I need to	Strongly disagree	Disagree	Neither disagree nor agree	Agree	Strongly agree

(Continued)

Table 8.1 (Continued)

Part 1. School Leader Experiences					
The physical environment in which I work promotes my physical and mental health and wellbeing	Strongly disagree	Disagree	Neither disagree nor agree	Agree	Strongly agree
Part 2. School Culture					
I have a clear understanding of the school's objectives	Strongly disagree	Disagree	Neither disagree nor agree	Agree	Strongly agree
I feel that my work contributes to the school's objectives	Strongly disagree	Disagree	Neither disagree nor agree	Agree	Strongly agree
I am treated with respect by the people I work with	Strongly disagree	Disagree	Neither disagree nor agree	Agree	Strongly agree
I feel valued for the work I do	Strongly disagree	Disagree	Neither disagree nor agree	Agree	Strongly agree
My work gives me a sense of fulfilment	Strongly disagree	Disagree	Neither disagree nor agree	Agree	Strongly agree
I feel a sense of belonging to the school community	Strongly disagree	Disagree	Neither disagree nor agree	Agree	Strongly agree
This school inspires me to do the best in my job	Strongly disagree	Disagree	Neither disagree nor agree	Agree	Strongly agree
I think that the school respects individual differences and promotes diversity (e.g., culture, race, gender, background, working styles)	Strongly disagree	Disagree	Neither disagree nor agree	Agree	Strongly agree

	Strongly disagree	Disagree	Neither disagree nor agree	Agree	Strongly agree
I feel that the school protects me from harm and abuse	Strongly disagree	Disagree	Neither disagree nor agree	Agree	Strongly agree
I feel that the school protects me from discrimination	Strongly disagree	Disagree	Neither disagree nor agree	Agree	Strongly agree
The leadership team shares a strong collective vision	Strongly disagree	Disagree	Neither disagree nor agree	Agree	Strongly agree
I feel valued as a member of the leadership team and have a sense of belonging to the team	Strongly disagree	Disagree	Neither disagree nor agree	Agree	Strongly agree
The leadership team is provided with opportunities for team-building and socialising to strengthen our relationships and improve team dynamics	Strongly disagree	Disagree	Neither disagree nor agree	Agree	Strongly agree
I have plenty of opportunities to express my views and contribute to decision-making	Strongly disagree	Disagree	Neither disagree nor agree	Agree	Strongly agree
I have positive relationships with the board of governors and feel we work well together	Strongly disagree	Disagree	Neither disagree nor agree	Agree	Strongly agree
I feel that the board of governors actively promotes and supports my wellbeing	Strongly disagree	Disagree	Neither disagree nor agree	Agree	Strongly agree
I feel the appraisal system works well and my performance is evaluated fairly	Strongly disagree	Disagree	Neither disagree nor agree	Agree	Strongly agree
Part 3. Mental Health Awareness and Support					
The school community understands the importance of school leader wellbeing to the success of the school	Strongly disagree	Disagree	Neither disagree nor agree	Agree	Strongly agree

(*Continued*)

Table 8.1 (Continued)

Part 3. Mental Health Awareness and Support					
I am actively encouraged and supported to take care of myself	Strongly disagree	Disagree	Neither disagree nor agree	Agree	Strongly agree
I receive regular training on managing and sustaining my own mental health and wellbeing	Strongly disagree	Disagree	Neither disagree nor agree	Agree	Strongly agree
I am provided with opportunities to engage in self-reflection on my mental health and wellbeing and develop a wellbeing plan	Strongly disagree	Disagree	Neither disagree nor agree	Agree	Strongly agree
There is someone I can go to in school to discuss my mental health and wellbeing needs and concerns	Strongly disagree	Disagree	Neither disagree nor agree	Agree	Strongly agree
I would feel comfortable to discuss my mental health and wellbeing needs with someone at school	Strongly disagree	Disagree	Neither disagree nor agree	Agree	Strongly agree
I am confident that if I needed the school's help with my mental health and wellbeing, I would be well supported	Strongly disagree	Disagree	Neither disagree nor agree	Agree	Strongly agree
As a leadership team we are open and honest with each other about our stress and mental health	Strongly disagree	Disagree	Neither disagree nor agree	Agree	Strongly agree
Members of the leadership team are open and honest with the community about their stress and mental health	Strongly disagree	Disagree	Neither disagree nor agree	Agree	Strongly agree
I have opportunities to network with leaders from other schools	Strongly disagree	Disagree	Neither disagree nor agree	Agree	Strongly agree

	Strongly disagree	Disagree	Neither disagree nor agree	Agree	Strongly agree
The school provides me with regular coaching with a trained coach	Strongly disagree	Disagree	Neither disagree nor agree	Agree	Strongly agree
I am provided with opportunities to seek support and debrief when involved in emotionally challenging situations or incidents at school	Strongly disagree	Disagree	Neither disagree nor agree	Agree	Strongly agree
My requests for flexible working or time off are considered fairly	Strongly disagree	Disagree	Neither disagree nor agree	Agree	Strongly agree
I feel run down and drained of physical or emotional energy	Strongly disagree	Disagree	Neither disagree nor agree	Agree	Strongly agree
I have negative thoughts about my job	Strongly disagree	Disagree	Neither disagree nor agree	Agree	Strongly agree
I feel lonely and isolated in my work	Strongly disagree	Disagree	Neither disagree nor agree	Agree	Strongly agree
I am harder and less sympathetic with people than perhaps they deserve	Strongly disagree	Disagree	Neither disagree nor agree	Agree	Strongly agree
I feel that I am in the wrong organisation or the wrong profession	Strongly disagree	Disagree	Neither disagree nor agree	Agree	Strongly agree
My work has a positive impact on my mental health	Strongly disagree	Disagree	Neither disagree nor agree	Agree	Strongly agree
What measures or changes in school would reduce your stress or improve your mental health the most?					

Notes

1 Leithwood, K. and Jantzi, D., 2006. Transformational School Leadership for Large-Scale Reform: Effects on Students, Teachers, and Their Classroom Practices. *School Effectiveness and School Improvement*, 17, 201–227.

2 Leithwood, K., Harris, A. and Hopkins, D., 2008. Seven Strong Claims about Successful School Leadership. *School Leadership and Management*, 28(1), 27–42.

3 Cole, M.S., Walter, F., Bedeian, A.G. and O'Boyle, E.H., 2012. Job Burnout and Employee Engagement: A Meta-analytic Examination of Construct Proliferation. *Journal of Management*, 38(5), 1550–1581.

4 Marquié, J.C., Duarte, L.R., Bessières, P., Dalm, C., Gentil, C. and Ruidavets, J.B., 2010. Higher Mental Stimulation at Work Is Associated with Improved Cognitive Functioning in Both Young and Older Workers. *Ergonomics*, 53(11), 1287–1301.

5 Salanova, M., Llorens, S., Cifre, E. and Martínez, I.M., 2012. We Need a Hero! Toward a Validation of the Healthy and Resilient Organization (HERO) Model. *Group & Organization Management*, 37(6), 785–822.

6 Bhui, K., Dinos, S., Galant-Miecznikowska, M., de Jongh, B. and Stansfeld, S., 2016. Perceptions of Work Stress Causes and Effective Interventions in Employees Working in Public, Private and Non-governmental Organisations: A Qualitative Study. *BJPsych Bulletin*, 40(6), 318–325.

7 Roberts, S.J., Scherer, L.L. and Bowyer, C.J., 2011. Job Stress and Incivility: What Role Does Psychological Capital Play? *Journal of Leadership & Organisational Studies*, 18, 449–458.

8 Matthiesen, S.B. and Einarsen, S., 2007. Perpetrators and Targets of Bullying at Work: Role Stress and Individual Differences. *Violence and Victims*, 22(6), 735–753.

9 Savill-Smith, C., 2019. *Teacher Wellbeing Index*. London: Education Support.

10 Health and Safety Executive (HSE), 2021. *Work-related Stress, Anxiety or Depression Statistics in Great Britain*. London: HSE.

11 Guharajan, N., 2018. Health Management at Unilever – Return on Investment: The Unilever Singapore Lamplighter Program (2009–2015). *Occupational and Environmental Medicine*, 75(2).

12 Barber, L., Hayday, S. and Bevan, S., 1999. *From People to Profits*. Brighton: Institute for Employment Studies.

13 Fink, D. and Brayman, C., 2006. School Leadership Succession and the Challenges of Change. *Educational Administration Quarterly*, 42(1), 62–89.

14 Henry, G.T. and Harbatkin, E., 2019. Turnover at the Top: Estimating the Effects of Principal Turnover on Student, Teacher, and School Outcomes. *Education Working Paper*, 19–95.

15 Laws, J., 2015. The Wellness Imperative. *Occupational Health & Safety (Waco, Tex.)*, 84(9), 68–69.

16 Hampson, E. and Jacob, A., 2020. *Mental Health and Employers: Refreshing the Case for Investment*. London: Deloitte.
17 Boyle, E., 2021. 4 Things Gen Z and Millennials Expect from Their Workplace. Accessed online www.gallup.com/workplace/336275/things-gen-millennials-expect-workplace.aspx.
18 Chartered Institute of Personnel and Development (CIPD), 2021. *Health and Wellbeing at Work Survey 2021*. London: CIPD.
19 Maslach, C., Jackson, S.E. and Leiter, M.P., 1997. *Maslach Burnout Inventory*. Washington, DC: Scarecrow Education.
20 Tennant, R., Hiller, L., Fishwick, R., Platt, S., Joseph, S., Weich, S., Parkinson, J., Secker, J., & Stewart-Brown, S. (2007). The Warwick-Edinburgh Mental Wellbeing Scale (WEMWBS): Development and UK validation. *Health and Quality of Life Outcomes, 5*, Article 63.
21 Cohen, S., Kamarck, T. and Mermelstein, R., 1994. Perceived Stress Scale. *Measuring Stress: A Guide for Health and Social Scientists*, 10(2), 1–2.

What Schools Can Do   9
Addressing Workload

In Part I, I discussed how the intensification of the school leader's role has led to increasing emotional demands and an ever-expanding workload. Headteachers and principals are working considerably longer hours than they used to, and their average working week is significantly longer than the average employee. Despite working long hours, many leaders find it impossible to complete their work in the time available. The emotional demands of the role are also placing a huge strain on leaders, making it difficult for them to switch off during non-work time, which is affecting their ability to recover. Consequently, growing numbers of headteachers and principals are finding their job to be unmanageable and unsustainable. The emotional demands and the heavy, relentless workload are factors closely associated with headteacher and principal burnout. If schools wish to prevent burnout, and support leaders to manage stress and improve wellbeing, it is crucial that they first find ways to address workload.

In this chapter, I consider interventions that schools can implement to address the workload of leaders. I first explore how school leadership can be reconceptualised, to reduce the demands placed on individual leaders and better meet the needs of 21st-century schools. Using Kagan's model of the leadership continuum, I examine ways in which school leadership may be more dispersed. Kagan's model, which places leadership on a continuum from sole leadership to supported leadership, dual leadership, and shared leadership,[1] is a useful construct to examine alternative approaches to leadership in schools. I begin by discussing *supported leadership* and examine the role that senior leadership teams (SLTs) play in school leadership. I then consider *dual leadership* in the form of co-headships and co-principalships. Finally, I examine *shared leadership* and consider the benefits of dispersing leadership more widely through a collaborative school culture. Later in the chapter,

DOI: 10.4324/9781003198475-12

I also look at other ways in which workload may be addressed, including the provision of more leadership time for teaching heads and principals, increased administrative support, and streamlining work processes.

Rethinking School Leadership

The current model of school leadership is largely built around the idea that power and responsibility are vested in a sole headteacher or principal. This model worked effectively in the past, but as the role of the school leader has expanded, the scope and intensity of the work and the complex and broad skills required have become too much for one person to manage. To make the work sustainable over the period of a whole career, it is necessary to consider alternative ways in which school leadership may be defined and practised.

There are many ways in which the power and responsibility of school leadership can be dispersed beyond the headteacher or principal. Since the 1990s, a huge body of literature has developed around what is often called *distributed leadership*. Other terms in less common use are *delegated leadership, democratic leadership, dispersed leadership, collaborative leadership*, and *shared leadership*. These terms are often used interchangeably, without clear definition, and can be confusing. They represent an increasing acknowledgement, however, that school leadership needs to move away from a reliance on a single individual towards alternative approaches.

In implementing interventions to address leader workload, schools should first review their leadership structures and practices, and consider whether there may be a better way of doing things that is more effective and sustainable. In a study of Ontario principals, a quarter found redefining the school leader's role to be effective in supporting their wellbeing, while 38% said this type of intervention was not available to them. Only 18% of principals felt this kind of initiative was ineffective.[1]

Supported Leadership – Building Effective Senior Leadership Teams

The intensification of the school leader's work has led many schools to delegate leadership tasks beyond the headteacher or principal, through the creation of new leadership roles and the development of larger SLTs. The SLT remains a source of untapped leadership potential in many schools. An effective SLT can offer valuable support to a headteacher or principal, provide opportunities to delegate tasks and responsibilities, and make a significant impact on workload. The potential of the SLT goes well beyond delegation, however, as a strong SLT empowers and improves the wellbeing of the whole team. Empowering team members by delegating substantial areas of responsibility increases self-esteem, enhances work engagement, motivation, and commitment. A strong SLT provides a source of collegial support for all team members and allows them to feel less isolated. Finally, an effective SLT allows members to achieve more together than they can do individually, improving job performance and satisfaction.

In planning interventions to reduce leader workload, schools should first review their approach to senior leadership and consider ways in which their SLT may be strengthened or used more effectively. In doing so, schools need to determine if they have the right conditions in place to foster a strong and effective senior team. To maximise SLT effectiveness, teams need to have an appropriate structure, a team dynamic, effective team leadership, and the appropriate skills and experience to manage the work.

Studies show that headteachers and principals spend too much of their day on managerial and specialised tasks that could be done by other people.[2] In recent decades, there has been a move towards increasing the number of supporting roles in school leadership teams to address this issue. This has manifested, most commonly, in an increase in the number of assistant headteachers or assistant principal positions to help with growing managerial responsibilities. Some forward-thinking schools, particularly in the independent sector, have also created new specialised roles focused on instructional leadership, and non-academic roles, such as director of business administration. In some systems, however, budgetary cuts have led to a reduction in the number of vice principal roles, which has increased the burden on the remaining members of the SLT.

Larger SLTs allow workload to be more widely dispersed and can be an effective approach to addressing workload issues. The creation of specialised roles also brings new expertise into the team, which may allow it to work more efficiently and effectively. The cost of creating additional roles should be viewed as an investment in the wellbeing and retention of headteachers and principals, and in the overall success of the school.

Structure and Size of SLT

While larger SLTs can bring many benefits to schools, very large teams may not always be successful. Studies from schools, and other organisations, show the optimum size of an SLT to be between five and eight members, irrespective of the size of the organisation.[3] Teams of this size ensure the number of interpersonal relationships within the team are kept to a minimum. This means there is less social complexity and scope for discord, making it easier to achieve alignment and unity among the team.

When considering the structure of an SLT, it is important to review how responsibilities are allocated across the team. Deputy headteachers, vice principals, and other supporting leaders have traditionally focused on managerial and administrative tasks. Power and authority commonly reside only in the headteacher or principal. Studies show that the most effective SLTs disperse leadership, with leaders at all levels playing a full role in the strategic and instructional leadership of the school.[4] Leadership is conducted on a much less hierarchical basis than in the past, as members are empowered to significantly influence school outcomes. This involves creating a culture where deputy headteachers, vice principals, and those in similar roles are given key portfolios and are granted real authority to make decisions autonomously or in collaboration with the rest of the team.

Empowering the SLT is an effective way to not only disperse workload but also draw on individual skills and collective excellence. Studies show that empowering employees brings considerable benefits to an organisation, by tapping into the potential of many. It also increases employee confidence, initiative, and creativity, and leads to increased retention.[5]

While empowerment is important, role clarity is also key. it is crucial that each SLT member has a well-defined set of responsibilities which is widely understood both within and outside the team.[6] Effective SLTs have clear job descriptions which accurately reflect their areas of responsibility and allocated tasks, while allowing for some flexibility. The most effective teams allocate these responsibilities based on individuals' expertise and what they can bring to the role. It is vital, however, to provide leaders with opportunities to carry out a full range of leadership tasks for professional development purposes and to support their career progression.

Team Dynamic

For an SLT to be most effective, they need to have a team identity and a team dynamic. This starts with a clear and compelling shared purpose. Schools should ensure that all SLT members are involved in the development of the vision and the direction of the school. The vision should be based around shared values that are clearly understood and regularly articulated. Effective SLTs also have clearly defined team tasks and goals, which are aligned to, but distinct from, the school's strategic goals, which they work to achieve together. Each team member regards the success of the team, and the achievement of team goals, to be more important than their individual success. They reject competitive individualism and personal self-interest in favour of their shared goals.

Effective SLTs also have agreed team norms, which govern their behaviour and allow them to operate effectively. These should include norms around collaborative working practices, dealing with conflict, and ensuring confidentiality.

Induction for new SLT members is an essential area that is often overlooked. It is important to transition new members into the team, providing them with information on each member's responsibilities, team norms, and operational systems and practices.

Strong interpersonal relationships among team members, based upon trust, mutual support, and respect, are also crucial to ensure an SLT's success. This is supported by high quality communication, dedicated SLT meeting time and opportunities for formal team building.[7] The most effective SLTs engage in collective decision-making, take joint responsibility for decisions, and maintain a united front even where there is discord. Opportunities should be provided to build relationships and a team dynamic through professional and social events.

The importance of leading the SLT is often overlooked by headteachers and principals. While tasks, responsibilities, and sometimes power are shared across the team, accountability usually remains with the headteacher or principal and they are looked to as the leader by other SLT members. They, therefore, carry the responsibility for building a strong team identity. Headteachers and principals must have sufficient understanding of the dynamic processes at work within the team and engage in appropriate team leadership behaviours and actions to get the most out of their SLT. Their responsibility includes fostering positive attitudes among the staff and the school community towards the SLT, to ensure there are strong links, based upon mutual respect.[8] As team leader, the headteacher or principal also needs to have an understanding of the individual characteristics, strengths and aspirations of each SLT member, to engage them in effective supervision and motivate and inspire them.

Regular self-evaluation by the SLT around its operation and progress towards team goals is essential to its effectiveness. Systems and protocols for review should be built into the annual cycle. Finally, continuity in team composition is essential to ensure SLT effectiveness. Individuals need to be in post long enough for relationships to develop and systems to be embedded.[8]

Developing SLT Skills and Expertise

A senior leadership team will only work effectively if all team members are competent, and have the skills and expertise required to carry out their role. As discussed in Chapter 7, it is widely acknowledged that the training made available to headteachers and principals often fails to prepare them for the breadth and complexity of their role. Studies also highlight the inadequacy of preparation for deputy headteachers, vice principals, and other similar roles.[9] In most systems there is no systematic training to support deputies and vice principals in making the transition to leadership, and they are often provided with insufficient opportunities for on-the-job, sequential skill building. In addition, most systems have no formal standards for deputies and vice principals and evaluation is not tailored to the role.

A study of Ontario principals shows conflict resolution, communication skills, emotional intelligence, and problem-solving to be the skills that leaders feel are the most important in their role. These skills are often not included in formal training programmes and must be learned on the job. Interventions which aim to fill gaps in leadership training and prepare SLT members for the demands of the role represent a worthwhile investment for schools. It is not always easy to find appropriate training, however, and the most effective courses are not always affordable for schools. The proliferation of online training during the COVID-19 pandemic has made many professional development programmes more accessible and cost-effective, but schools and leaders need to be sure that courses and programmes will be effective before they invest their time and money.

There is a small number of comprehensive school leader professional development programmes that receive consistently positive reviews from participants. The Principal's Centre at Harvard Graduate School of Education offers a range of online professional development courses designed to help leaders meet the challenges of modern-day school leadership. They are open to leaders worldwide. For UK leaders, the National Professional Qualification for Senior Leadership and National Professional Qualification for Headship have been recently revised to meet the needs of 21st-century leaders. For international school leaders, the Principals' Training Centre offers a full suite of excellent courses to support leaders in their work, including a full certification programme. International School Leadership also offers programmes for school leaders and school systems leaders, which include a globally recognised certification. Masters in educational leadership programmes have become increasingly popular in recent years and are considered by many leaders to be essential in improving their capability to carry out the role. These programmes can be tailored to the needs and interests of individual participants. Many offer the option to study part-time by distance learning.

As discussed in Part I, leading schools through a crisis can have a significant impact on the mental health and wellbeing of leaders. While it can be argued that the COVID-19 pandemic is a crisis that could not be prepared for, 42% of headteachers and principals worldwide report they had received no crisis leadership training prior to 2020. For crisis leadership training, I cannot recommend highly enough the PREPaRE training for school crisis response teams, developed by the US National Association of School Psychologists. They offer two workshops, with Workshop 1 focusing on comprehensive school safety planning and Workshop 2 covering mental health crisis interventions for students, staff, and the school community. Workshops are widely available across the United States but also elsewhere, including Australia, Germany, Oman, and Singapore. Trainers will visit schools to train whole crisis leadership teams and can deliver training online. Face-to-face training within schools is highly effective, but it can be expensive. The cost can be defrayed by inviting other local schools to join and share the expense. This also provides an opportunity to build connections with nearby schools and create a network willing to support each other during times of crisis.

The Council of International Schools (CIS) also offers child protection workshops for international school communities, which are highly recommended for school leaders. Leaders can attend the Child Protection Foundation Workshop and opt to follow this up with the Child Protection Deep Dive. These courses are now available for virtual attendance. All CIS workshop content is aligned with CIS international accreditation standards.

Many leaders report obstacles to attending professional development training, especially lack of time and funding. Schools reviewing SLT workload should consider time for professional development as essential. It has become the norm for leaders in many schools to fund the costs of expensive professional development, such as a masters or in-service certification programmes, sometimes with a small financial contribution from the school. This precludes many from participating or encourages them to put off further training until they can afford it. For many, the additional workload that high-level study brings is also a factor in their reluctance to participate. For those who do take on additional study, while the benefits are significant, the added workload can be detrimental to their wellbeing. Schools need to acknowledge the value of high-quality training for leaders and look for ways to prioritise this in their budgets, to enable them to make a substantial contribution to the costs and to provide leaders with regular study leave.

The paucity of formal training and preparation for deputy heads, vice principals, and similar roles makes it even more important that leaders are provided with professional learning opportunities within school through their supervision. Appraisal of SLT members plays a key role in ensuring the ongoing professional development of leaders. Schools need to develop evaluation frameworks tailored to SLT roles, which include clear standards by which individuals can be appraised.

SLTs also need to develop skills and expertise in teamworking and leading. Schools should seek out professional development opportunities that enhance teamwork and build understanding around how effective teams operate. They should also encourage headteachers and principals to access training on how to lead their team effectively and how to mentor and coach team members.

Dual Leadership – Co-headship and Co-principalship

Dual Leadership is an effective way to manage school leader workload that is gaining in popularity. Co-headship or co-principalship can take many forms, but models are usually built around either two full-time or two part-time headteachers or principals sharing one post. In the full-time model, both leaders are usually on-site at the same time, fulfilling different roles and responsibilities. In the part-time model, leaders divide the days, with one leader on-site at any time. Both models usually offer flexibility in the way that areas of responsibility are shared, basing this upon the strengths and preferences of the individual. In the full-time model, it is common for one leader to focus on student-facing areas, such as teaching and learning and pastoral care, while the other takes responsibility for finance, operations, and other administrative tasks. It is, however, equally common for co-leaders to each be involved in the full range of leadership responsibilities. In the part-time model, leaders normally fulfil all aspects of the headteacher or principal role while they are on-site but may still take overall responsibility for individual areas.

The Benefits of Dual Leadership

Studies have found co-leaders to be overwhelmingly positive about the dual leadership experience. Full-time co-headships or co-principalships allow leaders to have an increased presence on-site, which provides greater access for stakeholders and strengthens relationships.[10] This can lead to greater levels of trust in the school community and reduce conflict. Dual leadership has also been found to improve decision-making and problem-solving through high quality collegial conversations between co-leaders.[11] Co-leaders describe the benefits of working alongside a close peer, where they are able to learn from each other and play a role in each other's development.[12] Dual leadership also provides a model of collaboration and professionalism for staff, students, and parents. Studies show that teachers prefer working with co-leaders,[13] while those involved in co-leadership have greater job satisfaction than sole leaders.[7]

The greatest benefits of dual leadership are connected to workload sharing, with dual leadership being viewed as an important health and wellbeing resource. Many co-leaders describe feeling invigorated by dual leadership and find their workload more manageable and sustainable.[14] Co-leaders report decreased stress, better work-life balance, and reduced work-family conflict.[7] They also feel less isolated in their role, benefiting from debriefing after emotional interactions and receiving coaching from their co-leader. This allows them to gain perspective, reduces the amount of rumination that takes place following an incident, and enables them to manage the emotional demands of the role better.[15]

Clearly there are prerequisites to a successful dual leadership, and co-headships or co-principalships are not always successful. Several factors have been associated with successful co-leadership. These include shared values and beliefs, strong communication, clearly defined leadership responsibilities, and the development of trust. Successful co-leaders also present a unified front to the community, even where there is disagreement, rather than allowing stakeholders to play them off against each other.

Cost is of course a major concern for schools considering co-leadership. While the employment of two part-time headteachers or principals is likely affordable, the cost of two full-time co-leaders may seem prohibitive to many schools. Studies show that while some large schools pay two full-time leaders a full salary each, there are other ways to approach the cost issue. Schools are recommended to consider the whole cost of their SLT, which may allow them to find creative ways to restructure and make dual leadership affordable.[3] For example, many US schools that employ two full-time co-leaders divide the salary of one principal and one vice principal between the co-principals and dispense with the vice principal role. This provides a model where two individuals share the authority and responsibility of the principal role, rather than a hierarchical structure involving a principal and vice principal. Studies report that other schools have been able to mitigate the cost of a second principal by having one leader focus more closely on fundraising.

This all points to dual leadership as being an effective way to reduce headteacher and principal workload and improve leader wellbeing. To be successful, however, co-leadership needs the support of governance teams and the wider school community. This support includes positive expectations of governance towards co-leadership, open-mindedness of all stakeholders, and support from governance in bringing the school community on board.[8]

Planning for Dual Leadership

When considering a dual leadership model, schools should first inform themselves about co-leadership by contacting schools that have adopted the model. In England, the Shared Headship Network is a small organisation that works to promote co-headship and support schools and leaders interested in this approach. Schools should also consult with all stakeholder groups to discuss whether co-leadership may work for their school and seek input. Listening to initial concerns and considering drawbacks, and how they may be overcome, is key to gaining commitment and buy-in at this early stage. It is important that schools plan how co-leadership will work in practice, considering recruitment, the contractual position, and finances. Schools also need to seek external support from their local authority, district, or accreditation agency, or from professional associations.

Finally, it is important to understand that co-leadership is different for every school and is a journey for which there is no road map. Embarking on a co-headship or co-principalship requires a school to be bold and accept the challenges that will be encountered along the way. A growing body of research shows that, for many schools, this approach to leadership can be transformational, not only for the headteacher or principal but for the whole community.

Shared Leadership – Creating a Collaborative Professional Culture

Dispersing leadership beyond the senior leadership team is another approach to relieve the workload of school leaders. Studies have identified how headteachers and principals who report higher levels of shared responsibility tend to experience greater job satisfaction and wellbeing.[16] Researchers have also found a positive correlation between high levels of shared leadership and positive school culture.[17]

Effective shared leadership is complex to implement, however. It must not be used simply to offload leadership tasks onto others but should involve developing a collaborative professional culture. Redistributing workload without an underlying foundation of genuine collaboration is likely to have a negative impact on those to whom work is redistributed. It is also likely to rebound onto headteachers and principals, as middle leaders, and other colleagues who are bearing the burden of additional leadership tasks, become exhausted, detached, and increasingly ineffective in their roles.

Building a collaborative professional culture involves multiple areas of focus, which begins with a sense of shared purpose. This involves formulating and making visible a set of school values, creating and implementing a vision around these values, and developing a universal set of learning principles for the school. It also involves identifying priorities and working together to achieve the goals set out in the strategic plan and school improvement plan.

Shared practice is also a key aspect of a collaborative professional culture. Colleagues work together to plan and assess learning, share pedagogy, take part in shared teaching activities, and engage in peer observation and feedback. Finally, a collaborative culture focuses on shared decision-making and problem-solving. This involves drawing on the expertise in the building, in genuine collaboration, rather than just consultation.

For schools seeking to build a collaborative professional culture, there are often barriers in place. Lack of understanding of what collaboration is and what it looks like in practice, as well as insufficient understanding, or scepticism, about its benefits can stand in the way of developing a collaborative culture. Many schools also have difficulty providing the right structures or resources to support collaboration. Insufficient or inconsistent time to collaborate is a perennial problem that requires creative thinking and open-mindedness to solve. Poor investment in middle leaders, who play a key role in the collaborative process, is another common issue. For collaboration to be successful, schools need to ensure they provide adequate non-teaching time, training, and coaching for middle leaders. Finally, people-related issues can be tricky barriers to overcome. These include lack of team identity, personalities who prefer to work alone, relationship conflicts and lack of trust. All these matters need to be addressed if a collaborative professional culture is to be successfully developed.

Addressing Internal Workload Drivers

While many drivers of workload in schools are external, and outside of the school's control, there are also internal drivers that may unnecessarily increase workload. All schools have organisational inefficiencies and processes that can be more streamlined. These internal workload drivers will be different for every school but are likely to include meeting structures, intra-school communications, school calendar, timetabling, staff absences, and reporting to parents.

It is easy for schools to continue working with systems, processes, and procedures that are inefficient. Things are often done the same way for many years, if not decades, and there can be a reluctance by some to change. There may also be a lack of awareness of how a task can be done more efficiently or concern about the cost of bringing in new systems, both in hard cash and people hours. Leaders in many schools are simply too busy to give time and energy to considering how everyday tasks might be streamlined.

Streamlining Work Processes

To address internal workload drivers, schools need to identify key processes that may be inefficient and develop a strategic approach to improve efficiency.

This can be a complex process that requires schools to look at everyday systems and procedures through a new lens. In industry and commerce, techniques such as the Lean model, which has its roots in manufacturing, have been developed to help organisations to achieve greater efficiency and quality, by eliminating waste or activities that do not add value. This and other similar approaches, while not specifically designed for the education sector, have been used in schools to improve communication, budgeting, procurement, facilities management, transportation, human resources, and office administration.

The Lean methodology focuses on empowering staff to document current practice and identify opportunities to streamline tasks, reduce resource needs, and control costs through small, incremental changes. While many schools use consultants or proprietary software, or both, to support this process, the principles are easy to implement independently. In a study from Ontario, a third of principals reported finding streamlined work processes to be effective or very effective in supporting their well-being, while a fifth said this type of intervention was not available to them. Only a quarter found this type of initiative to be ineffective.[1]

Reducing Teaching Loads

In many schools, especially in the public sector, headteachers, principals, and, more commonly, deputy heads and vice principals still carry a significant teaching load. In Australia in 2017, 600 of 1,600 New South Wales primary school principals were teaching, with an average of 27% of their working week being spent in the classroom.[2] While it is desirable for senior leaders to stay connected to students and to the daily work of teaching colleagues, the expectation to teach represents a huge burden for many, as it provides insufficient time to carry out essential leadership duties. This significantly increases the challenges leaders face in managing their workload and leaves most with no alternative but to work unsustainably long hours to get everything done.

For some schools the cost of appointing additional teaching staff to relieve the teaching burden of leaders may be unaffordable. In this situation, it is worth bearing in mind that even a slight reduction in the teaching load of a busy school leader can have a significant impact on their workload and wellbeing. The reduction of one hour of teaching per week probably represents three hours given back to leaders for leadership tasks, when planning, preparation, marking, feedback, and assessment are all taken into consideration. In a study from Ontario, a third of principals found a reduction in teaching time to be effective in improving their wellbeing, while 43% said this kind of intervention was not available to them. Only 15% found this kind of initiative to be ineffective.

Studies show that the appointment of additional administrative support can make a real difference in a school leader's workload. Employment of a personal assistant to carry out high-level administrative duties has been found to have a significant impact on headteachers and principals.[18] In recent years, it has also become more common for schools to appoint a bursar or business manager to address financial matters. The independent sector has also seen growing roles in the areas of operations, admissions, human resources, marketing, and fundraising.

Administrative and Specialised Support

For many schools, the cost of creating new support roles may seem prohibitive. There is, however, sufficient evidence of the financial benefits to consider them to be a shrewd investment. Research has found that the appointment of a business manager can help schools make significant savings and tap into new sources of income, as well as maximise the use of local government finance. The National College for School Leadership estimates that, on average, a school business manager can recover their salary costs over a three-year period.[19] The Independent Schools Council calculated that, in 2015, school development offices had raised £150 million in funds from donors over the previous year, with the amount forecast to double by 2020. The return on investment for schools with a development office is estimated to be £3.75 in philanthropic income for every £1 invested.[20] An experienced admissions officer or head of marketing can significantly increase student enrolment and bring in additional school fees, while a skilled director of operations can reduce a school's costs in key areas, including procurement, and maximise income from the renting of facilities and other activities.

Where restricted budgets completely prevent schools from creating additional roles, there are alternatives. Some schools have succeeded in appointing shared business managers to work across several neighbouring sites. In England, especially in multi-academy trusts, shared services are becoming an increasingly popular way to pool expensive skills, making economies of scale across several sites.

Flexible Working

While dual leadership has already been discussed, there are other forms of flexible working that can make the workload of school leaders more manageable. The UK Department for Education identifies 14 different flexible working practices. These include compressed hours, which involves working full-time hours over fewer days and flexi, or lieu time, involving paid time off to compensate for long working hours. They also include phased retirement, which allows for a gradual reduction of working hours or responsibilities during transition to retirement from full-time work.

There is no research yet on the benefits of flexible working for school leaders, but plenty of studies highlight the benefits flexible working practices for teacher wellbeing. School leaders report that teachers who work flexibly feel supported and valued, are perceived as working harder and more efficiently, are less tired or stressed, and have reduced rates of sickness absence.[21] Most teachers report that flexible working has improved their work-life balance, allowing them to spend more time with their families and increase their job satisfaction.[22]

Flexible working remains much less common among school leaders, and there is a perception that flexible working is not compatible with senior leadership. In a study conducted by NASUWT, a fifth of women teachers said they did not think that flexible working was compatible with leadership, while 81% did not know any senior leaders who worked flexibly. Yet there are many examples of headteachers and principals around the world being involved in successful flexible working initiatives.[23]

Flexible working practices can bring significant benefits to headteachers and principals, providing them with opportunities to rest and recover, or to experience a better work-life balance. In my own research from 2020, more than half of participants identified time to attend to their own needs as the support they most wanted.[24] Lieu days, working from home days, and discretionary leave are ways that schools can recognise the long hours that leaders work and provide them with opportunities to get away from the school environment, to engage in self-care activities, or to work without the interruptions that are a common feature of their normal working day.

Identifying Workload Issues

As discussed in Chapter 8, leaders' stressors and their wellbeing needs will vary considerably from school to school and need to be identified before interventions can be planned and implemented. While there are studies that highlight general trends in how school leaders spend their days, the workload issues that may need addressing will be unique in every context. For workload interventions to have maximum effect, it is important for schools to know how leader workload is currently distributed and the specific workload issues experienced by their SLT.

While workload surveys can be used for this purpose, and more targeted questions on workload can be added to School Leader Wellbeing Insights, workload surveys can be flawed, as they rely upon a participant's memory to provide an accurate picture of their working week. A more effective way to establish a clear picture of leader workload is to conduct a work study across the leadership team. This can help identify the categories of tasks that leaders are expected to fulfil in an average week and the amount of time spent on each category.

Technology enables real-time work studies that are both time efficient and accurate. A messaging service such as WhatsApp or text messages can be used to prompt leaders to complete a very brief survey several times a day, for a period of a few weeks, stating where they are and what they are doing. These brief surveys can be created in Google Forms or other survey creation tools, such as Survey Monkey. Data can easily be analysed, using the tools available in the software, and can provide a comprehensive overview of how leaders, in different roles, spend their time.

A work study of this kind is a valuable tool to allow schools to review leaders' workloads and identify areas where work may be reduced and is highly recommended in most contexts. This approach needs to be handled with care, however, especially in schools with low levels of trust among the leadership and governance team. Some individuals may feel uncomfortable with this process and view it as an opportunity for supervisors to check up on them. To avoid this perception and to ensure full participation, leaders need to be fully briefed and involved in the design of the study prior to implementation. This will help ensure they understand the purpose of the work study, how data will be collected, analysed, and utilised, and that they are given opportunities to contribute their ideas, ask questions, and raise concerns.

Chapter Summary

- Finding ways to reduce headteacher and principal workload is key to improving the health and wellbeing of school leaders.
- Different ways of dispersing leadership can reduce workload and provides leaders with increased support.
- Building more effective senior leadership teams is a meaningful way to disperse leadership. This involves empowering SLT members to have real authority, ensuring there is a team dynamic, and providing all senior leaders with the skills they need to do the job well.
- Dual leadership, in the form of co-headship or co-principalship, may also be an effective way to disperse leadership for some schools. Studies show co-leadership models to be highly effective in supporting headteacher and principal wellbeing and providing schools with a sustainable leadership model.

- Shared leadership involves dispersing leadership across the wider school community through a culture of professional collaboration. This can be a highly effective way to empower others and place decision-making and problem-solving into the hands of the many, rather than the few.
- Reducing organisational inefficiencies and streamlining key systems and processes can have a real impact on reducing leader workload.
- Alleviating the teaching and administrative burden on leaders is also an effective way to make more time for core leadership duties.
- Providing leaders with opportunities for flexible working, including compressed hours, flexi and lieu time, discretionary days, and phased retirement can help them to manage their workload more effectively and improve work-life balance.
- It is important that schools have access to hard data around the specific workload demands of leaders in their school before they embark on interventions to address workload. Workload surveys or work studies are the most effective way to achieve this.

Recommended Resources – Leadership Training

There is a small number of comprehensive, school leader professional development programmes that receive consistently positive reviews from participants.

The Principal's Centre at Harvard Graduate School of Education
For UK leaders, the National Professional Qualification for Senior
    Leadership and National Professional Qualification for Headship
For international school leaders, the Principals' Training Centre and
    International School Leadership

Recommended Resources – Crisis Leadership Preparation and Training

The US National Association of School Psychologists' PREPaRE training offers two workshops, focusing on comprehensive school safety planning and mental health crisis interventions. Workshops are widely available across the United States and in Australia, Germany, Oman, and Singapore. Trainers will visit schools to train whole crisis leadership teams and can deliver training online.

Notes

1 Pollock, K. and Wang, F., 2020. *School Principals' Work and Well-Being in Ontario: What They Say and Why It Matters.* Toronto, ON: Western University.

2 Deloitte, 2017. *The Principal Workload and Time Use Study.* Sydney: New South Wales Government.

3 Lahti, R., 2017. Four Ways to Accelerate Your Executive Team's Productivity. Accessed online www.forbes.com/sites/forbescoachescouncil/2017/04/27/four-ways-to-accelerate-your-executive-teams-productivity/?sh=329296a821d5.

4 Day, C. and Sammons, P., 2016. *Successful School Leadership.* London: Education Development Trust.

5 Robertson-Smith, G. and Markwick, C., 2009. *Employee Engagement: A Review of Current Thinking.* Brighton: Institute for Employment Studies.

6 Bush, T. and Glover, D., 2012. Distributed Leadership in Action: Leading High-performing Leadership Teams in English Schools. *School Leadership & Management,* 32(1), 21–36.

7 Court, M., 2003. Towards Democratic Leadership. Co-principal Initiatives. *International Journal of Leadership in Education,* 6(2), 161–183.

8 Bush, T. and Glover, D., 2012. Distributed Leadership in Action: Leading High-performing Leadership Teams in English Schools. *School Leadership & Management,* 32(1), 21–36.

9 Rintoul, H.M. and Kennelly, R., 2014. The Vice Principalship: The Forgotten Realm. In *Pathways to Excellence: Developing and Cultivating Leaders for the Classroom and Beyond* (Advances in Educational Administration, Vol. 21). Bingley: Emerald Group.

10 Slater-Sanchez, J., 2020. The Efficacy of the Co-principal Model of School Administration as Viewed Through the Lens of the California Professional Standards for Education Leaders. Brandman University, Ed.D.

11 Wexler Eckman, E., 2006. Co-principals: Characteristics of Dual Leadership Teams. *Leadership and Policy in Schools,* 5(2), 89–107.

12 Thomson, P. and Blackmore, J., 2006. Beyond the Power of One: Redesigning the Work of School Principals. *Journal of Educational Change,* 7(3), 161–177.

13 Hewitt, P.M., Denny, G.S. and Pijanowski, J.C., 2012. Teacher Preferences for Alternative School Site Administrative Models. *Administrative Issues Journal,* 2(1), 8.

14 Eckman, E. and Kelber, S.T., 2009. The Co-principalship: An Alternative to the Traditional Principalship. *Planning and Changing,* 40(1), 86-102.

15 Döös, M., Wilhelmson, L., Madestam, J. and Örnberg, Å., 2018. The Shared Principalship: Invitation at the Top. *International Journal of Leadership in Education,* 21(3), 344–362.

16 Chaplain, R.P., 2001. Stress and Job Satisfaction among Primary Headteachers: A Question of Balance? *Educational Management & Administration,* 29(2), 197–215.

17 Çobanoğlu, N. and Bozbayindir, F., 2019. A Study on Shared Leadership and Positive Psychological Capitals of Teachers at Primary and Secondary Schools. *Universal Journal of Educational Research*, 7(5), 1265–1274.

18 Greene, K., Lee, B., Springall, E. and Bemrose, R., 2002. *Administrative Support Staff in Schools: Ways Forward*. London: National Foundation for Educational Research.

19 National College for School Leadership (NCSL), 2009. *Discover The Benefits of School Business Managers*. Nottingham: NCSL.

20 Baines Cutler Solutions, 2015. *National Independent Schools' Financial Benchmarking Survey 2015*. London: Independent Schools Council.

21 Department for Education (DfE), 2020. *Exploring Flexible Working in Schools*. London: Cooper Gibson Research.

22 Sharp, C., Smith, R., Worth, J. and Van den Brande, J., 2019. *Part-Time Teaching and Flexible Working in Secondary Schools*. London: National Foundation for Educational Research.

23 National Association of Schoolmasters and Union of Women Teachers (NASUWT), 2016. *Flexible Working: The Experiences of Teachers*. London: NASUWT.

24 Kelly, H., 2020. School Leader Wellbeing During the COVID 19 Pandemic 2020. Accessed online https://drhelenkelly.com/2020/12/13/school-leader-wellbeing-during-the-covid-19-pandemic-the-2020-report/.

What Schools Can Do   **10**

Supporting Leaders' Mental Health and Wellbeing

In the previous chapter, I outlined ways in which schools can reduce the demands placed on headteachers and principals by addressing workload. In this chapter, I look at how schools can provide support for leaders to help them to cope with the demands. I begin by discussing awareness raising and culture change around workplace mental health. I then consider proactive training to provide leaders with information and tools to support wellbeing. Later in the chapter, I discuss the importance of social support and examine three forms of social support, mentoring, coaching, and networking. Finally, I consider a range of health and wellbeing benefits that schools can provide for their leaders.

Research shows that many school leaders feel unsupported in their role and would like more support from both inside and outside the school community. In a 2019 study, nearly two-fifths of Ontario principals, reported feeling unsupported,[1] whereas in my own 2020 research only a third of leaders said they were receiving enough support.[2] While there is now a great deal of research around the stressors school leaders encounter, there is much less evidence on the types of support they receive and which are the most effective. This reflects what is happening outside of the education sector, where there is also a paucity of reliable evidence on the effectiveness of support interventions. From the studies available, we know that two categories of workplace support have the greatest impact. They are interventions which focus upon raising awareness and changing culture around mental health, and proactive, early interventions that support employees' mental health, such as training and social support.

DOI: 10.4324/9781003198475-13

Awareness Raising and Culture Change

In the corporate world, the success of workplace wellbeing interventions is measured by return on investment (ROI). Researchers have found that raising awareness and changing culture around mental health can provide an ROI of £6 for every £1 invested.[3] Raising organisational awareness is not only a key stand-alone strategy to improve workplace wellbeing but is also integral to the success of other wellbeing interventions. There is evidence to show that the stigma around mental ill health makes employees more reluctant to disclose stress-related issues or actively seek support, which reduces the number of employees willing to take part in work-based well-being interventions. Raising awareness and destigmatising mental ill health can increase participation levels in a range of support-based interventions.[3]

Studies show that there is a significant stigma attached to the mental ill health of school leaders, which needs to be overcome if leaders are to seek and accept support. Over half of senior leaders who participated in the 2021 UK Teacher Wellbeing Index said they did not feel confident discussing unmanageable stress or mental health problems with their employer. A third said there was a stigma that stopped them from discussing their mental health with anyone at school, while 42% felt mental health issues would be perceived as a sign of weakness by others.[4]

The US National Academy of Medicine identifies three forms of stigma around mental health – self-stigma, public stigma, and structural stigma.[5] Workplace stigma is a form of structural stigma that is rooted in system-level discrimination around mental health. This stigma is manifested in cultural norms, institutional practices, and a disparity between physical and mental healthcare policies. While in recent years many schools have taken steps to reduce mental health stigma, efforts have been primarily focused upon the mental health of students, although growing attention is also being paid to promoting staff mental health. While headteachers and principals benefit from general awareness raising, there is a need to specifically address the issue of school leaders' mental health. There is still a long way to go before we see significant and widespread change in this area.

There are several ways in which schools can move mental health up the agenda. A good starting point is the use of government standards around employee mental health. In the UK, the government's review *Thriving at Work* led to the creation of six core and four enhanced standards to tackle mental ill health at work.[6] The standards focus upon areas such as developing a mental health at work plan, building mental health awareness, encour-aging open conversations about mental health, and providing support when employees are struggling. They also focus on providing employees with good working conditions, a healthy work-life balance, and opportunities for professional development. Similar standards have been introduced in Canada[7] and are also currently being developed in California.

Guidelines of this kind provide useful frameworks and ideas, not only for schools operating within those jurisdictions but also for schools in countries where no standards exist. They can inform and underpin interventions to raise awareness, change culture, and reduce stigma around the impact of leader stress.

These standards, and other literature from the field, emphasise the importance of leading awareness-raising initiatives from the top, as without the high-profile involvement of leaders and supervisors, culture change cannot occur. Just as school leaders play a key role in addressing stigma around staff mental health, shifting perceptions around school leader stress requires commitment from those responsible for supervising leaders. For executive heads, headteachers, and whole school principals, this is likely to be the governing body. For those in other leadership positions, it will be line managers and others above them in the leadership hierarchy.

Awareness-raising initiatives in schools should include the provision of mental health literacy training for leaders and their supervisors. This should involve guidance on recognising signs of distress in leaders, how to raise concerns, facilitating conversations around mental ill health and connecting individuals with practical support. Interventions could also involve encouraging leaders and supervisors to share their mental health challenges and building conversations about stress and mental wellbeing into regular leadership meetings. It is also essential to eliminate discriminatory behaviour in school by ensuring there is parity between mental and physical ill health in all policies and practices. This includes access to healthcare and employee-assistance programmes, paid sick leave and return to work support. It also involves committing to the use of non-stigmatising language around mental health across all school communications.

Proactive Training and Support

Research in the corporate world has found that the most effective workplace wellbeing interventions combine awareness raising and culture change with proactive training and support. Proactive training and support provide an average ROI of £5 for every £1 invested, whereas reactive support, such as treatment for current mental health conditions, provides a return of only £3 for every £1 invested.[3]

In the context of school leaders, proactive training and support may include workshops around managing stress and wellbeing; social support in the form of mentoring, coaching, and networking; and the provision of health and wellbeing benefits.

Mental Health and Wellbeing Training

While training focused on school leaders' mental health and wellbeing is slowly gaining popularity, it is still not widely available. Three-quarters of Ontario principals consider stress management skills to be among the most important skills needed for the job.[1] Eighty-five percent of UK senior leaders feel their training has not prepared them to manage their own mental health, with only a quarter having been involved in professional learning of this kind.[5] While training can vary in quality, a recent study of Ontario principals found only 11% of participants report this kind of professional learning to be ineffective.[1]

Studies show that many headteachers and principals also wish to receive training focused on supporting the wellbeing of others. Three-quarters of UK leaders feel unprepared to manage the health and wellbeing of students and staff, while fewer than a quarter have been involved in training in this area.[5]

There is an increasing number of courses available that focus on supporting mental health and wellbeing in schools. *Mental Health First Aid*, a course first developed in Australia for a variety of workplaces, is becoming increasingly popular with schools. It provides training on identifying early signs of mental ill health, helping someone experiencing a problem, preventing mental illness from deteriorating, and guiding someone to the right support. It also covers how to reduce stigma around mental ill health in the workplace. This course is available from a wide range of providers internationally and can be accessed online.

The UK-based Anna Freud National Centre for Children and Families offers a range of online courses to support school wellbeing. This includes *Leading a Mentally Healthy School, Supporting Staff Wellbeing in Schools and Colleges*, and *Senior Mental Health Lead Training*. Also based in the UK, the professional development provider The National College provides on-demand webinars and certified courses focused on mental health and wellbeing, and Leeds Beckett University offers a one-year, part-time, online *MA Leadership of School Mental Health and Wellbeing*, which is open to educators around the world.

In the United States, the Mental Health Technology Transfer Center network (MHTTC) provides a free five-hour online training course, *Classroom Wellbeing Information and Strategy for Educators* (WISE). The National Center for School Mental Health, at the University of Maryland, also offers a range of online courses and pre-recorded webinars. The Australian National Excellence in School Leadership Institute (NESLI) has developed *The*

Principal's Wellbeing Programme, in collaboration with Dr Philip Riley, the chief author of the Australian Principal Occupational Health, Safety and Wellbeing Survey. This comprehensive programme offers the option of fully online learning or a blended model and can be accessed by individual leaders or tailored to the needs of school leadership teams. It includes four modules targeted specifically at the needs of school leaders. These are Organisational Wellbeing and Psychological Safety, Conflict and Communication, Managing Emotional Demands, and Coping Strategies. For international schools, the Council of International Schools (CIS) provides wellbeing workshops focused on their specific challenges and needs.

Social Support

As discussed in Chapter 2, the headteacher's and principal's role can very isolating, with many leaders experiencing professional and personal loneliness. There is plenty of evidence from the field of education to show the positive impact of work-related social support on the stress levels and mental health of school leaders. The burnout literature shows lack of community to be a significant contributor to headteacher and principal burnout, while supportive workplace relationships can mitigate burnout.[8] Research has also highlighted how social support can directly reduce the negative impact on leaders of working long hours.[9]

Social support can take the form of informal, school-based support or formal support. For maximum effect, school leaders should have access to both kinds of support. The availability of informal, in-school support can have a significant impact on headteacher and principal wellbeing. Studies show support from colleagues, supervisors, and other school leaders to be highly effective in reducing stress.[10] This includes providing opportunities to debrief and receive immediate support when urgent issues arise, mentoring, and opportunities for reflection with others facing similar challenges. Positive and nurturing relationships among senior colleagues are key to preventing school leader loneliness and provide valuable succour for leaders. The benefits of developing supportive senior leadership teams have already been discussed in the previous chapter. Fostering positive relationships across the school community with staff, parents, and supervisors also plays an important role reducing in leader stress and improving wellbeing. This is discussed in the next chapter.

Sadly, the culture in many schools fails to provide the informal social support that leaders need. When this occurs, the provision of formal support takes on a greater importance, although all leaders can benefit from participating in formal support. Formal social support takes three main forms: mentoring, coaching, and networking.

There has been increasing attention paid to the benefits of mentoring and coaching as forms of support for employees across a range of sectors and workplaces. Over the last 25 years, a growing body of research has shown how both mentoring and coaching provide opportunities for leaders to reflect on their practice, explore ideas, and set goals while receiving support and feedback. Mentoring and coaching are often confused, as they serve a similar purpose and have common features.

Fenwick and Pierce define a mentor as a "professional colleague and critical friend who helps the principal understand professional norms and job expectations and provides helpful advice about professional challenges."[11] While not always the case, mentors are usually more experienced leaders who provide advice and guide less experienced colleagues along their professional journey. Coaching differs from mentoring as it involves more intentional conversations focused on the challenges, strengths, and attributes of the coachee, with the purpose of achieving change and growth. The coaching process emphasises goal setting and provides support, feedback, and advice to help leaders achieve their goals. Coaching commonly involves a relatively short period of interaction, rather than the long-term relationship that is common in mentoring. While peer coaching among school leaders is a well-accepted model, the most effective coaching often takes place with a professional, trained, and accredited coach, who may come from outside the education system.

Mentoring

Mentoring programmes are most often implemented to support new school leaders and have been a common feature of headteacher and principal induction across many public-school systems, including in the UK, United States, and Singapore, since the mid-nineties. Mentors act as a catalyst or sounding board for mentees, assist them in solving problems, provide links to people and other resources, and give emotional support. Evaluative studies of school leader mentoring programmes suggest that mentoring of novice leaders can result in a wide range of benefits for the mentee and their schools, including reduced feelings of isolation and stress. Mentoring can also increase confidence and self-esteem, bring an accelerated rate of learning, improve personal skills, and increase technical expertise.[12]

Despite these well-documented benefits, mentoring has fallen out of fashion in recent years, with only 11% of senior leaders in the UK taking part in a mentoring programme.[4] To capitalise on the benefits of mentoring, schools need to ensure opportunities to work with a mentor are made available to all novice leaders. Programmes can be established in school, where more experienced leaders mentor less experienced colleagues.

Research has identified a range of factors which may affect the effectiveness of mentoring, including the availability of time, the matching of mentors and mentees, the qualities and attributes of mentors, and the nature and quality of mentor training.[13] In-school mentoring programmes are more likely to be successful if they are actively endorsed by key stakeholders and there is an administrator formally designated to oversee the programme. Where possible, training should be provided for mentors and protocols established to ensure mentoring sessions are purposeful. Care also needs to be taken to ensure that pairings are a good match and that both mentor and mentee have the same expectations of the process.[14]

As an alternative to in-school programmes, schools can invite leaders to appoint a mentor from outside of the organisation. This may be someone with whom they already have a relationship. Where there is access to formal mentoring programmes, established by school districts or local authorities, schools need to ensure that leaders register to take part. In all cases, the provision of time is a key factor in the success of mentoring. Formal mentoring sessions, whether in-house or with external mentors, should be regularly scheduled and built into the working day, wherever possible. Discussions on mentoring should be included as part of the mentee's appraisal, to provide opportunities to reflect on the process and provide some level of accountability. Schools with in-house programmes also need to ensure that mentors do not become overwhelmed by their mentoring responsibilities by allocating no more than one mentee to each mentor.

Roughly half of US school districts have adopted mentoring requirements for new principals. In the UK, the Association of School and College Leaders (ASCL) offers a mentoring programme for new headteachers and executive heads, while the National Association of Head Teachers (NAHT) also offers mentoring for senior leaders at various stages of their careers. In Australia, many states provide principal mentoring programmes. The Girls' Schools Association (GSA), offers *The Global Mentoring Network for Aspiring Leaders* programme, which is open to leaders in any state school. For international schools, *EARCOS Leadership Mentoring* is a well-regarded programme that has over 100 leaders involved in mentoring and peer-to-peer relationships across the East Asia region. The Academy for International School Heads (AISH) *Mentoring and Coaching Programme* also offers mentoring to new or experienced international school leaders.

Coaching

Despite the well-documented benefits of mentoring, coaching has become a more popular approach to providing social support for leaders. Recently, there has been a huge proliferation in coaching in schools, particularly school-based peer coaching programmes, where teaching staff form collegial coaching relationships with others working in similar roles. While such initiatives most commonly focus on improving teacher performance through reflection, professional dialogue, and collaboration, there is some evidence that they also positively affect staff wellbeing. Despite the popularity of coaching for teaching staff, only 13% of UK senior leaders report having been coached.[4]

Research on the effectiveness of coaching emphasises the importance of sufficient time and quality of coaching training. It also highlights the importance of high levels of trust between coaching partners and the use of contextually and culturally appropriate coaching models.[15]

For many school leaders, school-based peer coaching is a challenge, due to issues of trust, confidentiality, and stigma, as well as time constraints. For executive heads, headteachers and whole school principals, there are often no school-based peers with whom they can establish a trusting coaching relationship. Establishing a coaching partnership with a leader from another school can be a highly effective tool to support leader wellbeing, but relationships of this kind tend to be informal and ad hoc.

Engaging a professional coach may be the most effective way for school leaders to participate in coaching and there is a growing body of research around the benefits of professional coaching. One recent study by Leeds Beckett University demonstrates how specialist coaching can make a real difference in the professional and personal lives of headteachers.[16] Participants in the study were provided with a programme of six two-hour coaching sessions with a specialist executive coach, which took place across one school year and was funded by their trade union. During the sessions, headteachers discussed the challenges and complexities of their role, were provided with space and time to reflect, and received professional and emotional support. The effect of the sessions was evaluated via a survey, focus groups, and interviews with participants, coaches, and the programme leader.

The findings of the study indicate that the programme had a significant impact on the resilience, wellbeing, and work-life balance of participants. Coaching improved their self-belief and confidence and helped them to prioritise their own physical health. It also helped them to address feelings of isolation and influenced the way they worked with colleagues and the wider school community. The sessions supported leaders in having more balanced emotions at work, which resulted in them being less reactive with others. They also allowed leaders to reconnect with their values and sense of vocation. Participants were able to prioritise their wellbeing more effectively and became bolder in advocating for their own needs. There is evidence that the intervention also had an effect on the retention of participants in their schools.

The Leeds Beckett study highlights the importance of trusting relationships between leaders and coaches and guaranteed confidentiality. The independence of coaches, who were not connected in any way to a participant's school, was a crucial element to the success of the programme, allowing leaders to talk openly and honestly, without fear of repercussions. The study also emphasises the value of using highly skilled, professional coaches with significant coaching expertise. While coaching of this kind is expensive, all participants viewed coaching as a justifiable investment, despite the high cost, and many sought to continue with professional coaching when the initial programme ended.

All schools wishing to support the wellbeing of their leaders should provide opportunities for coaching. The main takeaway from the research is that any coaching is better than no coaching, but that school-based peer coaching is likely to be the least effective form of coaching, followed by informal coaching partnerships with leaders from other schools.

Peer coaching will be more effective if participants receive training in both the theories of coaching and practical coaching expertise. There are several organisations that offer this kind of training, specifically aimed at school leaders. They include the British School of Coaching's *Coaching for Effective School Leadership* programme, the UK-based Integrity Coaching *Coaching for SLTs* course, the Ontario Principals' Council *Foundational Coaching Skills Training*, the Australian Victorian Academy of Teaching and Leadership *Coaching with Confidence* programme, and the Association of California School Administrators *Leadership Coaching Training*.

As with mentoring, peer coaching can only be effective if time is set aside for regular, intentional, and well-defined coaching sessions. Building opportunities to reflect upon peer coaching outcomes into headteacher and principal appraisal, or performance management, can be an effective way to ensure coaching is prioritised by both the school and leaders.

Professional coaching, despite the cost, represents the best investment of time and money. In recent years, there has been such a huge proliferation of providers offering executive coaching for school leaders that it is hard to know which are likely to be effective. The cost of highly qualified and accredited coaches precludes most headteachers and principals from personally funding this kind of support. Many of the most high-profile coaching firms require a commitment to several two-hour sessions across a school year, at a significant cost. There are cheaper and more flexible options, as scores of former school leaders are now training to become accredited coaches and the market is growing. Schools should seek recommendations, and educate themselves on the different coaching accreditation programmes, to enable them to assess the level of experience and expertise of individual coaches. The International Coaching Federation is the leading and most globally renowned accrediting body, which offers three levels of credentialling – *Associate Certified Coach, Professional Certified Coach*, and *Master Certified Coach*. The International Association of Coaching, also operating worldwide, has two levels of individual accreditation – *Certified Masteries Coach* and *Master Masteries Coach*. The European Mentoring and Coaching Council provides training and accreditation across Europe and offers four levels of individual accreditation – *Foundation, Practitioner, Senior Practitioner*, and *Master Practitioner*. Each level of coaching certification requires increasing amounts of training and hours spent coaching in the field. All good coaches should offer a free, no-obligation initial conversation to potential clients to discuss a leader's needs and establish a common understanding of the format of the programme. Most coaching now takes place virtually or by telephone and does not require face-to-face attendance.

Networking

School leader networking is a term used to refer to a wide variety of exchanges between and among headteacher and principal peers. These can include informal social gatherings, regular meetings among peers to discuss practice, seeking advice from other school leaders, and more formal meetings through a wide range of organisations. Professionally facilitated networks, organised by school districts, local authorities, professional development providers, and organisations specialising in school leader coaching, are also growing in popularity. While networking formats may vary considerably, they all provide opportunities for mutual support, where participants can reflect upon their work and context; share information, ideas, and stories; discuss matters of practice; consult with others; and give and receive feedback.

Given the complexity of the school leader role and the inadequacy of training, leaders need to find ways to continuously develop their capacity and skills to meet the daily challenges they encounter. Networking provides a community with which to have real-time discussions, build expertise through situation-based learning, and receive moral support in a safe environment of critical colleagues and friends.[17]

While incidental and informal networks can bring considerable benefits for leaders, research has mainly focused on deeper, more deliberate networking opportunities that are purposefully developed and cultivated as a resource for professional learning. This kind of networking engages the social and intellectual resources of members and builds the skills and knowledge of all participants. Studies show that it reduces leader isolation and provides a valuable source of professional development and support.[18] Despite the clear benefits, only 4% of UK senior leaders report having taken part in facilitated peer group support.[4]

As with mentoring and coaching, the most successful networks are built on a foundation of trusting relationships. Networking is also most successful when leaders connect with others working in similar contexts.

Schools should view networking opportunities as important interventions to support the wellbeing of their leaders and should ensure they are pro-active in helping headteachers and principals to access networks. Rather than relying upon leaders to develop their own networks, governing bodies can reach out to similar schools in their locality to encourage and facilitate networks of leaders at all levels. This should include deputy or assistant headteachers and vice or assistant principals, in addition to headteachers and principals. This is particularly important in areas where there are no existing networks or where leaders are new to the school or area.

In international schools, where leaders are more vulnerable to isola-tion, and receive little local government support, networks can be a lifeline for leaders. Where schools operate in a highly competitive environment, there may be more of a tendency to reject the idea of networking with competitor schools. This is short-sighted, as there are many ways in which schools can collaborate and allow leaders to receive support from each other that do not compromise confidentiality. Such issues can also be overcome by establishing networks across a wider geographical area with schools of a similar nature.

Health and Wellbeing Benefits

Employee health and wellbeing benefits have been a common aspect of cor-porate packages for many years but are much less common in the field of education, despite the positive effects they bring. Research from the cor-porate world shows that wellness packages for employees bring an average return on investment (ROI) of £1.50 for every £1 spent, across a wide range of benefits. Some benefits bring a much greater ROI, with disease man-agement initiatives bringing an ROI of 3.8, for example. In addition to ROI, studies show that employee health and wellbeing benefits also bring value on investment (VOI) in the form of increased employee engagement, improved morale, decreased presenteeism, and higher staff retention rates.[3] A study of Ontario principals found health and wellbeing benefits to be one of the most effective methods of support available to principals, with only 18% finding them ineffective.[1]

In countries which do not have socialised medicine, employee healthcare is often part of the normal package of benefits provided to school leaders. In the independent school sector, especially in international schools, health insurance is also a common feature of the headteacher's or principal's package. The quality and coverage of these packages, and access to other health and wellbeing benefits, varies considerably and often lags behind what is available outside the education sector.

There is a growing body of evidence, from the corporate world, on both the ROI and VOI of a wide range of health and wellbeing benefits that schools should consider providing for senior leaders. These include comprehensive private healthcare, offering cover for dental, eyecare, physiotherapy, and psychotherapy, in addition to standard cover. They also include disease management initiatives, such as health screening, regular health assessments, and interventions such as healthy heart support for those at high risk of cardiovascular disease.

Benefits such as stress and wellbeing counselling, health club membership, personal training, and employee assistance programmes have also been shown to be successful. Work-based benefits commonly include access to healthy meals, initiatives to improve the physical environment, provision of access to light and fresh air, and ergonomic workstations. Employer-funded social and team-building events also bring strong ROI and VOI.

Employers should seek to maximise employee participation rates by promoting the availability of benefits. Studies highlight the importance of increasing employee awareness about the benefits available to them and how to access these benefits.[3]

While the benefits discussed above may seem unaffordable for many schools, based on the potential ROI and VOI, improving health and wellbeing benefits for school leaders is something that all schools should consider. Even small changes to a leader's benefits packages can bring tangible improvements to their health and wellbeing, including a sense of being valued by their school.

Chapter Summary

- There are many interventions that schools should consider implementing to support the health and wellbeing of their leaders.
- Research shows that raising awareness and reducing stigma around mental health issues, combined with proactive training and support, is likely to bring the best return on investment.
- It is crucial that schools begin by addressing structural stigma and reducing discrimination around mental health by reviewing cultural norms, institutional practices, and school policies.

- Proactive training to provide school leaders with information and guidance around workplace mental health will enable leaders to attend to their own mental health needs and those of others. There is now a wide range of courses available, many of which can be accessed online.
- Work-based social support is key to improving school leaders' mental health and wellbeing. Leaders should have access to both informal support and some type of formal support, such as mentoring, coaching, or facilitated networking.
- Research shows that mentoring is a highly effective way to provide headteachers and principals with support. All novice leaders should be provided with access to a mentor in the first few years of their career. Studies highlight the best conditions to ensure mentoring has the greatest impact.
- Coaching has become popular in recent years. While peer coaching models can be successful given the right conditions, studies show professional leadership coaching to have the most impact on leaders' health and wellbeing. While it is expensive, professional coaching represents an excellent return on investment for schools. Schools should ensure that all senior leaders have access to a professional coach.
- Schools should review the health and wellbeing benefits provided for leaders. Improved health and wellbeing benefits have been shown to bring a good return on investment in the corporate world. Even small improvements can make a difference to leaders.

Recommended Resources Mental Health First Aid Training

Mental Health First Aid (MHFA) provides training on reducing stigma around mental ill health in the workplace, identifying early signs of mental ill health and guiding someone to the right support. This course is available from a wide range of providers internationally and can be accessed online.

MHFA England

MHFA USA

MHFA Australia

MHFA Canada

MHFA New Zealand

MHFA International

Recommended Resources Wellbeing Training

The UK-based Anna Freud National Centre for Children and Families offers a range of online courses for school staff. This includes *Leading a Mentally Healthy School, Supporting Staff Wellbeing in Schools and Colleges*, and *Senior Mental Health Lead Training*.

In the United States, the Mental Health Technology Transfer Center (MHTTC) network provides a free five-hour online training course *Wellbeing Information and Strategy for Educators* (WISE). The National Center for School Mental Health, at the University of Maryland, also offers a range of online courses and pre-recorded webinars.

Notes

1 Pollock, K. and Wang, F., 2020. *School Principals' Work and Well-Being in Ontario: What They Say and Why It Matters*. Toronto, ON: Western University.

2 Kelly, H., 2020. School Leader Wellbeing During the COVID 19 Pandemic 2020. Accessed onlinehttps://drhelenkelly.com/2020/12/13/school-leader-wellbeing-during-the-covid-19-pandemic-the-2020-report/.

3 Hampson, E. and Jacob, A., 2020. *Mental Health and Employers: Refreshing the Case for Investment*. London: Deloitte.

4 Savill-Smith, C., 2019. *Teacher Wellbeing Index*. London: Education Support.

5 National Academies of Sciences, Engineering, and Medicine, 2016. *Ending Discrimination against People with Mental and Substance Use Disorders: The Evidence for Stigma Change*. Washington, DC: National Academies Press.

6 Stevenson, D. and Farmer, P., 2017. *Thriving at Work: The Independent Review of Mental Health and Employers*. London: Department of Work and Pensions.

7 Canadian Standards Association, 2013. *Psychological Health and Safety in the Workplace*. Toronto, ON: Canadian Standards Association.

8 Friedman, I.A., 2002. Burnout in School Principals: Role Related Antecedents. *Social Psychology of Education*, 5, 229–251.

9 Nahum-Shani, I. and Bamberger, P.A., 2011. Explaining the Variable Effects of Social Support on Work-based Stressor – Strain Relations: The Role of Perceived Pattern of Support Exchange. *Organizational Behavior and Human Decision Processes*, 114(1), 49–63.

10 Juneja, H. and Malhotra, M., 2015. Exploring the Relationship and Impact of Working Hours on Work-family Conflict and Social Support among Doctors. *International Journal of Science and Research*, 5(9), 1583–1588.

11 Fenwick, L.T. and Pierce, M.C., 2002. *Professional Development of Principals*. New York: ERIC Digest.

12 Yirci, R. and Kocabas, I., 2010. The Importance of Mentoring for School Principals: A Conceptual Analysis. *International Journal of Educational Leadership Preparation*, 2(5), 1–7.

13 Hobson, A.J. and Sharp, C., 2005. Head to Head: A Systematic Review of the Research Evidence on Mentoring New Head Teachers. *School Leadership & Management*, 25(1), 25–42.

14 Bush, T. and Coleman, M., 1995. Professional Development for Heads: The Role of Mentoring. *Journal of Educational Administration*, 33(5).

15 Zepeda, S.J., Parylo, O. and Ilgan, A., 2013. Teacher Peer Coaching in American and Turkish Schools. *International Journal of Mentoring and Coaching in Education*, 2(1).

16 Lofthouse, R. and Whiteside, R., 2019. *Sustaining a Vital Profession: Evaluation of a Headteacher Coaching Programme* (Project Report). Leeds: Beckett University.

17 Wassmer, G., 2011. Supporting New School Leaders: The Benefits of Online Peer Communities. Ontario Institute for Studies in Education University of Toronto, Ed.D.

18 Drago-Severson, E., 2012. The Need for Principal Renewal: The Promise of Sustaining Principals through Principal-to-Principal Reflective Practice. *Teachers College Record*, 114(12), 1–56.

What Schools Can Do   **11**

Building Community

Studies show that community is the area of work life most closely associated with headteacher and principal burnout.[1] Relationships with adults in school can be highly stressful for leaders. If the emotional demands of these relationships are not balanced by positive social connections, then leaders are more vulnerable to burnout. As discussed in Chapter 2, many school leaders experience isolation in their work. This loneliness can play a significant part in the sustainability of their roles, as strong social connections can mitigate the effects of burnout and affect wellbeing positively.

In the school context, community is most effectively built through developing a positive culture. The wellbeing of school leaders cannot be viewed in isolation from the rest of their community. The culture of a school affects the wellbeing of everyone. Schools with a positive culture will experience more trusting relationships, less conflict and greater harmony than schools without. This enhances wellbeing for the entire community and positively affects school leaders, as problems are more easily resolved, the work is less emotionally draining, and leaders feel more supported. A large body of evidence shows how positive school culture benefits both adults and children. For staff, it increases morale, motivation, and productivity, improves wellbeing, drives retention, and reduces burnout. For students, it increases self-esteem, motivation, and engagement, and improves behaviour, wellbeing, and academic success.[2] In considering interventions to improve headteacher and principal wellbeing, schools should reflect on their culture.

Studies show that despite the benefits that a positive school culture brings, many schools are struggling with a poor organisational or workplace culture. Research from the UK shows that nearly half of all staff working in schools

DOI: 10.4324/9781003198475-14

feel the culture of their school has a negative effect on their wellbeing, while fewer than a quarter feel it has a positive effect.[3] This is echoed in my own 2021 study of international school teachers, where only 20% of participants felt the culture of their school has a positive influence on their wellbeing.[4]

In this chapter, I examine the main elements of a positive school and workplace culture and consider how schools can improve their culture to enhance their community. I focus upon two main ideas, creating a sense of belonging and building positive relationships. While developing and maintaining a positive culture involves the whole school community, in this chapter, I focus mainly on relationships between and among staff, leadership, and governance. Creating a sense of belonging for leaders and staff and fostering positive, collegial relationships forms the bedrock of a positive workplace culture. From this foundation schools can move on to build community across all stakeholder groups.

> A positive school culture has the strange dual function of enabling people to be both more energised and relaxed; more vulnerable and more resilient. It is found in the relational micro-moments that build trust and respect. It exists not so much in policy documents but in the thousands of interactions and conversations that take place every day.[5]

Creating a Sense of Belonging

A positive workplace culture is about creating a sense of belonging for all staff. Feeling a sense of belonging to a social group is a basic psychological need that governs much of human behaviour, thought, and emotion. Social connection is a key element of human survival, as it brings reliable physical support and emotional security in the face of adversity. A significant body of research demonstrates how a sense of belonging increases happiness, improves mental and physical health, and increases longevity. Supportive social networks can act as buffers against stress and depression and high levels of workplace belonging are linked to an increase in job performance, a reduction in staff turnover, and a significant reduction in absenteeism.[6]

Feeling excluded from a group can have a significant negative impact on individuals. Neuroscientists suggest that humans may be hardwired to experience suffering when there is an absence of social connection. Brain imaging shows that we experience social exclusion in the same region of the brain as we experience physical pain.[7] Researchers have found that being ignored at work is worse for physical and mental wellbeing than harassment or bullying. People who have experienced workplace exclusion are significantly more likely to report a low sense of workplace belonging, job dissatisfaction, an intention to leave their job, and poor health.[8]

Schools provide opportunities for colleagues to experience belonging through the web of relationships and sense of community they offer. Belonging is, however, more than just being part of a group; it is about identifying as a member of that group, sharing values and beliefs with the other members, and feeling accepted by them.

Shared Values

Creating belonging in school is about building a unique school identity and developing a feeling of unity that makes individuals feel proud to be part of it. This encourages stakeholders to be tolerant and respectful of each other's views, strengths, and differences, and to recognise the contributions and skills that everyone brings. This sense of identity starts with a set of shared values, around which the school's guiding statements and goals can be built, giving everyone a common purpose. A unique set of values can define and influence a school community by setting expectations for the behaviour and attitudes of students and adults. Developing a set of school values that reflect the values of the community and promote a person-centred, caring, respectful and inclusive culture can bring significant benefits to a school, strengthening relationships, increasing community engagement, and driving commitment.

To build a positive workplace culture, schools need to develop and then embed a set of values that are truly shared by the staff community. Ideally, these values will be developed as part of an open and collaborative process involving staff at all levels, as well as other stakeholder groups. Once a set of shared values has been agreed, schools need to ensure these values are embedded and reinforced in day-to-day practice.

Embedding Values – Vision and Mission

The development of a school's guiding statements, a clear mission and vision built around the community's shared values plays an important role in implementing and embedding values. A school's mission is a declaration of its day-to-day purpose and describes the organisation's core objectives and commitments. The school's vision summarises its high-level goals and unites and motivates the community around achieving those goals. Together the mission and vision articulate the community's shared beliefs and principles, provide a focus for all aspects of school life, and form the foundation for actions that lead to school improvement.

For a mission and vision to be effective in embedding a school's values, and in driving positive workplace culture, they need to be developed as part of a collaborative process involving the whole staff community. This process commonly begins with the governance and leadership teams and cascades down to involve staff in all roles.

Embedding Values – Making Them Visible

Making a school's mission, vision, and values visible around school is not enough to ensure they will become embedded into day-to-day life, but it is an important starting point. A mission and vision will never become ingrained if stakeholders are not aware of them. It is important that schools take steps to display the guiding statements around the school building, in public areas and in classrooms, so that the school community, and visitors alike, are constantly reminded of what the school stands for. The guiding statements must also be fed into internal and external communications, such as the school's website, social media, community newsletters, and staff and student handbooks. They should be included in communications aimed at recruiting new students and staff, such as prospectuses, job advertisements, and job descriptions. School events and meetings, such as student assemblies, staff meetings, and parent evenings also represent key opportunities to remind the community not only of what the guiding statements are but to highlight evidence of how they are being put into practice and underpin the day-to-day life of the school.

Embedding Values – Planning and Policies

If a school is to live its mission and vision, then the guiding statements need to be embedded into all strategic, development, and operational planning and decision-making. This will ensure that the school's priorities, goals, and decisions reflect the agreed values and systematically align with the guiding statements. Procedures should also be established to allow for regular evaluation of the extent to which the guiding statements influence decision-making.

Too often in schools, policy development is something that happens in isolation from the staff community and fails to align with practice or represent the stated values and aspirations of the school. Individual policies also fail to become living documents that guide administrative and academic practice. For shared values to become embedded, policy development must take place collaboratively. Only through this approach can a school be certain that policy represents who they truly are, or want to be, and that what is written on the page reflects what is happening around the building.

Embedding Values – Recruitment, Induction, and Training

Filling the school with employees who can support the vision and mission is central to embedding the school's values in daily practice. This starts at the recruitment stage and continues through induction and training. An induction process focused on the guiding statements helps new colleagues understand and embody the school's values. Likewise, every in-house training programme provides an opportunity for reinforcing the vision, mission, and values.

Embedding Values – Staff Appraisal

Ongoing, one-to-one discussions with colleagues during appraisal meetings play a key role in recognising the positive behaviours that embody the schools' values or challenging negative behaviours. Staff professional growth targets should be aligned with the school's strategic goals, which are aligned with the guiding statements. Opportunities should also be provided for staff to reflect upon how they embody the values of the school through their classroom practice and collegial relations.

Embedding Values – Teams and Groups

Team meetings are one of the most effective forums for reinforcing the school's guiding statements. The most effective teams set group goals that align with the school's goals and provide a direct link back to the vision, mission, and values. All regular team meetings and committee or group discussions should be viewed as an opportunity to focus on the guiding statements in a positive way, by celebrating successes or focusing together on the next steps towards improvement.

Building Positive Relationships

Building positive relationships plays a crucial role in creating and maintaining a positive workplace culture. Studies show there are striking similarities between what teachers want from their relationships with colleagues and what children want from their relationships with teachers.[9] Both adults and children wish to be recognised by others, have their efforts acknowledged and strengths valued, and be treated with respect.

The quality of the relationships that teachers have with leaders and colleagues is a key factor in school effectiveness. Relationships that offer support, encouragement, opportunities for collaboration, and positive communication are associated with higher levels of teacher and school efficacy.[10] Where teachers lack a shared sense of commitment and connection, however, they are much less likely to manage challenges and hardships well and their effectiveness is diminished.[11]

Most collegial relationships in schools are positive, but studies show that a significant minority of teaching staff and leaders would like to improve the quality of their relationships with colleagues. In a recent UK study, more than a quarter of teachers and teaching assistants said their relationships with senior leadership negatively affected their wellbeing. A third of teachers felt that better relationships with leaders would improve the mental health of the workforce, while a quarter want colleagues to be more understanding and accommodating of each other's needs and feelings.[3] Principals in Australia,[12] New Zealand,[13] and Ireland[14] identify interpersonal conflicts as being one of their greatest workplace stressors. Studies in these countries have found that while social support from colleagues is on a par with that experienced by other professions, social support from supervisors is significantly lower than the average workplace. This matches findings from Ontario, where principals report relationships with superintendents and trustees to be among the least positive they experience.[15]

The Role of Trust

Trust is a key element in building positive relationships in any organisation and plays a vital role in organisational success. In this context, trust is defined as an employee's willingness to be vulnerable, based on confidence that others are benevolent, reliable, competent, honest, and open.[16] Trusting relationships allow individuals to have positive expectations regarding each other's conduct. While trust exists at both the organisational and individual level, micro-interactions between individuals influence an employee's trust in the organisation. Studies show that when trust is intact, employees are more willing to contribute and commit to the organisation and to relationships with others.[17] Trust is, therefore, key to building community in schools.

Workplace trust has also been found to have a significant impact on employee wellbeing. A 2015 study of 2.5 million employees, across 195 countries, found there to be 40% less employee burnout in high-trust organisations and 74% less stress. High levels of workplace trust also helped workers to feel closer to their colleagues and brought a greater sense of accomplishment. The study found that employees in high-trust environments reported double the amount of energy at work and a third more life satisfaction than those in low-trust organisations. They also had higher levels of job performance and were 50% more productive.[17]

In schools, trust is fundamental to building and maintaining positive collegial relationships. Four key factors have been identified that influence levels of trust between teacher colleagues. These are sharing a common vision for students, the belief in colleagues' competence, emotional safety, and nurturing relationships.[18] Strong relationships between teaching colleagues have been likened to those of friendship or familial ties.[19] while trusting relationships are crucial to teacher motivation, successful teacher development and school improvement.[18]

School leadership plays a key role in building trust between leaders and staff and among teaching colleagues. Researchers have found that in schools where leaders are considered trustworthy, they set a tone that extends to teachers, making teachers more likely to trust each other, as well as trust students and parents.[20]

Barriers to Trust Building

Studies have identified common barriers to trust building between leaders and teachers and among teacher colleagues, which schools need to overcome if a positive workplace culture is to be developed. These include top-down decision-making that is perceived by staff to be arbitrary, misinformed, or not in the school's best interests; lack of transparency; and poor information-sharing. Other barriers include lack of shared understanding around the fundamentals of teaching practice and policy, which can undermine confidence in the competence of colleagues and lead to conflict. Leaders' expectations for staff and colleagues' expectations for each other are often highly diverse, based on norms and practices brought from previous schools. When expectations are largely unspoken, it becomes impossible for individuals to live up to them. This can create not only uncertainty about the competence of others but also anxiety, as teachers are unclear about whether they are meeting others' expectations.

Teacher isolation, ineffective communication, and lack of leader follow-through on support can also erode trust, as teachers feel alone, misunderstood, or unsupported by those around them. Trust is also undermined when funding for basic resources is inadequate or unreliable and where staff feel insecure in their employment, due to staffing cuts. Failure to remove ineffective leaders, or teachers, can stand as a major barrier to trust building, as can frequent turnover of teachers and leaders. Poor retention levels create uncertainty and instability among staff and undermine the long-term relationships that are essential to the development of trust.

Trust Building

Studies have identified a range of approaches and behaviours that headteachers and principals can adopt to promote the development of trust between leaders and staff.[21] Leaders build trust by ensuring that teachers have the basic tools and resources they need to do their jobs well. Demonstrating personal and professional integrity in dealings with staff by being honest and following through on the commitments is also key. Leaders need to be accessible to staff, by making themselves available to everyone, and showing they care, by taking a genuine interest in everyone's wellbeing and personal life. Collaboration is an important aspect of trust building. This involves including staff in decision-making and treating them as capable professionals whose opinions are valued and who can be trusted to do what is best for students. This also involves embracing conflict, by welcoming dissenting views, and encouraging risk-taking to allow teachers to innovate and develop their practice, without fear of reprisal.[22]

Effective communication is key to trust building. Leaders need to make expectations clear to all staff and establish norms and guidelines to avoid relying on assumptions. They should also facilitate and model positive interactions and open and honest communication. This involves leaders sharing information and being transparent about both the decision-making process and the challenges involved in decision-making. It also involves being prepared to have courageous conversations with staff who are not meeting expectations. Finally, leaders should be prepared to replace ineffective teachers if trust is to be developed. This should be done with sensitivity and regard for due process if it is to build rather than undermine trust.

Studies suggest there are many activities that schools can take part in that promote trusting relationships. Leaders should begin by setting clear intentions to prioritise relationship building by working collaboratively with staff to set goals around improving relationships and fostering trust. Engaging staff in developing the school's guiding statements, as discussed earlier, is not only an effective way to create a sense of belonging but it also builds trust. Developing a set of learning principles that aligns with the school's guiding statements is also an effective trust-building strategy. Trust among teachers is rooted in common understandings of what exceptional learning and student conduct looks like. Trusting relationships are enhanced when teachers share common principles around these areas and perceive that colleagues act in accordance with them.

Creating the right conditions to foster a collaborative professional culture, as discussed in Chapter 9, is also fundamental to trust building. This involves establishing a shared understanding of what collaboration is, identifying and overcoming the main barriers to effective collaboration, and providing meaningful opportunities for staff to collaborate. It also involves developing a professional learning model that promotes collaboration, such as professional learning communities, peer coaching, and team planning and teaching.

Improving communication skills among leaders and staff is key to ensure that interactions are positive. Communication skills training can increase self-awareness, improve relationship behaviour, and help individuals to manage challenging interactions. Training that focuses on developing listening skills and other communication techniques, such as Nonviolent Communication[23] and Active Constructive Responding,[24] can have a significant impact. Establishing norms around written communication, such as emails and instant messaging, can also bring significant benefits. Finally, schools should consider reviewing induction programmes with recent hires, to ensure that new staff feel welcome and supported, and know where to go to ask for help.

Fostering Workplace Civility

Feeling valued by colleagues is a key element of determining whether workplace relationships are positive. The need to be valued is rooted in the role that group membership played in evolutionary survival, and people care deeply how others value them.[25] We demonstrate that we value others by showing them respect, through conducting our day-to-day interactions in a courteous and considerate manner.

Civil interactions are of central importance in creating a positive workplace culture, as they build trust and a sense of psychological safety. Workplace civility is manifested through colleagues' personal interest in each other, cooperation and teamwork, the valuing of difference, and fair resolution of conflicts. High levels of workplace civility bring considerable benefits, protecting employees from the negative effect of work demands,[26] building greater organisational commitment, and increasing job satisfaction.[27] It also improves employee mental health,[28] reduces burnout, and increases employee retention.[26]

Workplace incivility can lead to a range of negative emotions and behaviours, including fear, sadness, guilt, hostility, and a desire for retaliation, which can perpetuate further incivility.[29] In workplaces where poor behaviour is prevalent, the norms for mutual respect have often been abandoned and a culture of incivility has become established. This can lead to spirals of incivility, where those who experience or witness poor behaviour become more likely to engage in the poor treatment of others.[30] While isolated acts of disrespect may seem innocuous, such acts can be highly contagious and can spread distrust and dissatisfaction. Even micro-level negative behaviours can affect the health and happiness of individual employees.[31]

Uncivil behaviour can take many forms, including ignoring colleagues, gossiping, discounting a colleague's contribution, sabotaging another's efforts, or poor etiquette in verbal and written communication. It may also involve more serious negative behaviour, such as abusive language, bullying, intimidation, and discrimination. Studies have found that incivility is more likely to occur when colleagues are encouraged to pursue individualism at the expense of team goals, where workers fail to practice self-restraint, or feel they will not be held accountable for their behaviour.[28] Incivility is also linked to levels of workplace stress, with the highest levels of poor behaviour occurring in the most stressful environments.[31]

A growing body of research around workplace culture shows that poor behaviour is much more likely to be prevalent when individuals experience injustice or perceive they have been treated unfairly.[32] When an employee joins an organisation, they enter into a psychological contract with their employer, where they trust the organisation to facilitate a balanced relationship. In this context, perceived unfairness is seen by an employee as a breach of trust. This may cause a negative emotional reaction, including feelings of anger, disappointment, or betrayal, and may lead some individuals to engage in incivility directed towards the organisation, supervisors, or co-workers as a form of retaliation or a demonstration of power. Perceptions of injustice may hinge on issues of pay, autonomy, and other working conditions. They can also be precipitated when an employee senses unequal treatment of colleagues by leaders. Studies highlight how workers who feel that colleagues are treated better than them are more likely to experience high levels of team conflict and have poor wellbeing.[33] Leaders need to seek to minimise feelings of workplace injustice and understand that the quality and nature of their relationships with each individual employee matters. Minor issues of fairness, or favouring some colleagues over others, may seem small and inconsequential but can have seriously negative effects, both for individuals and for overall school culture.

Interventions to Tackle Incivility

Developing approaches to create more respectful workplaces, by intentionally tackling incivility, has become increasingly popular in recent years. One approach, Civility, Respect and Engagement in the Workplace (CREW), has been used in organisations across the world to improve collegial relations and workplace culture.[34] CREW is not a prescriptive programme but provides a framework to develop interventions in response to the needs of the individual workplace.

CREW emphasises improving the culture within work groups, rather than organisation-wide. Depending on the school's size, structure, and organisation, this could involve the whole school, a section of the school, or individual departments, grade levels, or other teams. It involves a commitment of time, space, and resources to facilitate weekly meetings for work groups. Meetings are focused on discussing the importance of civility and determining customised interventions on specific areas of focus identified by the work groups. In some organisations, the process is facilitated by an expert consultant, but this is not essential. Interventions chosen by the group may include establishing norms around appropriate workplace behaviour, clarifying procedures for addressing poor behaviour and improving communication skills. Other interventions may involve the development of policies to address inclusion and diversity, or the provision of training in conflict management.

Organisations using CREW report a significant impact on workplace civility.[34] Progress can be evaluated using one of several civility scales that have been developed for this purpose.[35] Questions on civility can be built into staff and leader wellbeing surveys or schools can implement workplace culture surveys that address a range of workplace culture factors.

The Role of Leaders

It is important to note the role that leaders play in building a positive workplace culture. School leaders function as role models, set behavioural standards and organisational objectives, and communicate expectations to all stakeholder groups. The expression of emotions by leaders also influences the moods and emotions of others through what is called *emotional contagion*. Neuroscientists define this as a process by which humans synchronise their emotions and moods with those around them. Studies show that the emotions, moods, and behaviours of leaders have a particular influence on their followers, can rapidly spread through a group and have a significant impact on the quality of relationships within an organisation.[36] School leaders, therefore, play a key role in determining whether the school has a culture of civility and respect or a negative culture, where disrespectful behaviour and maltreatment is common.

It is important to acknowledge that headteachers and principals are not the only leaders within a school community. Governing bodies also play an important role in determining whether a school has a positive culture. Just as headteachers and principals model and establish behavioural expectations for staff, influence their emotions, and affect their levels of trust, so members of the governing body and other supervisors play a similar role for leaders. In Chapter 2, I discussed the effect that poor relationships between governors and other supervisors have on the wellbeing and retention of headteachers and principals. Disrespectful behaviour, poor communication, bullying, and conflict between supervisors and leaders is often at the heart of these poor relationships. Schools are recommended to address this by prioritising relationship building between senior leadership and the governance team. This should involve promoting greater levels of collaboration between governance and leadership, including working collaboratively on activities that promote a sense of belonging and build trust. The governance team should also be encouraged to take part in communication skills training and work with senior leaders to facilitate more respectful interactions.

Positive Emotions

Over the last 20 years, increasing attention has been paid to the role of positive emotions in creating a positive workplace culture. Positive emotions in the workplace have been found to improve collegial relationships and strengthen community, as well as enhance workers' engagement, increase job satisfaction, and reduce employee turnover.[37] Research from the field of positive psychology has found that to flourish, individuals need to experience three times as many positive emotions as negative. High-performing work teams have an average positivity ratio of 6 to 1.[38] Unfortunately, our evolutionary survival mechanisms mean we are hardwired to experience more negative emotions than positive. This *negativity bias* means that we are more likely to hold on to negative feelings, while letting go of the positive. The plasticity of the brain means that we can overcome negative bias by intentionally generating and acknowledging positive emotions, allowing the brain to form new neural pathways. Studies have identified a range of approaches that can enable us to generate and hold on to positive emotions in the workplace.[39]

Character Strengths

Character is viewed as the part of an individual's personality that other people admire, respect, and cherish. Studies have found character strengths to be central to who we are and how we perceive ourselves.[40] When individuals use their character strengths, they are happier, more connected, and more productive. In the workplace, the use of character strengths is associated with greater employee health and wellbeing; improved job performance, productivity, and satisfaction; and lower staff turnover.[41]

Two different frameworks are commonly used to identify an individual's character strengths. The Values in Action (VIA) strengths classification, from the VIA Institute, includes 24 strengths, grouped into six classes of virtues, and Clifton Strengths, distributed by the Gallup Organization, defines 34 talents in four domains. Both are equally well researched and provide invaluable tools to support workplace wellbeing. The VIA strengths framework is more commonly used in schools, as the VIA Survey of Character Strengths is free of charge and comes with some free resources and activities. The VIA Institute also provide a youth survey that is gaining in popularity for use with students of all ages.

A wide range of strengths-based activities and interventions have been used in the workplace to increase positive emotions and build a positive culture. These include finding new ways to use an individual's top five to seven strengths, known as signature strengths, in the course of daily work. Using signature strengths increases an employee's feelings of excitement and motivation around work and leads them to be more energised and engaged. Team-level strengths-based interventions can also be highly effective. These focus on creating mutual awareness of each other's signature strengths and developing a team plan to harness these strengths for the benefit of the team.

Savouring

Savouring is another technique developed by positive psychologists to increase positive emotions. Savouring helps us to counteract our negative bias by intentionally noticing, appreciating, and intensifying positive experiences. This can involve savouring in anticipation of future pleasure, savouring present experiences, or reminiscing about the past. The regular practice of savouring can have long-term benefits by strengthening an individual's capacity to notice and attend to positive experience. Studies show that savouring in the workplace can strengthen positive emotions by boosting and accentuating positive work experiences. It can also enhance interpersonal relationships by helping colleagues to bond.[42]

Two main savouring techniques have been used successfully in the workplace. The first is basking, which allows individuals and teams to feel pride in achievements and receive recognition and praise. The second is focused on jointly expressing gratitude. Savouring activities can involve individuals sharing successes with their work group, celebrating team achievements, and acknowledging the role of individuals. It can also involve thinking or reminiscing together about positive events or reflecting on acts of kindness.

Chapter Summary

- The quality of the school community can have a significant impact on a school leader's wellbeing. A school community can be strengthened by building a positive school culture.
- Fostering a sense of belonging for all stakeholders is key in creating a positive school culture. This is most effectively achieved through developing a set of shared values that are reflected in the school's guiding statements and goals and are embedded into policy and practice.
- Positive relationships are at the heart of a positive workplace culture. They are fostered through building trust and ensuring high levels of workplace civility.
- Trust between colleagues is built through a common vision for students, a belief in others' competence, emotional safety, and nurturing relationships.
- Barriers to trust building include top-down decision-making, poor transparency, and a lack of shared understanding around teaching and learning. Trust is also undermined by ineffective communication, poor resourcing, and failure to hold underperforming colleagues to account.
- Workplace civility plays a major role in building positive relationships. Interventions such as CREW can help schools prioritise civil interactions between colleagues.
- Leaders play a key role in modelling civil interactions in school and promoting positive relationships between staff. Leader supervisors, such as governors, fulfil a similar role for the leaders they supervise.
- The culture of a school can be enhanced through the regular experience of shared positive emotions. Positive emotions can be fostered through the use of character strengths in the school's daily work and through approaches such as savouring and gratitude.

Notes

1 Friedman, I.A., 2002. Burnout in School Principals: Role Related Antecedents. *Social Psychology of Education*, 5, 229–251.
2 Span, W., 2019. The Benefits of All Stakeholders of a Positive School Climate and Culture. *National Youth Advocacy and Resilience Conference*, 106.
3 Savill-Smith, C., 2019. *Teacher Wellbeing Index*. London: Education Support.
4 Kelly, H., 2020. School Leader Wellbeing During the COVID 19 Pandemic 2020. Accessed online https://drhelenkelly.com/2020/12/13/school-leader-wellbeing-during-the-covid-19-pandemic-the-2020-report/.

5 Roffey, S., 2019. Relationships and Social Capital at School. In S. Roffey, ed. *Positive Relationships Evidence Based Practice across the World*. Dordrecht: Springer.

6 BetterUp, 2021. *The Value of Belonging at Work: New Frontiers for Inclusion in 2021 and Beyond*. San Francisco, CA: BetterUp.

7 Macdonald, G. and Leary, M.R., 2005. Why Does Social Exclusion Hurt? The Relationship between Social and Physical Pain. *Psychological Bulletin*, 131(2), 202–223.

8 O'Reilly, J., Robinson, S.L., Berdahl, J.L. and Banki, S., 2015. Is Negative Attention Better Than No Attention? The Comparative Effects of Ostracism and Harassment at Work. *Organization Science*, 26(3), 774–793.

9 Fattore, T., Mason, J. and Watson, E., 2009. When Children Are Asked about Their Well-being: Towards a Framework for Guiding Policy. *Child Indicators Research*, 2(1), 57–77.

10 Day, C., Sammons, P. and Stobart, G., 2007. *Teachers Matter: Connecting Work, Lives and Effectiveness*. London: McGraw-Hill Education.

11 Gu, Q., 2014. The Role of Relational Resilience in Teachers' Career-long Commitment and Effectiveness. *Teachers and Teaching*, 20(5), 502–529.

12 Riley, P., See, S.M., Marsh, H. and Dicke, T., 2021. *The Australian Principal Occupational Health, Safety and Wellbeing Survey 2020*. Sydney: Institute for Positive Psychology and Education, Australian Catholic University.

13 Riley, P., Rahimi, M. and Arnold, B., 2021. *The New Zealand Primary Principal Occupational Health, Safety and Wellbeing Survey 2020*. Melbourne: Research for Educational Impact (REDI), Deakin University.

14 Riley, P., 2015. *Irish Principals' and Deputy Principals' Occupational Health, Safety and Wellbeing Survey*. Melbourne: Research for Educational Impact (REDI), Deakin University.

15 Pollock, K. and Wang, F., 2020. *School Principals' Work and Well-Being in Ontario: What They Say and Why It Matters*. Toronto, ON: Western University.

16 Hoy, W.K. and Tschannen-Moran, M., 1999. Five Faces of Trust: An Empirical Confirmation in Urban Elementary Schools. *Journal of School Leadership*, 9(3), 184–208.

17 Zak, P., 2017. *Trust Factor: The Science of Creating High-performance Companies*. New York, NY: AMACOM.

18 Bryk, A.S. and Schneider, B., 2002. *Trust in Schools: A Core Resource for Improvement*. New York, NY: Russell Sage Foundation.

19 Hong, J., Cross Francis, D., Wang, Q., Lewis, L., Parsons, A., Neill, C. and Meek, D., 2020. The Role of Trust: Teacher Capacity During School Leadership Transition. *Frontiers in Education*, 5, 108.

20 Tschannen-Moran, M., 2014. *Trust Matters: Leadership for Successful Schools*. London: John Wiley & Sons.

21 Barlow, V., 2001. *Trust and the Principalship*. Calgary: University of Calgary.

22 Brewster, C. and Railsback, J., 2003. *Building Trusting Relationships for School Improvement: Implications for Principals and Teachers*. Portland, OR: North Western Regional Educational Laboratory.

23 Rosenberg, M.B., 2002. *Nonviolent Communication: A Language of Compassion*. Encinitas, CA: Puddle Dancer Press.

24 Passmore, J. and Oades, L.G., 2022. Positive Psychology Techniques – Active Constructive Responding. *Coaching Practiced*, 47.

25 Turner, J.C. and Reynolds, K.J., 1987. A Self-categorization Theory. Rediscovering the Social Group. In P. Van Lange, A. Kruglanski and E. Higgins, eds. *In Handbook of Theories of Social Psychology Self-categorization Theory*. London: SAGE.

26 Leiter, M.P., Laschinger, H.K.S., Day, A. and Oore, D.G., 2011. The Impact of Civility Interventions on Employee Social Behavior, Distress, and Attitudes. *Journal of Applied Psychology*, 96(6), 1258.

27 Chiaburu, D.S. and Harrison, D.A., 2008. Do Peers Make the Place? Conceptual Synthesis and Meta-Analysis of Coworker Effects on Perceptions, Attitudes, OCBs, and Performance. *Journal of Applied Psychology*, 93, 1082.

28 Lim, F.A. and Bernstein, I., 2014. Civility and Workplace Bullying: Resonance of Nightingale's Persona and Current Best Practices. *Nursing Forum*, 49(2), 124–129.

29 Yao, J., Lim, S., Guo, C.Y., Ou, A.Y. and Ng, J.W.X., 2022. Experienced Incivility in the Workplace: A Meta-analytical Review of Its Construct Validity and Nomological Network. *Journal of Applied Psychology*, 107(2), 193.

30 Andersson, L.M. and Pearson, C.M., 1999. Tit for Tat? The Spiraling Effect of Incivility in the Workplace. *Academy of Management Review*, 24(3), 452–471.

31 Johnson, P.R. and Indvik, J., 2001. Slings and Arrows of Rudeness: Incivility in the Workplace. *Journal of Management Development*, 20(8), 705–714.

32 Day, A., Kelloway, E.K. and Hurrell Jr, J.J., (eds.), 2014. *Workplace Well-being: How to Build Psychologically Healthy Workplaces*. London: John Wiley & Sons.

33 Hooper, D.T. and Martin, R., 2008. Beyond Personal Leader – Member Exchange (LMX) Quality: The Effects of Perceived LMX Variability on Employee Reactions. *The Leadership Quarterly*, 19(1), 20–30.

34 Osatuke, K., Leiter, M., Belton, L., Dyrenforth, S. and Ramsel, D., 2013. Civility, Respect and Engagement at the Workplace (CREW): A National Organization Development Program at the Department of Veterans Affairs. *Journal of Management Policies and Practices*, 1(2), 25–34.

35 Ferriss, A.L., 2002. Studying and Measuring Civility: A Framework, Trends and Scale. *Sociological Inquiry*, 72(3), 376–392.

36 Snaebjornsson, I.M. and Vaiciukynaite, E., 2016. Emotion Contagion in Leadership: Follower Centric Approach. *Business and Economic Horizons*, 12, 53–62.

37 Fredrickson, B.L., 2000. Why Positive Emotions Matter in Organizations: Lessons from the Broaden-and-Build Model. *The Psychologist-Manager Journal*, 4(2), 131.

38 Fredrickson, B.L., 2013. Updated Thinking on Positivity Ratios. *American Psychologist*, 268(9), 814–822.

39 Staw, B.M., Sutton, R.I. and Pelled, L.H., 1994. Employee Positive Emotion and Favorable Outcomes at the Workplace. *Organization Science*, 5(1), 51–71.

40 Niemiec, R.M. and McGrath, R.E., 2019. *The Power of Character Strengths: Appreciate and Ignite Your Positive Personality*. Cincinnati, OH: VIA Institute on Character.

41 Pang, D. and Ruch, W., 2019. Fusing Character Strengths and Mindfulness Interventions: Benefits for Job Satisfaction and Performance. *Journal of Occupational Health Psychology*, 24(1), 150.

42 Davenport, L.J., Allisey, A.F., Page, K.M., LaMontagne, A.D. and Reavley, N.J., 2016. How Can Organisations Help Employees Thrive? The Development of Guidelines for Promoting Positive Mental Health at Work. *International Journal of Workplace Health Management*, 9(4), 411–427.

What Leaders Can Do   **12**

Managing Stress

In the previous three chapters, I discussed what schools can do to reduce the demands on headteachers and principals, support their wellbeing, and help mitigate stress. In this chapter, I look more closely at how leaders can improve their own wellbeing and consider a range of evidence-based strategies that will help leaders manage stress more effectively. I begin by focusing on the concept of self-care and the importance of viewing self-care as a leadership attribute. I then consider the concepts of rest and recovery and the central role they play in health and wellbeing. I discuss work recovery and the importance to effective stress management of recovering during non-work time. Later in the chapter, I examine the relationship between sleep and stress and discuss how poor sleep can be addressed. Finally, I look at ways to prioritise rest and recovery and consider a range of strategies that may help leaders in establishing new habits and routines to support more effective stress management.

Stress is a biological survival mechanism that enables humans to react to life-threatening situations. When we are exposed to a threat, the body rapidly releases the hormones adrenaline, noradrenaline, and cortisol into the bloodstream, which causes an instantaneous cascade of physiological changes. These changes help us fight off the threat or run to safety, and once the threat is past, the body returns to normal. Although in the modern world we are exposed to few life-threatening situations, our brain is unable to distinguish these kinds of threats from more common, everyday stressors. This results in the stress response being repeatedly activated, leading to chronically high levels of stress hormones, which, over time, cause our biological systems to become dysregulated. Chronic stress can take a significant toll on the body, contributing to obesity, high

DOI: 10.4324/9781003198475-15

blood pressure, and the clogging of arteries, which raise the risk of heart attacks and stroke. Persistent hormone surges also cause changes to the brain that may contribute to a range of mental health issues and affect cognitive functioning. Prolonged stress impairs the prefrontal cortex, which controls logic, analysis, and decision-making, while the amygdala, which is associated with our emotional processes, becomes hyperactive. This affects our executive functioning, including decision-making, rationalising, planning, and organisation – all key aspects of the school leader's role.

Chronic stress is not only a precursor of ill health and occupational burnout in school leaders but can severely affect their ability to perform their job. If stress can be effectively managed, the likelihood of it becoming chronic can be reduced and the risk of burnout decreased. Stress management involves a set of mental, emotional, or behavioural approaches that may reduce stress and its negative effects.

In recent years, literature and resources on stress management have proliferated and it has become a multibillion-dollar industry. While research in the field is growing, it can be challenging to evaluate the effectiveness of various stress management techniques, as the amount and quality of evidence varies greatly. This makes it hard for the individual to identify the most effective techniques from the multitude of options available. Stress management also places an onus on the individual to make changes to their routines, which they may find challenging to implement consistently. It is for this reason that stress management often has limited effect. Most stress management approaches begin with understanding the need to take greater care of oneself and making a commitment to improve self-care. For many school leaders, focused on the needs of others, this can prove highly challenging.

Self-care is a broad concept, based on the fundamental principles of self-reliance and personal responsibility. Self-care involves self-recognition, self-monitoring, and self-management of the symptoms of disease; making healthy lifestyle choices; and committing to a work-life balance. Many school leaders feel they do not have time for self-care. They fail to value it, or prioritise it, and many feel they should not need it. Yet self-care is about ensuring our basic human needs are met – our need for rest, recovery, nutrition, exercise, and human connection, needs which are hard to deny. Failure to engage in self-care practices can exacerbate stress, make leaders less effective, and increase the risk of burnout. For these reasons, care of self should be seen as an investment in sustained leadership and a desirable leadership attribute that supports effective performance and benefits the whole school community.

Rest and Recovery

Rest and recovery are basic biological processes, vital to our functioning, which allow our bodies to repair and our thoughts to reorganise. Rest is a state where the body ceases work or movement and is characterised by minimal functional and metabolic activity. This occurs primarily when we sleep, but also at other times. Recovery is a return to a normal state of health, mind, or strength, which may be achieved through rest but also through other processes. Recovery from work refers to reducing symptoms associated with the physical and psychological strain caused by the work. A model called the *effort-recovery model* assumes that psychological and physiological systems, activated during the working day, will return to a baseline value once an employee takes a break from work activities.[1] Recovery allows an individual to replenish resources and ensures they are ready for the next challenge. Research shows that if workers are regularly unable to take recovery breaks, they will over time develop chronic stress and fatigue, which may affect wellbeing, motivation, and performance at work.[2]

In recent decades, work has increasingly become the central measure of our value. Overwork is applauded, and stress and burnout are considered the unfortunate by-products of success. If we are defined by our work, then when we stop working, we lose a sense of who we are or our purpose in life. In this paradigm, recovery time is viewed as the adversary of our commitment to and effectiveness in the workplace. For those engaged in emotionally and cognitively demanding jobs, the lines between work and leisure have become increasingly blurred. Individuals find it hard to detach from work when they are away from the workplace, and the proliferation of technology has created a situation where we are always available, which makes it even harder to take time to recover.

Work Recovery

School leadership is highly demanding work. Headteachers and principals need to be in an optimal physical and psychological state to maintain the levels of energy, focus, and engagement that the job requires. Recovery from work is an important mechanism in achieving this. Work recovery allows leaders to reduce the symptoms of physical and psychological strain caused by their daily job demands and stressful events at work. Researchers have identified four experiences that are essential to effective work recovery. These are *psychological detachment, relaxation, mastery experiences*, and *control*.[2]

Psychological Detachment

Studies show the most important component of work recovery is psychological detachment. This involves fully disengaging from work, both mentally and physically, during non-work time. Psychological detachment is strongly associated with decreased levels of exhaustion and psychological strain, as well as improved sleep. It is also positively linked to job performance.[3]

For headteachers and principals, psychological detachment can be difficult to achieve. Long working hours, including evenings and weekends, reduce opportunities for leaders to switch off. The proliferation of technology has blurred the boundaries between work and home for leaders. Studies have also found that individuals working in intensive conditions have the most difficulty disengaging from work-related thoughts, as those in high-stress jobs tend to ruminate on the events of the working day during non-work time.[4] Research shows that ruminating on a difficult interaction with a colleague has the same psychological effect as the actual interaction and causes stress reactions to be sustained over a longer period.[4] Work-related rumination not only prevents an individual from disengaging from work but is also associated with an increased risk of cardiovascular disease,[5] cortisol secretion,[6] sleep disturbance, and poorer executive functioning.[4] It is, therefore, essential that headteachers and principals find ways to detach from work-related thinking during non-work time.

A growing body of research highlights how psychological detachment can be learned, and studies have identified a small number of interventions that can support individuals in disengagement. These include creating plans at the end of the working day to describe where, when, and how unfulfilled work goals will be completed.[7] Mindfulness is also an effective way to address a tendency to ruminate. An online, instructor-led mindfulness intervention was found to significantly reduce work-related rumination, with effects maintained at both three- and six-month follow-up.[8] A three-week, online, self-training intervention in mindfulness was also found to increase psychological detachment in participants.[9]

Studies on the effect of cognitive behavioural therapy (CBT) on disengagement from work-related thoughts have shown positive results. A one-day CBT-based workshop, focused on work rumination, chronic fatigue, and sleep quality, was found to significantly reduce levels of rumination in participants at six-month follow-up.[8] While short duration interventions can have a positive effect, interventions of longer duration and higher dosage have been found to be more effective in helping participants to switch off.[10] Finally, studies show that a reduction in smartphone use during non-work time significantly increases an individual's ability to disengage from work-related thinking.[11]

Relaxation Experiences

Relaxation is essential for employees to recover from the demands of work and allow bodies and brains to be restored to pre-stress levels. The idea of the *relaxation response* was developed by Dr Herbert Benson in the 1960s as a counter to the stress response. The relaxation response is an individual's ability to release chemicals and brain signals that make muscles and organs slow down and increase blood flow to the brain. Practising relaxation has been found to lower heart rate, blood pressure, and oxygen consumption and alter genomic activity, which all counteract the effect of stress on the body. Regular relaxation reduces the risk of a wide range of mental and physical health conditions, including cancer, heart disease, stroke, and insomnia. Individuals who report an inability to relax after work have been found to have a threefold increased risk of heart disease[12] and are three times more likely to experience sleep disturbance. They are also significantly more likely to experience a wide range of neurotic symptoms.[13]

A huge body of literature has developed around relaxation, not all of which is well researched. It is generally accepted that relaxation can be achieved through engagement in both leisure activities and specific relaxation techniques. Activities such as massage, sauna, interaction with pets, knitting, or listening to music have all been found to initiate the relaxation response. Studies have also found a wide range of specific relaxation techniques to be effective. These include meditation, deep breathing, progressive muscle relaxation, visualisation, and self-hypnosis. Autogenic training, a set of mental exercises focused on the body's experience of relaxation, and biofeedback, which uses an electronic device to monitor and manage heart rate, blood pressure, and other body responses, have also been shown to be highly effective.

Mastery Experiences

While both psychological detachment and relaxation are key components of work recovery, effective recovery also involves mastery experiences. Mastery provides opportunities for individuals to be successful at things unrelated to work and experience feelings of achievement and competence. The completion of challenges leads to neurochemical reactions in the brain, including the release of dopamine, that leave individuals feeling uplifted. Engaging in mastery experiences enhances feelings of wellbeing, positive emotions, and life satisfaction.[14] A wide range of activities can provide mastery experiences, including sport and hobbies that become progressively more challenging, such as learning a language or playing a musical instrument.

Control

Control refers to the level of autonomy that individuals have over how they spend their non-work time. Studies show that freedom to decide how to spend leisure time is key to an individual's recovery process. High levels of control are associated with decreased emotional exhaustion and high levels of positive emotion.[2]

Recovery at Weekends

A growing body of research highlights how recovery time at weekends is crucial to reducing stress, allowing for the regeneration of physical and psychological resources. Weekend experiences have a significant impact on general wellbeing and job performance in the immediate days following the weekend.[15] More specifically, the extent of an individual's psychological detachment, relaxation, mastery, and control experiences at the weekend all influence their state of being at the start of the working week. They account for fluctuations in weekly task performance and a range of constructive work-based behaviours, including altruism, courtesy, and conscientiousness.[16] Studies show that social activity during the weekend improves work engagement and general wellbeing during the following week and reduces the risk of burnout.[6] Absorption in joint weekend activities with a spouse or partner have also been shown to aid recovery from work and increase positive emotions after the weekend.[17]

Engaging in weekend activities that include all four recovery experiences is, therefore, highly beneficial to school leaders. While weekend recovery experiences have a significant impact on workers' job performance and wellbeing at the beginning of the working week, research has found that the effects diminish as the week progresses, fading out more quickly where individuals fail to engage in recovery activities at the end of each workday.[18] Occasional work-free weekends will therefore have limited benefits, and the greatest recovery is experienced when frequent weekend recovery is combined with regular workday recovery.

Holiday Recovery

Holidays from work provide longer breaks to facilitate the replenishment of resources and are essential to work recovery. Vacations have been shown to have positive effects on people's health and wellbeing, with people reporting less exhaustion and fewer health complaints when returning from holiday. Holidays also increase an individual's engagement on return to work and decrease levels of burnout.[19] Taking annual vacations reduces the overall risk of death by about 20%, and the risk of death from heart disease by as much as a third.[20]

Studies show that the benefits of a holiday gradually fade in the weeks following return and disappear completely after around one month.[21] For school leaders, there is often a tendency to put off recovery until the longer vacations and hope that a good break over the summer will provide sufficient replenishment of resources to keep them going through the following school year. Research findings point to regular short breaks, coupled with work-free weekends and recovery time each workday, to be a much more effective way to ensure that work recovery occurs.

Work-Home Boundaries

Effective work recovery during non-work time is influenced by an individual's work-home boundaries. Boundary theory is a growing field of research that has proliferated since the onset of the COVID-19 pandemic. Studies have found that the boundaries employees set between work and home fall along a continuum ranging from *segmentation*, where work and non-work are strictly separated, and *integration*, where they are completely blended.[22] Most workers fall somewhere between the two ends of the continuum. Work-home boundaries are shaped by organisational and cultural practices, but they are also influenced by an individual's preferences.[23] Studies show that individuals are likely to feel more effective in their work and non-work roles when their boundary preferences are fulfilled.[24] This would seem to indicate that a school leader who prefers a high level of integration between work and home will benefit from a blurring of work and non-work boundaries.

Another body of research, however, points to there being a detrimental effect on health and wellbeing for *integrators* compared to *segmenters*. Those who have blurred home-work boundaries find it harder to psychologically detach from work during non-work time and experience higher levels of work-related rumination than those who see work and home as two distinct spheres.[25] Studies have also found that *segmenters* have lower levels of stress and exhaustion than integrators.[26]

Recovery During the Workday

The literature on work recovery shows that workers involved in cognitively demanding work, such as headteachers and principals, benefit from participating in recovery experiences not only during non-work time but also during the working day. Psychologists have found that an individual's capacity to exert cognitive effort is limited and that, without regular breaks, cognitive resources become depleted due to mental overexertion.

Taking breaks not only provides time to replenish resources but allows the unconscious brain to establish new connections and see patterns that are not obvious to the conscious mind. When we take a break and let the mind wander, the brain shifts to inward-focused cognition and switches on the default mode network (DMN). During this time, the brain is not inactive but integrates new information with existing knowledge and enables the unconscious mind to find creative solutions to problems that the conscious brain cannot see. This all points to the brain performing more effectively if regular breaks are taken.

Studies have found that breaks taken during the workday not only improve performance but can help manage stress, decrease exhaustion, and reduce the need for a long recovery at the end of the working day.[27] Breaks at work can take multiple forms, but the literature on recovery has focused on *micro-breaks* as an effective strategy for sustaining employee resources. Micro-break activities are short, informal activities taken voluntarily between tasks, at an employee's discretion, and can last from just a few seconds to several minutes. Studies show that frequent micro-breaks reduce physical and mental fatigue and increase positive emotions.[28]

Micro-breaks provide an opportunity to psychologically detach from work, relax, and rebuild psychological resources. Relaxation micro-breaks, such as meditating, daydreaming, or stretching have been shown to help individuals' physical and psychological systems return to pre-stress levels.[29] Short breaks to engage in physical activity are also highly beneficial in improving mental health and personal relationships among workers.[30] Likewise, cognitive micro-break activities that facilitate a mental break from work demands, such as casual reading, browsing the internet for entertainment, or personal learning are also effective. Individuals who participate in social micro-breaks experience increased feelings of recovery compared to those who take solitary breaks.[31] Social micro-breaks that involve talking about common interests with colleagues or checking in with a friend or family member increase feelings of vitality more than breaks that involve chatting about work-related matters. Regardless of the activity involved, the voluntary and autonomous nature of micro-breaks is key to their effectiveness, as self-initiated micro-breaks allow employees to choose optimal timing and preferred activities to accommodate their individual needs and daily rhythms.[32]

The fast pace and relentless nature of the headteacher's and principal's work can provide little opportunity for them to take breaks during the school day. School leaders need to understand, however, that regular short breaks can have a considerable effect on their ability to manage stress, as well as improve their job performance and productivity. Studies that involved only a 40-second relaxation or cognitive microbreak were found to improve task performance and concentration immediately following the break.[33] It is, therefore, essential that headteachers and principals build regular micro-breaks into the pattern of their working day. Strategies could include scheduling breaks, agreeing break times with close colleagues, or setting an alarm to prompt breaks. Implementing tools such as the Pomodoro technique,[34] which allows for five minutes of break time every 30 minutes using either a Pomodoro timer or an app such as BeFocused, can help individuals to adopt new routines.

Sleep

Sleep is a primary human function, as important as breathing, water, or food. Yet our need for sleep is severely neglected, and we constantly devalue the seriousness of sleep deficiency. In the context of life's challenges, getting enough sleep takes a low priority for many. Both the UK National Health Service and the US Centers for Disease Control and Prevention (CDC) report that one in three adults has problems sleeping.

We know that headteachers and principals experience more sleep problems than the general population. Participants in the Australian Principal Occupational Health, Safety and Wellbeing Survey have consistently reported a much greater incidence of sleeping troubles over the last decade than the public at large.[35] A pre-COVID survey of UK senior leaders reported that over half experienced insomnia or sleeping difficulties,[36] while only 16% of leaders in my 2020 mid-pandemic survey reported getting enough sleep.[37] Over half of Ontario principals feel their work has a considerable effect on their sleep.[38]

Sleep plays a significant role in our health, wellbeing, and performance. When we sleep, the body repairs cells, grows new tissue, restores energy, and releases essential hormones and proteins. Neurons are reorganised, which supports brain function in key areas, including learning, memory, problem-solving, creativity, decision-making, and concentration. Sleep also helps moderate activity in the amygdala, the emotional control centre of the brain, allowing us to respond less emotionally when faced with a stressful situation. It helps regulate weight, by controlling hunger hormones, protects against insulin resistance, and fights infection through the production of proteins, antibodies, and immune cells.

When we are deprived of sleep, these benefits are quickly lost. Even a sleep deficit of a couple of hours can lead to lack of alertness, impaired memory, relationship conflicts, and a reluctance to participate in normal daily activities.

Chronic sleep deficiency can be much more serious, causing changes at a genetic level, and contributing to a wide range of physical and mental health conditions and early death. It also affects our emotional functioning, influences our interactions with others, and reduces job performance.[39]

Humans are biologically programmed to spend a third of their adult lives asleep, with seven to nine hours of quality sleep per night being ideal. Researchers have found that when the duration of sleep regularly drops below seven hours, and especially when it starts to move towards six and half hours or less, negative effects become significantly more prevalent.[40] While many of these effects will become apparent quite quickly, especially in cognitive and emotional functioning, others may not take effect for years or even decades. The US CDC has found that those who sleep less than seven hours a night are 50% more likely to have heart disease, stroke, depression, and chronic kidney disease than those who sleep for seven hours or more. They are also more likely to have asthma, diabetes, arthritis, and cancer. Sleep deprivation is also linked to a higher mortality risk, with an individual that sleeps on average less than six hours a night having a 13% higher mortality risk than someone sleeping between seven and nine hours.[41] Chronic lack of sleep can, therefore, be a ticking time bomb of which most school leaders are completely unaware.

Sleep and Stress

Prioritising sleep is crucial in the management of stress. High levels of stress reduce sleep duration and decrease REM and deep sleep, leading to poor sleep quality. Adults who sleep less than eight hours a night are more likely to report symptoms of stress in the past month, such as feeling irritable, angry, or overwhelmed. They are also more likely to say their stress has increased in the past year. Of adults who are already highly stressed, 45% report that lack of sleep makes their stress worse, compared to only 5% of those who are mildly stressed.[42]

Likewise, feeling stressed increases the chances of having a poor night's sleep. On average, adults with lower reported stress levels sleep one hour more each night than adults with higher stress levels. They are also much more likely to say they have excellent or very good-quality sleep. Half of high-stress individuals report not having enough sleep compared to only 10% of those with low stress. Impairments in daily functioning, brought about by lack of sleep, can cause or contribute to stress. These include fatigue, difficulty concentrating, irritability, mood disturbances, decreased motivation, and impaired performance, all of which are significantly raised in those who have less sleep.[42]

The relationship between sleep and stress creates a vicious circle of inadequate sleep and increasing stress. If the cycle can be broken, then stress will be reduced and sleep improved. Getting enough sleep on a nightly basis can alleviate stress quite effectively. It is, therefore, important to prioritise sleep to improve stress management, as well as to manage stress to improve sleep. Studies shows that most Americans would be happier, healthier, and safer if they were to sleep an extra 60 to 90 minutes per night.[43]

Improving Sleep

School leaders who are experiencing sleep difficulties can feel bombarded with information about how to improve their sleep. There is a wealth of literature and a wide range of products on the market targeted at improving sleep and tackling insomnia. It is hard for leaders to know what really works, and where to invest their money and efforts to take control of their sleep performance. Fortunately, there is a significant body of research developing around sleep interventions, which help us to identify what approaches are most effective.

Following several meta-analyses of peer reviewed studies on treatments for insomnia, the American College of Physicians has officially endorsed cognitive behavioural therapy for insomnia (CBT-I) as the best treatment for chronic insomnia disorder.[44] CBT-I is a multi-component treatment that combines several different approaches, involving cognitive, behavioural, and educational elements. It focuses on recognising and changing beliefs that affect an individual's ability to sleep, by controlling or eliminating negative thoughts and worries that keep them awake.

A CBT-I programme will draw upon a range of strategies and techniques, which vary depending on the needs of each patient. Sleep education involves informing patients about healthy sleep patterns and lifestyle habits. Sleep hygiene focuses on increasing behaviours that improve sleep, while eliminating behaviours that cause sleep problems, such as creating an optimal sleep environment, increasing exercise, moderating caffeine, alcohol, and nicotine, and making changes to evening food intake. CBT-I may also include stimulus control therapy, a series of steps to reduce anxiety around sleep, and develop a positive relationship with the sleep area, such as lying down only when feeling tired, using the bed only for sleep and sex, setting an alarm for the same time each morning, and avoiding napping during the day. Other elements of CBT-I include light therapy, which involves going outside during daylight hours or using a light box, and a wide range of relaxation techniques, including breathing exercises, progressive muscle relaxation, hypnosis, yoga, and meditation.

CBT-I has been found to improve sleep experiences in 70% to 80% of insomnia patients, with results maintained over time. These include falling asleep more quickly, increased time asleep, and reduced periods of wakefulness.[44] Research on the effectiveness of CBT-I has mainly focused on face-to-face programmes, delivered by qualified CBT-I therapists, usually in a course of six to eight sessions. There is also a growing body of research to support the effectiveness of self-help approaches to CBT-I, which can be worked through independently by patients.[45] Such programmes are usually delivered by booklet, audio, video, internet, or specialised apps. Patients find self-help CBT-I to be effective in improving various sleep measures, and programmes involve low drop-out rates.[46]

Examples of self-help CBT-I programmes include a number of peer-reviewed apps, such as *SHUTi, Sleepio, RESTORE,* and *CBT-I Coach.* Online options include *Conquering Insomnia Programme, FreeCBT-I,* and *Sleep.8Coaching.* A range of self-help resources, including books, websites, apps, and online therapists are available at MySleepwell.ca, a not-for-profit initiative from Dalhousie University in Canada; UK-based Talkplus; the Government of Western Australia's Centre for Clinical Interventions; and NHSInform Scotland.

Prioritising Rest and Recovery

In this chapter so far, I have examined the importance of adequate rest and recovery to stress management. This involves getting enough sleep, taking breaks during and at the end of the workday, ensuring work-free weekends, and taking regular, short holidays. To ensure they are taking sufficient breaks, school leaders need to consider a range of actions. These may include scheduling microbreaks, managing work commitments to ensure sufficient evening recovery, and establishing boundaries between work and personal life. This requires high levels of personal organisation and a commitment to self-care. For most leaders this also requires a change in habits.

Establishing New Habits

Habits are automatic mental or behavioural responses to environmental cues or triggers. We generally underestimate the role that habits play in our everyday lives, yet around half of the actions and choices that make up our daily routines are likely to be habits. We acquire a habit by repeated experiences that create neural connections in the brain, allowing us to perform the habit automatically and minimise the mental energy we expend.

Studies show that habits help maintain behaviour patterns that contribute to stress. Researchers have found that stressed individuals are more likely to repeat habitual behaviour and find it more difficult to break out of bad habits than those who are less stressed.[47] Stress inhibits the brain's neural circuitry that allows us to make conscious choices and activates the circuitry of impulse. This affects our ability to make good choices and suppresses our thinking about the consequences of poor choice. Changing our stress physiology by reducing stress hormones can facilitate a break from habitual behaviour and have a positive effect on the choices we make.

Like the relationship between sleep and stress, habits and stress can form a vicious circle. Bad habits increase stress, and stress increases our chances of defaulting to those habits. Small steps that reduce stress can help activate our self-awareness circuitry and lead to us making better choices. This reduces stress further and perpetuates a more positive cycle of behaviour, which over time can have a significant effect on health and wellbeing.

Paying greater attention to rest and work recovery requires the establishment of new habits. School leaders often feel they are often not able to make large-scale changes in their lives. They also commonly dismiss the value of small changes. Research in the field of habit formation has found, however, that incremental changes in behaviour can have a significant effect on the behaviours that contribute to stress.[48]

Habits can be broken by controlling the cues that trigger behaviour. Researchers have found context to be a key trigger in habit formation. This includes location, time of day, the people you are with, and prior actions performed. If the context remains the same, it is harder to break old habits.[49]

Building new habits requires the repetition of behaviour in a context until it becomes automatic. Techniques to support habit formation include combining a desire to form a new habit with an intention to regularly perform it in a specific place and at a specific time. Stacking a new habit on top of a current good habit is another effective technique. This involves setting an intention to perform the new behaviour immediately after performing the current habit, with the current habit acting as the trigger for the new habit.[50]

Studies show that adding friction, by making a bad habit harder to do, can be highly effective. Reducing friction, to make a new habit easy to perform, is also effective. Making a behaviour more or less rewarding will affect how habit forming it becomes. Forming new habits is also easier if behaviours are aligned with an individual's natural strengths.[49]

Individuals can become easily deterred from their intentions to establish new habits, or break old ones, when progress is perceived as slow. Researchers have found that it takes on average 66 days for new habits to become automatic, although two to three months is considered by most psychologists to be a realistic time frame to create new habits.[50]

Breaking habits that negatively affect rest and work recovery or establishing new ones that will support this process begins with a process of self-reflection. This helps build awareness around current behaviours that are supportive and those acting as barriers to rest and recovery. Leaders should evaluate their sleep, their work-home boundaries, and the amount of time they allocate for recovery during the workday, evenings, weekends, and holidays. They should reflect upon how they spend their non-work time and the opportunities they create for psychological detachment, relaxation, control, and mastery experiences. Small changes in these areas can make a significant effect on a leader's wellbeing, over time, as they facilitate a route out of the cycle of stress, poor sleep, inadequate recovery, and unhealthy habits.

Chapter Summary

- Rest and recovery are the most effective approaches to stress management.
- Work recovery reduces the symptoms of physical and psychological strain caused by the demands of school leaders' work.
- Four experiences are essential to effective work recovery – psychological detachment, relaxation, mastery experiences, and control.
- Switching off from work-related activities and thinking is the most important component of work recovery. This can be learned and supported by a range of interventions.
- The large body of literature around relaxation makes it hard for leaders to establish what works best. Studies highlight the effectiveness of a wide range of leisure activities and specific relaxation techniques.
- Mastery experiences provide leaders with opportunities to be successful in the non-work domain. Mastery experiences include sport and interests that are progressively more challenging.
- Leaders need to have control over how they spend their leisure time for work recovery to be most effective.
- Leaders should seek regular and consistent opportunities for work recovery during the working day, at evenings and weekends, and during frequent, short holidays.
- Clear work-home boundaries support psychological detachment and reduce stress and exhaustion.
- Sufficient sleep plays a key role in stress management. CBT-I is psychologists' preferred treatment for chronic insomnia.
- Leaders will need to break old habits and establish new ones that support adequate rest and work recovery. This process begins with self-reflection to establish what needs to change.

- Small, incremental changes can make a big impact over time.
- Research into habit formation provides a wealth of strategies and tools to support changing habits.

Recommended Resources for Improving Sleep

Psychologists consider CBT-I to be the most effective way to address insomnia and other sleep problems. Examples of online self-help CBT-I programmes include *Conquering Insomnia Programme, FreeCBT-I,* and *Sleep.8Coaching.*

A range of self-help resources, including books, websites, apps, and online therapists, is available at MySleepwell.ca, a not-for-profit initiative from Dalhousie University in Canada.

Notes

1 Bennett, A.A., Bakker, A.B. and Field, J.G., 2018. Recovery from Work-related Effort: A Meta-analysis. *Journal of Organizational Behavior*, 39(3), 262–275.

2 Sonnentag, S., Cheng, B.H. and Parker, S.L., 2022. Recovery from Work: Advancing the Field Toward the Future. *Annual Review of Organizational Psychology and Organizational Behavior*, 9.

3 Sonnentag, S., Kuttler, I. and Fritz, C., 2010. Job Stressors, Emotional Exhaustion, and Need for Recovery: A Multi-source Study on the Benefits of Psychological Detachment. *Journal of Vocational Behavior*, 76(3), 355–365.

4 Cropley, M. and Zijlstra, F.R., 2011. Work and Rumination. In C. Cooper and J. Langan-Fox, eds. *Handbook of Stress in the Occupations*, pp. 487–503. Cheltenham, UK: Edward Elgar.

5 Kivimäki, M., Virtanen, M., Elovainio, M., Kouvonen, A., Väänänen, A. and Vahtera, J., 2006. Work Stress in the Etiology of Coronary Heart Disease: A Meta-analysis. *Scandinavian Journal of Work, Environment & Health*, 431–442.

6 Rystedt, L.W., Cropley, M., Devereux, J.J. and Michalianou, G., 2008. The Relationship Between Long-term Job Strain and Morning and Evening Saliva Cortisol Secretion among White-collar Workers. *Journal of Occupational Health Psychology*, 13(2), 105.

7 Smit, B.W., 2016. Successfully Leaving Work at Work: The Self-regulatory Underpinnings of Psychological Detachment. *Journal of Occupational and Organizational Psychology*, 89(3), 493–514.

8 Querstret, D., Cropley, M. and Fife-Schaw, C., 2017. Internet-based Instructor-led Mindfulness for Work-related Rumination, Fatigue, and Sleep: Assessing

Facets of Mindfulness as Mechanisms of Change. A Randomized Waitlist Control Trial. *Journal of Occupational Health Psychology*, 22(2), 153.

9 Althammer, S.E., Reis, D., van der Beek, S., Beck, L. and Michel, A., 2021. A Mindfulness Intervention Promoting Work – Life Balance: How Segmentation Preference Affects Changes in Detachment, Well-being, and Work – Life Balance. *Journal of Occupational and Organizational Psychology*, 94(2), 282–308.

10 Karabinski, T., Haun, V.C., Nübold, A., Wendsche, J. and Wegge, J., 2021. Interventions for Improving Psychological Detachment from Work: A Meta-analysis. *Journal of Occupational Health Psychology*, 26(3), 224.

11 Derks, D. and Bakker, A.B., 2014. Smartphone Use, Work – Home Interference, and Burnout: A Diary Study on the Role of Recovery. *Applied Psychology*, 63(3), 411–440.

12 Suadicani, P., Heina, H.O. and Gyntelberg, F., 1993. Are Social Inequalities as Associated with the Risk of Ischaemic Heart Disease a Result of Psychosocial Working Conditions? *Atherosclerosis*, 101(2), 165–175.

13 Lusa, S., Häkkänen, M., Luukkonen, R. and Viikari-Juntura, E., 2002. Perceived Physical Work Capacity, Stress, Sleep Disturbance and Occupational Accidents among Firefighters Working During a Strike. *Work & Stress*, 16(3), 264–274.

14 Sonnentag, S., Binnewies, C. and Mojza, E.J., 2008. "Did You Have a Nice Evening?" A Day-level Study on Recovery Experiences, Sleep, and Affect. *Journal of Applied Psychology*, 93(3), 674.

15 Fritz, C., Sonnentag, S., Spector, P.E. and McInroe, J.A. 2010. The Weekend Matters: Relationships between Stress Recovery and Affective Experiences. *Journal of Organizational Behavior*, 31(8), 1137–1162.

16 Fritz, C. and Sonnentag, S., 2005. Recovery, Health, and Job Performance: Effects of Weekend Experiences. *Journal of Occupational Health Psychology*, 10(3), 187.

17 Hahn, V.C., Binnewies, C. and Haun, S., 2012. The Role of Partners for Employees' Recovery During the Weekend. *Journal of Vocational Behavior*, 80(2), 288–298.

18 Binnewies, C., Sonnentag, S. and Mojza, E.J., 2010. Recovery During the Weekend and Fluctuations in Weekly Job Performance: A Week-level Study Examining Intra-Individual Relationships. *Journal of Occupational and Organizational Psychology*, 83(2), 419–441.

19 Kühnel, J. and Sonnentag, S., 2011. How Long Do You Benefit from Vacation? A Closer Look at the Fade-out of Vacation Effects. *Journal of Organizational Behavior*, 32(1), 125–143.

20 Gump, B.B. and Matthews, K.A., 2000. Are Vacations Good for Your Health? The 9-year Mortality Experience after the Multiple Risk Factor Intervention Trial. *Psychosomatic Medicine*, 62(5), 608–612.

21 Yu, J., Smale, B. and Xiao, H., 2021. Examining the Change in Wellbeing Following a Holiday. *Tourism Management*, 87, 104367.

22 Nippert-Eng, C., 1996. *Home and Work: Negotiating Boundaries in Everyday Life.* Chicago, IL: University of Chicago Press.

23 Methot, J.R. and LePine, J.A., 2016. Too Close for Comfort? Investigating the Nature and Functioning of Work and Non-work Role Segmentation Preferences. *Journal of Business and Psychology*, 31(1), 103–123.

24 Chen, Z., Powell, G.N. and Greenhaus, J.H., 2009. Work-to-family Conflict, Positive Spillover, and Boundary Management: A Person-environment Fit Approach. *Journal of Vocational Behavior*, 74(1), 82–93.

25 Cropley, M. and Millward, L.J., 2009. How Do Individuals 'Switch-off' from Work During Leisure? A Qualitative Description of the Unwinding Process in High and Low Ruminators. *Leisure Studies*, 28(3), 333–347.

26 Sonnentag, S., Kuttler, I. and Fritz, C., 2010. Job Stressors, Emotional Exhaustion, and Need for Recovery: A Multi-source Study on the Benefits of Psychological Detachment. *Journal of Vocational Behavior*, 76(3), 355–365.

27 Coffeng, J.K., van Sluijs, E.M., Hendriksen, I.J.M., van Mechelen, W. and Boot, C.R.L., 2015. Physical Activity and Relaxation During and After Work Are Independently Associated with the Need for Recovery. *Journal Physical Activity and Health*, 12(1), 109–115.

28 Henning, R.A., Jacques, P., Kissel, G.V., Sullivan, A.B. and Alteras-Webb, S.M., 1997. Frequent Short Rest Breaks from Computer Work: Effects on Productivity and Well-being at Two Field Sites. *Ergonomics*, 40(1), 78–91.

29 Kim, S., Park, Y. and Niu, Q., 2017. Micro-break Activities at Work to Recover from Daily Work Demands. *Journal of Organizational Behavior*, 38(1), 28–44.

30 Michishita, R., Jiang, Y., Ariyoshi, D., Yoshida, M., Moriyama, H. and Yamato, H., 2016. The Practice of Active Rest by Workplace Units Improves Personal Relationships, Mental Health, and Physical Activity among Workers. *Journal of Occupational Health*, 59(2).

31 Waber, B.N., Olguin Olguin, D., Kim, T. and Pentland, A., 2010. Productivity Through Coffee Breaks: Changing Social Networks by Changing Break Structure. Available online SSRN 1586375.

32 Kühnel, J., Zacher, H., De Bloom, J. and Bledow, R., 2017. Take a Break! Benefits of Sleep and Short Breaks for Daily Work Engagement. *European Journal of Work and Organizational Psychology*, 26(4), 481–491.

33 Lee, K.E., Williams, K.J., Sargent, L.D., Williams, N.S. and Johnson, K.A., 2015. 40-second Green Roof Views Sustain Attention: The Role of Micro-breaks in Attention Restoration. *Journal of Environmental Psychology*, 42, 182–189.

34 Cirillo, F., 2018. *The Pomodoro Technique: The Life-changing Time-management System.* London: Random House.

35 Riley, P., See, S.-M., Marsh, H. and Dicke, T., 2019. *The Australian Principal Occupational Health, Safety and Wellbeing Survey 2020.* Sydney: Institute for Positive Psychology and Education, Australian Catholic University.

36 Savill-Smith, C., 2019. *Teacher Wellbeing Index*. London: Education Support.

37 Kelly, H., 2020. School Leader Wellbeing During the COVID 19 Pandemic 2020. Accessed online https://drhelenkelly.com/2020/12/13/school-leader-wellbeing-during-the-covid-19-pandemic-the-2020-report/.

38 Pollock, K. and Wang, F., 2020. *School Principals' Work and Well-Being in Ontario: What They Say and Why It Matters*. Toronto, ON: Western University.

39 Carskadon, M.A., 2004. Sleep Deprivation: Health Consequences and Societal Impact. *Medical Clinics*, 88(3), 767–776.

40 Watson, N.F., Badr, M.S., Belenky, G., Bliwise, D.L., Buxton, O.M. and Tasali, E., 2015. Recommended Amount of Sleep for a Healthy Adult: A Joint Consensus Statement of the American Academy of Sleep Medicine and Sleep Research Society. *Journal of Clinical Sleep Medicine*, 11(6), 591–592.

41 Center for Disease Control Sleep Statistics. Accessed online www.cdc.gov/sleep/data_statistics.html.

42 American Psychological Association, 2020. *Stress in America Survey 2020*. Washington, DC: AMA.

43 American Psychological Association, 2004. More Sleep Would Make Most Americans Happier, Healthier and Safer. Accessed online www.apa.org/research/action/sleep-deprivation.

44 Mitchell, L.J., Bisdounis, L., Ballesio, A., Omlin, X. and Kyle, S.D., 2019. The Impact of Cognitive Behavioural Therapy for Insomnia on Objective Sleep Parameters: A Meta-analysis and Systematic Review. *Sleep Medicine Reviews*, 47, 90–102.

45 Irish, L.A., Veronda, A.C., van Lamsweerde, A.E., Mead, M.P. and Wonderlich, S.A., 2021. The Process of Developing a Sleep Health Improvement Plan: A Lab-Based Model of Self-Help Behavior. *International Journal of Behavioral Medicine*, 28(1), 96–106.

46 Morin, C.M., Beaulieu-Bonneau, S., LeBlanc, M. and Savard, J., 2005. Self-help Treatment for Insomnia: A Randomized Controlled Trial. *Sleep*, 28(10), 1319–1327.

47 Schwabe, L. and Wolf, O.T., 2009. Stress Prompts Habit Behavior in Humans. *Journal of Neuroscience*, 29(22), 7191–7198.

48 Schwabe, L., Höffken, O., Tegenthoff, M. and Wolf, O.T., 2011. Preventing the Stress-Induced Shift from Goal-Directed to Habit Action with a β-Adrenergic Antagonist. *Journal of Neuroscience*, 1(47), 17317–17325.

49 Pine, K. and Fletcher, B., 2016. *Changing People's Habits Is Associated with Reductions in Stress, Anxiety and Depression Levels*. Brighton: Do Something Different.

50 Lally, P., van Jaarsveld, C.H.M., Potts, H.W.W. and Wardle, J., 2010. How Are Habits Formed: Modelling Habit Formation in the Real World. *European Journal of Social Psychology*, 40, 998–1009.

What Leaders Can Do **13**

Addressing Self-Sabotage Behaviours

While burnout is primarily a condition of the workplace, rather than of the individual, there may be personality traits, characteristics, or behaviours that render some leaders more vulnerable to burnout than others. These individual factors are commonly overestimated, but they can play a role in exacerbating a leader's stress levels and contribute to them becoming overwhelmed. In the field of psychology, self-sabotage is a well-recognised phenomenon that results from counterproductive mindsets or behaviours. This can lead to an individual becoming stuck in negative or self-destructive cycles, which may damage them physically, mentally, or emotionally and hinder their success or wellbeing.[1]

Self-sabotage behaviours may be conscious or unconscious and emanate from biological responses once necessary for survival. They are commonly rooted in an individual's previous emotional experiences, often from childhood, which affect their self-perception and may be linked to low self-esteem. Studies show that past insecurities can be triggered when an individual approaches something they truly desire, such as workplace goals. Dysfunctional habits can develop to protect an individual from the emotions associated with failure. These unconscious behaviours fill a deep-seated need and become repeated over time until they form a habit of which the individual is usually unaware.

Working with hundreds of headteachers and principals, in my capacity as colleague, consultant and coach, I have observed a range of self-sabotage behaviours commonly found in leaders, which may be responsible for exacerbating their work-related stress. I have identified ten behaviour types that may help us understand the kinds of self-sabotage that school leaders engage in. Many of these types are widely recognised in the field of psychology.

DOI: 10.4324/9781003198475-16

In this chapter, I use these behaviour types as a construct to help leaders identify and understand their own unhelpful behaviours and how they might be detrimental to their wellbeing. This is intended to facilitate a process of self-reflection and build self-awareness that will help individuals to understand internal factors that may be contributing to their workplace stress. This understanding will enable them to manage stress more effectively and mitigate burnout. When practised in moderation, most of the behaviours discussed in this chapter would commonly be considered positive, aspirational, and characteristic of effective leadership. If allowed to go unchecked, however, they can sometimes develop into dysfunctional habits that may be damaging to physical, mental, and emotional health and can undermine the pursuit of a leader's goals.

I want to acknowledge that, while large elements of my thinking are rooted in psychology theory, and supported by a strong body of research, the ten behaviour types I discuss here are not rigorously researched in relation to school leaders. I have, however, used this material in workshops and coaching sessions in recent years, and I have found that this approach resonates deeply with leaders. Most leaders can identify several of the self-sabotage behaviours in themselves and find them a useful tool to reflect upon their emotions, needs, and drivers.

The Imposter

Many school leaders I have worked with easily recognise the signs of imposter syndrome in themselves. Imposter syndrome was first described by psychologists Imes and Clance in the 1970s and is a phenomenon that occurs among high achievers who experience exaggerated levels of self-doubt despite their education, experience, and accomplishments. Feelings of being an imposter are more common among individuals embarking on a new endeavour, such as those in the early stages of a school leadership career, and those working in competitive environments.

The Imposter experiences frequent feelings of incompetence and inadequacy that will be reinforced by their shortcomings or failures, no matter how minor. They write off their successes to chance, unable to believe they have earned them on their own merit. They live in fear of being found out and worry that others will eventually unmask them as a fraud.

Those with imposter syndrome are likely to work harder than others, and hold themselves to higher standards, to make up for their perceived lack of prowess. These behaviours help them to feel more worthy of their role, assuage feelings of guilt about their inadequacy, and prevent others from recognising their shortcomings. This puts the Imposter under an incredible amount of pressure to perform, which can eventually take a toll on an their wellbeing, affecting mental health and leaving them vulnerable to burnout. Recent studies have identified links between imposter syndrome and significantly increased levels of emotional exhaustion, cynicism, and detachment.[2]

It is believed that around 25% to 30% of high achievers may suffer from imposter syndrome. Possible causes, or contributing factors, include family dynamics and family or cultural expectations. Research suggests that it may be more prevalent in certain populations, including those from minority and marginalised groups. Certain social and environmental factors can also increase the prevalence of imposter syndrome, including having less support, consistency, and positive reinforcement within the workplace. Imposter syndrome is linked to depression, social anxiety, generalised anxiety disorders, and neuroticism.[3]

The Perfectionist

The Perfectionist sets unattainable standards for themselves, is driven by a fear of failure and will accept nothing less than perfection. They find it easy to identify mistakes and flaws in themselves and their work and tend to wallow in negative feelings when their high expectations are not met. The Perfectionist often procrastinates, as their fear of failure puts them off attempting things, which can further perpetuate feelings of failure. This fear of failure makes it hard for them to relax, concentrate, or delegate. The Perfectionist is defensive and takes constructive criticism badly.

Many factors can contribute to whether an individual develops perfectionism. These factors often emanate from childhood, including poor early attachment to caregivers, unrealistic parental expectations, or fear of disapproval. The high level of control and predictability that perfectionism provides can also be a defence against a chaotic or unsafe home environment. For some, high achievement is a route to self-worth and a way to prove worth to others. Those who have a history of high achievement may engage in ongoing perfectionist behaviour to live up to previous achievements. Some cultures or educational institutions may actively promote a perfectionist mindset.

Perfectionism has been linked to workaholism, as well as a wide range of mental health disorders, including depression, anxiety, self-harm, eating disorders, and obsessive-compulsive disorder. Studies show clear links between perfectionism and all three dimensions of burnout, in a range of different professions, including teachers.[4]

The People Pleaser

The People Pleaser is an individual who feels the need to constantly meet the expectations of others. People-pleasing is associated with a personality trait known as *sociotropy*, which is characterised by a strong need for social acceptance and a consequent excessive investment in interpersonal relationships. The People Pleaser constantly agrees with people, even when they do not believe in what they are saying. They find it hard to say no and feel guilty or anxious when they refuse to take on a commitment. This means they often agree to do things that they do not like or do not want to do, and commonly make excuses to get out of a commitment rather than refusing from the start.

The People Pleaser feels responsible for how other people feel and will do anything to avoid conflict, often apologising for things that are not their fault. They frequently regret not having the strength to stand up for themselves. The People Pleaser may also change their personality to fit those around them, shifting their behaviour and attitude to match that of others. This can lead them to act in ways which are out of character.

The People Pleaser may experience anger, frustration, and built-up resentment towards others, which can lead to passive-aggressive behaviours and a tendency to pull away from relationships, rather than make their feelings known. People-pleasing may also lead to an individual forming superficial or inauthentic relationships as they deny their own needs and hide their true emotions.

Low self-esteem is a common cause of sociotropy. The People Pleaser seeks validation from others to feel good about themselves, and their self-esteem rises and falls depending on how others see them. People-pleasing is also rooted in insecurity and the desire to be liked by others, which may be connected to painful or difficult past experiences. Sociotropy has been linked to a range of mental health conditions, including anxiety, depression, avoidant personality disorder, borderline personality disorder, and co-dependency.

Constant people-pleasing behaviour can lead to an individual's resources being stretched too thin, which may reduce the time they have to attend to their own needs. It is common for people-pleasers to neglect self-care, which may result in them becoming stressed, drained, and exhausted. Although there is no research to confirm a link between people-pleasing behaviours and burnout, it is not hard to see how these behaviours may render an individual more vulnerable to stress and burnout.

The Driven

The Driven is ambitious, persistent, and wants to succeed. They demonstrate high levels of personal commitment to want to make a difference.

They are highly passionate about their work or mission focused. The Driven constantly sets targets and is prepared to put in incredible amounts of work to achieve their goals. They project power and need to be in control of the work environment. They admire, and prefer to be surrounded by, others who are equally driven and tend to lack respect for those with less drive. The Driven is motivated by challenging tasks but can become demotivated if work becomes tedious or repetitive.

Researchers have found that driven individuals have higher levels of dopamine in the reward and motivation centres of the brain.[5] High levels of drive may also be rooted in childhood experiences and may, for some, be linked to fear of failure or self-esteem issues. Success in the public eye is seen as a desirable way to increase self-worth.

The Driven is vulnerable to workaholism and to exhausting themselves by constantly pushing their limits. This can have a long-term effect on their health and wellbeing and make them susceptible to burnout. Research has found that employees driven by purpose are significantly more stressed and score lower for wellbeing, resilience, and self-efficacy than those who are not. They are also more vulnerable to experiencing burnout, as they drive themselves too hard and prioritise the mission over their own needs.[6]

The Servant Leader

Current literature on school leadership highlights the benefits of servant leadership for the school community, but few acknowledge the potentially damaging impact of servant leadership on leaders themselves. The Servant Leader is a servant first and leader second. Their leadership prioritises meeting the needs of others and focuses on the wellbeing and growth of their community, rather than accumulating and exercising power. They work hard to create a sense of belonging and empower others to develop and perform to their potential.

While this style of leadership is associated with high levels of employee engagement, collaboration, wellbeing, and a reduction in workplace incivility, it encourages leaders to abnegate their own needs in preference to the needs of others.

The literature on servant leadership emphasises the importance of listening, empathy, and healing. Empathy has been shown to be a finite resource, and numerous studies suggest a link between over-empathising and occupational burnout, particularly when empathy is practiced repeatedly, with little or no expectation of reciprocation. Studies also show how individuals practising high levels of empathy in the workplace are more vulnerable to experiencing emotional exhaustion and compassion fatigue, which can in turn lead to the feelings of detachment and cynicism indicative of burnout.[7]

The Loner

While a degree of loneliness may be a normal consequence of the school leader role, the Loner compounds this through self-isolation behaviours. There are several reasons why headteachers and principals may seek to isolate themselves from others in the workplace. Most leaders are aware, on some level, that at least some of their employees may not enjoy being with them and may be guarded or act in inauthentic ways when interacting with them. This causes leaders to feel uncomfortable and may lead to them maintaining a distance from their staff. The situation may be exacerbated by the knowledge that colleagues have rich and supportive relationships with each other, causing the leader to feel left out.

Headteachers and principals may also be more likely to isolate themselves during challenging periods when there is a need to make unpopular decisions, resulting in criticism being directed at them. During these times, their leadership practice comes under scrutiny, and leaders may feel misunderstood or unfairly judged by employees. The weight of increasing pressure during these times may cause leaders to recede into themselves, not only to avoid potential conflict but also as a coping mechanism. This can create not only a cognitive and emotional distance but may also cause leaders to retreat to the safety of their office to physically distance themselves. Aspects of the school leader's role that require them to make difficult decisions about staff, or appraise their performance, may also encourage headteachers and principals to purposely distance themselves from others to maintain objectivity.

An imbalance between a leader's desired level of social connection and their relationships on the ground may be more commonly experienced by new headteachers and principals. Those who are new to their school have yet to build trust and may be self-conscious and wary of others as they strive to constantly prove themselves. Those new to senior roles, especially those who are promoted from within their school, may experience sudden changes in relationships and may separate themselves from colleagues as they seek to come to terms with the new dynamic.

Loneliness, both on a professional and personal level, may be aggravated by the time commitments of leadership, which often leaves little opportunity for nurturing collegial relationships or for friends and family. Building new relationships, inside or outside of work, can be challenging for those burdened with long working hours and high stress levels.

Researchers at the University of California, Berkeley, have identified a connection between lack of sleep and social withdrawal. Those who are sleep-deprived feel lonelier and are less inclined to socially engage with others. They also found that the sleep-deprived are more likely to be socially shunned by others, as individuals who lacked sleep are less socially attractive.[8]

Lack of community has been found to be closely associated with headteacher and principal burnout.[9] Loneliness is also closely associated with a range of mental health problems, including anxiety, depression, and suicide, as well as physical ill-health issues, such as hypertension, heart disease, and stroke.[10]

The Validation Seeker

The need for validation is something that most school leaders experience in their work life. From an evolutionary perspective, humans are hardwired to seek inclusion, as rejection by the group could have significant implications for survival. Our behaviour has adapted to constantly seek validation from others. In the workplace, this need for validation is likely to express itself as a desire to have our work and accomplishments recognised by our team, leaders, and others around us. For the Validation Seeker, this behaviour has become maladapted, as they become caught up in a constant cycle of approval seeking. This is characterised by highs of self-importance when validated, and lows of self-pity, anger, and shame when invalidated.

The Validation Seeker is often defined by their work successes. They work harder than others and shows excessive levels of commitment to their role. They overinvest in the acquisition of workplace skills and qualifications and are more likely than others to feel slighted when a colleague disagrees with them.

Dysfunctional validation seeking is often rooted in a sense of inferiority that stems from upbringing, cultural experience, education, or work life. Studies have found women to be more likely to overinvest in workplace skills and qualifications than men.[11]

While there is no research to directly link excessive validation seeking with burnout, it is easy to see connections between the extra workload that validation-seeking behaviours bring and stress and exhaustion. Validation seekers may also be more likely to feel undervalued or unfairly treated at work, leading to imbalances in the work areas of fairness and rewards, both of which are known contributors to burnout.

The Hero Leader

The Hero Leader has been the dominant paradigm in school leadership for decades. It reflects a traditional, hierarchical approach to leadership, rooted in the hero myth. It taps into the unconscious need of followers for the psychological security of a strong leader. The Hero Leader thinks they are better and more important than their followers. They relish being the brightest person in the room and believe that it is this superiority that makes them a good leader. They use their authority to persuade or force others to conform to their wishes.

While they can be arrogant and self-centred, The Hero Leader also feels a need to keep others happy, as solving challenges and rescuing others makes them feel good about themselves. They have an unconscious need to be needed, appreciated, and valued and encourage others to become dependent upon them.

The demands placed on the Hero Leader can cause them to abnegate their own needs, or even deny their own humanness, by taking on a super-human quality. They hide their true selves and fear others will discover their weaknesses and struggles. This may lead not only to exhaustion but also to resentment building towards followers who view them as a panacea. Over time, this may lead to detachment and cynicism.

The Mask Wearer

Most school leaders wear a mask at times, especially in the early years of their career before they are comfortable with the role. The Mask Wearer has an inability to shed the mask and reveal their true selves in the workplace. The Mask Wearer plays the role of the leader, based on their ideas of what a leader is and how they behave, formed from their prior experience of leaders.

The Mask Wearer acts a part to hide their true thoughts and feelings. The mask acts as a defence, protecting leaders and helping them to hide their fears and insecurities. The mask enables them to remain detached when evaluating underperforming staff or to maintain composure in times of crisis. The mask hides the uncertainty and vulnerability that they do not want others to witness.

Mask wearing is linked to emotional labour, a suppression or faking of feelings to meet the expectations of a work role. Masking or faking feelings in the workplace has been found to cause emotional dissonance between one's inner and outer feelings that drain an individual's emotional resources over time and can lead to emotional exhaustion. A significant body of research shows a clear connection between emotional labour and occupational burnout in a wide range of professions and roles.[12]

The Job Lover

The Job Lover feels passionately about their work. They are so closely connected to the job, and so strongly identify with it, that they fail to set boundaries between their professional and personal lives. This high level of engagement creates a temptation to work all the time, leading an individual to become consumed by work and creating conflict with their other life activities. Research shows that while in some circumstances, this passion can support employee wellbeing, in others it can lead to an elevated risk of burnout.

Burnout researchers, Vallerand and colleagues, have developed a Dualistic Model of Passion to explain how some job-loving behaviours protect employees from burnout while other behaviours predispose them to it.[13] They distinguish between *obsessive passion*, which increases risk of burnout, and *harmonious passion*, which is protective. Obsessive passion involves relentlessly pursuing one's passion for work so that it becomes a compulsion and the central focus of one's life. An individual with obsessive passion for work so strongly identifies with their job that they have difficulty knowing who they are outside of a work context. They demonstrate an inability to step away from work-related activity or thinking without experiencing negative emotions, such as anxiety or guilt. Their constant rumination about work makes it difficult for them to switch off and be fully present in their personal life. This renders them unable to enjoy activities unconnected with work and may create significant conflict with family and friends. Obsessive passion is often associated with contingent self-esteem, where an individual relies heavily upon their work to produce feelings of self-worth.

Harmonious passion is a more balanced approach, where an individual chooses to passionately engage in work-related activity of their own volition and is not controlled by it. They can master and enjoy multiple areas of interest, inside and outside of work, and step away from work, free of guilt or anxiety.

Studies have found employees who engage in obsessive passion to be more highly disposed to burnout. This is due to conflict between their work and other life activities and to low levels of work satisfaction. Engagement in harmonious passion has been found to offer protection from burnout and bring a range of other wellbeing benefits.[14]

Overcoming Self-Sabotage Behaviours

Self-sabotage behaviours are often rooted in deep-seated feelings of inadequacy and insecurity that affect our self-perception. They can be addressed through practising self-compassion, a well-defined and well-researched concept that fosters positive attitudes towards oneself. Self-compassion is a way of relating positively to oneself that is not based on positive judgments or evaluations but on an acceptance that we are all flawed human beings.

A growing body of evidence shows a wide range of benefits for those who practice self-compassion. Self-compassionate individuals suffer less, thrive more, and report more happiness than others.[15] They experience less extreme reactions to failure, loss, and humiliation.[16] They are more able to sustain caregiving and experience less compassion fatigue.[17] Self-compassion is associated with lower levels of depression and anxiety[18] and less rumination, perfectionism, and fear of failure.[19] It is also connected to lower stress levels and a reduced incidence of burnout.[20] Researchers have found that those who lack self-compassion tend to subordinate their own needs to those of others more than self-compassionate individuals.[18]

The work of Kristin Neff, foremost self-compassion researcher, defines self-compassion as comprising three elements – self-kindness, common humanity, and mindfulness. Self-kindness is about accepting that being imperfect, failing, and experiencing difficulties in life is inevitable. It focuses on acknowledging distress and looking for ways to care for or soothe oneself, as we would comfort loved ones. Common humanity emphasises our own human experiences, imperfections, and failures as part of the broader human condition. We are not alone in being flawed and are able to forgive our imperfections. Mindfulness is about taking a balanced approach to our negative emotions and not getting swept away by reactivity. It is about acknowledging and labelling our thoughts without magnifying their significance or ruminating. This allows us to maintain perspective and change our inner narrative to something more positive.

Self-compassion allows us to make mistakes and helps us refrain from judging ourselves too harshly. It supports us in letting go of our need for validation. When we practice self-compassion, we are kind to ourselves in the face of personal failing, we care for ourselves, and we can reach out to others for connectedness.

Studies have shown that self-compassion can be learned and training in self-compassion can enhance psychological wellbeing.[21] Two major programmes have developed a comprehensive approach to building self-compassion. The Compassionate Mind Foundation offers a range of training opportunities to foster self-compassion in self and others. Their *Compassion-Focused Therapy* includes mindfulness training, visualisation, and the development of a range of self-compassion skills and habits. The Center for Mindful Self-Compassion (CMSC) offers the *Mindful Self-Compassion* (MSC) course, combining the skills of mindfulness and self-compassion, in a range of formats and lengths, online and in person at locations worldwide. Kristin Neff, co-founder of the CMSC, has an excellent website, which provides a range of free resources, including guided practise and self-compassion exercises, as well as details of self-compassion workshops.

Chapter Summary

- Self-sabotage behaviours, which may be rooted in deep-seated insecurities, can make a school leader more vulnerable to stress and burnout.
- These behaviours can manifest in a range of behaviour types that provide a useful construct for self-reflection and self-awareness building.
- The Imposter, the Perfectionist, and the Validation Seeker all hold themselves to high standards, which are hard to sustain and render them vulnerable to burnout.
- The People Pleaser, the Servant Leader, and the Hero Leader all tend to abnegate their own needs for others and have insufficient time to attend to their own wellbeing.
- The Job Lover and the Driven are motivated by ambition and passion to achieve at the highest level. This can cause them to push themselves too hard and pay the price in depleted resources.
- The Loner and the Mask Wearer hide their vulnerability and fail to seek social support. This puts them at an increased risk of burnout.
- Leaders can address self-sabotage behaviours by increasing their self-compassion. Self-compassion fosters positive attitudes towards oneself and reduces the negative attitudes and mindsets associated with self-sabotage behaviours.
- Self-compassion comprises three elements – self-kindness, common humanity, and mindfulness. It is associated with a range of benefits, including lower stress and a decreased incidence of mental ill health and burnout.
- Self-compassion can be learned, and a range of training programmes and workshops are available to help leaders to develop self-compassion skills and practices.

Notes

1 Selby, E.A., Pychyl, T., Marano, H.E. and Jaffe, A., 2014. Self-sabotage: The Enemy within. *Psychology Today*, 10 September 2011. Accessed online https://www.psychologytoday.com/gb/articles/201109/self-sabotage-the-enemy-within

2 Villwock, J.A., Sobin, L.B., Koester, L.A. and Harris, T.M., 2016. Impostor Syndrome and Burnout among American Medical Students: A Pilot Study. *International Journal of Medical Education*, 7, 364.

3 Bravata, D.M., Madhusudhan, D.K., Boroff, M. and Cokley, K.O., 2020. Prevalence, Predictors, and Treatment of Imposter Syndrome: A Systematic Review. *Journal of Mental Health & Clinical Psychology*, 4(3).

4 Fairlie, P. and Flett, G.L., 2003. Perfectionism at Work: Impacts on Burnout, Job Satisfaction, and Depression. In *Poster Presented at the 111th Annual Convention of the American Psychological Association*, Toronto, ON. Accessed online www.researchgate.net/publication/316249114_Perfectionism_at_work_Impacts_on_burnout_job_satisfaction_and_depression.

5 Treadway, M.T., Buckholtz, J.W., Cowan, R.L., Woodward, N.D., Li, R., Ansari, M.S. and Zald, D.H., 2012. Dopaminergic Mechanisms of Individual Differences in Human Effort-based Decision-making. *Journal of Neuroscience*, 32(18), 6170–6176.

6 Moss, J., 2019. When Passion Leads to Burnout. *Harvard Business Review*. Accessed online https://hbr.org/2019/07/when-passion-leads-to-burnout.

7 Briggs, R., 2021. "What About Me?": Teachers' Psychological Wellbeing and How It Can Be Supported When Teaching Pupils Experiencing Vulnerabilities and/or Trauma. University of Bristol, Ed.D. thesis.

8 Ben Simon, E. and Walker, M.P., 2018. Sleep Loss Causes Social Withdrawal and Loneliness. *Nature Communications*, 9(1), 1–9.

9 Friedman, I.A., 2002. Burnout in School Principals: Role Related Antecedents. *Social Psychology of Education*, 5, 229–251.

10 Bruce, L.D., Wu, J.S., Lustig, S.L., Russell, D.W. and Nemecek, D.A., 2019. Loneliness in the United States: A 2018 National Panel Survey of Demographic, Structural, Cognitive, and Behavioral Characteristics. *American Journal of Health Promotion*, 33(8), 1123–1133.

11 Risse, L., 2020. Leaning In: Is Higher Confidence the Key to Women's Career Advancement? *Australian Journal of Labour Economics*, 23(1), 43–78.

12 Kinman, G., Wray, S. and Strange, C., 2011. Emotional Labour, Burnout and Job Satisfaction in UK Teachers: The Role of Workplace Social Support. *Educational Psychology*, 31(7), 843–856.

13 Vallerand, R.J., Blanchard, C., Mageau, G.A., Koestner, R., Ratelle, C., Léonard, M. and Marsolais, J., 2003. Les Passions de L'ame: On Obsessive and Harmonious Passion. *Journal of Personality and Social Psychology*, 85(4), 756.

14 Vallerand, R.J., Paquet, Y., Philippe, F.L. and Charest, J., 2010. On the Role of Passion for Work in Burnout: A Process Model. *Journal of Personality*, 78(1), 289–312.

15 Barnard, L.K. and Curry, J.F., 2011. Self-compassion: Conceptualizations, Correlates, & Interventions. *Review of General Psychology*, 15(4), 289–303.

16 Shapiro, S.L., Brown, K.W. and Biegel, G.M., 2007. Teaching Self-care to Caregivers: Effects of Mindfulness-based Stress Reduction on the Mental Health of Therapists in Training. *Training & Education in Professional Psychology*, 1(2), 105–115.

17 Ringenbach, R., 2009. *A Comparison Between Counselors Who Practice Meditation and Those Who Do Not on Compassion Fatigue, Compassion Satisfaction, Burnout and Self-compassion*. Doctoral dissertation, The University of Akron.

18 MacBeth, A. and Gumley, A., 2012. Exploring Compassion: A Meta-analysis of the Association between Self-compassion and Psychopathology. *Clinical Psychology Review*, 32(6), 545–552.

19 Neff, K.D., 2011. Self-compassion, Self-esteem, and Well-being. *Social and Personality Psychology Compass*, 5(1), 1–12.

20 Shapiro, S.L., Astin, J.A., Bishop, S.R. and Cordova, M., 2005. Mindfulness-based Stress Reduction for Health Care Professionals: Results from a Randomized Trial. *International Journal of Stress Management*, 12(2), 164–176.

21 Germer, C.K. and Neff, K.D., 2013. Self-compassion in Clinical Practice. *Journal of Clinical Psychology*, 69(8), 856–867.

What Leaders Can Do **14**
Recovering From Burnout

In Part II, I set out strategies to reduce school leader stress and address the increasing incidence of burnout. In this chapter, I discuss what happens when burnout occurs and how leaders can recover from burnout. As discussed in Chapter 6, once an individual is on the burnout continuum, a burnout is not inevitable, and it is possible to prevent a burnout occurring. A school leader is likely to move both up and down the burnout continuum, and if signs and symptoms are recognised in time and steps are taken to considerably reduce stress, they may not reach crisis point. Once burnout occurs, however, the situation becomes much more serious, and it is unlikely that stress reduction alone will have a significant impact. A burnt-out school leader needs opportunity for substantial rest and reflection and may take many months, or even years, to feel well again. For some, the passion and drive that was the hallmark of their leadership may never return.

Recognising Burnout

It is important to understand that burnout is not the same as a short-term stress disorder that requires an individual to take extended time off work. Studies show that 80% of those experiencing short-term stress conditions will be back at work within 6–12 weeks and will be completely recovered within a few months.[1] Burnout involves a much longer and more complex recovery process. Initially, it may be difficult to distinguish a short-term stress condition from burnout, however, and an individual may find it hard to know what it is they are experiencing and what to expect.

As already discussed, Maslach and Leiter's model identifies three dimensions of burnout – exhaustion, detachment/cynicism, and ineffectiveness. Under

DOI: 10.4324/9781003198475-17

this model, a full burnout is recognised when all three dimensions are present. This is one way to distinguishes burnout from a short-term stress disorder. While the WHO does not recognise burnout as a clinical diagnosis, in some countries, such as Sweden and the Netherlands, it is recognised as such. In these countries researchers and medical practitioners have sought other ways to distinguish between a short-term stress disorder and what they term a *clinical burnout*. They focus largely on the extent of the exhaustion experienced by the sufferer and their physical and mental health symptoms. They also focus on the burnout process, which offers useful indicators that a clinical burnout has occurred, rather than a less serious stress-related condition.

Studies have found that employees who are forced to take extended time off work due to short-term stress disorders experience a different process leading up to their work absence than those who burnout.[1] For those with short-term stress disorders, there is most commonly a short lapse in time between an incidence of increased stress and the occurrence of mental or physical health problems. Increased stress may be acute and caused by specific changes in their working conditions, such as a new supervisor or a sudden increase in workload. Individuals commonly notice the onset and increase of stress-related symptoms and respond to them by seeking help.[2]

Those experiencing burnout are more likely to have ignored stress symptoms for several years prior to reaching a crisis. They commonly experience chronic lack of work recovery over a long period of time and report that living a stressful life has become the norm.[3] Their stress physiology adapts to these conditions, meaning they may not be aware of the severity of their stress until they reach crisis. While they may not recognise high stress levels, their stress system remains activated whether they are stressed or not, and they experience a chronic inability to relax.[4] They are likely to suffer from a range of physical and mental health symptoms but usually fail to seek professional help.[5] Instead, they cope by pushing themselves harder, which further exacerbates their condition.[2] They also commonly fail to seek social support and may withdraw and become more isolated.[5] When they eventually experience collapse, the trigger for the crisis may be something minor that pushes them over the edge.

This accurately describes my own experience of a burnout crisis. I largely ignored chronic stress that was building up over a period of around ten years, before I reached collapse. Most of this stress was related to the demands of my daily role as a school principal, compounded by the multiple crisis situations I had encountered in the schools where I worked. My work recovery was generally poor and opportunities for recovery were hindered by challenges in my family life, such as the illness and death of my mother, the inevitable ups and downs of married life, and the draining effects of menopause. Moving to three new countries over a ten-year period also brought significant challenges, as did studying for a masters and then a doctorate in quick succession. The combination of these factors meant that my life was always highly stressful. I sometimes wondered what impact this stress might be having on my health and wellbeing, but I pushed those concerns aside and pressed on in pursuit of my goals.

After ten years of almost daily stress, I no longer recognised its signs and symptoms. I had a chronic inability to relax and a feeling of being constantly hunted that had gone on for so long that it had become normal. I also experienced a range of health problems that magically disappeared within a year of retiring from my work as a principal. These problems, combined with chronic exhaustion, left me feeling close to breaking point at times. Yet I pushed on until I drained my resources dry.

There were times when I knew I was struggling. In 2015, following the death of a young member of our school community, I realised that I had no more to give and took a year out between jobs to complete my doctoral thesis. During this time, I travelled across the United States and Central America on a motorbike with my husband to rediscover the joy of life, replenish my resources, and rekindle my passion for school leadership. On returning to work 14 months later, in a new school, in an unfamiliar country, and with a bigger role, the demands began to overwhelm me all too quickly. But the situation eventually eased, and I found my stride. I loved what I did and felt energised, so I began to push myself harder than ever, seeking new challenges, pursing my passions, and enjoying the validation. There were huge highs and many lows. Over the next three years, the stress mounted, and I began putting my health and wellbeing at serious risk.

Throughout this whole process, it never occurred to me to seek social or professional support. When I was at my most drained, I isolated myself. I did not recognise this behaviour, but my husband observed how I changed during times of extreme stress. I worked harder, withdrew from family life, and retreated into my office at school, rather than slowing down and seeking sustenance.

Reaching a Burnout Crisis

Studies show that when approaching a burnout crisis, an individual will continue to try to fulfil their work obligations despite severe fatigue and distress. They may experience any number of physical, cognitive, mental, emotional, and behavioural signs and symptoms. Physical symptoms may include increasing headaches; gastrointestinal symptoms; chest pain or palpitations; hormonal symptoms, such as changes in libido, or issues with menstruation or menopause; and increasing colds, flu, and other infections. Cognitively, they may experience issues with concentration, working memory, forgetfulness, or impaired executive functioning. Mental health symptoms may include increased or fresh onset of anxiety and depression. Emotionally, individuals may experience frustration, anger, and emotional instability. This can manifest in conflict with colleagues, becoming easily agitated with family and friends, and self-medicating with alcohol, drugs, food, gambling, or shopping. They may also withdraw from others, both at work and socially, and give up their normal hobbies, pastimes, and sports.[6]

The final onset of my own crisis came after many months of building stress, exhaustion, and frustration. I was experiencing conflict with my senior colleagues and had begun to feel unfairly treated and disrespected. I could not gain perspective on the situation and became increasingly unable to keep a lid on my emotions, allowing my frustrations to spill over into several unpleasant confrontations. It was not my finest hour. I realise now how unstable and difficult I must have seemed at times.

The chest pain began in January 2019, five months before I eventually sought medical advice. The pain was brought on by stressful situations only occurring at first during SLT meetings. Yet I failed to consider that the stress might be seriously affecting me. In the following months, leading up to my collapse, I pushed myself harder than I ever had before. I was in overdrive and unable to stop. I knew I was exhausted but thought I could push through to the Easter holiday.

Just before the Easter break, something happened unexpectedly, a wonderful opportunity that brought extra work that needed to be completed before the return to school. While I had a few days off, I was not able to fully detach from work during the break, and when I returned to school my exhaustion had reached new levels. The frustration and anger I felt escalated as my energy levels plummeted. I had begun to lose faith in what we were trying to achieve as a school months before, but these feelings became magnified. I realised I had lost my sense of purpose and I tried to focus on getting through to the end of the year. At this point, just days before my collapse, I took the decision to take early retirement in two more years. I knew by then I would be done. I did not know I would not make it that far.

By May, the chest pain had increased and now came on during the evenings when I was relaxing. It was just before my 55th birthday, and I was conscious that my father had died of a heart attack when he was 54. I decided to seek medical help and was sent for a raft of scans and tests. Within a week, I was informed I had major blockages in my arteries and was in hospital for further investigations and treatment. Five days after being discharged from hospital, my GP informed me that I had likely experienced a burnout. I was signed off from work for the remainder of the school year. It happened so fast, yet I can see now that once the burnout was acknowledged, there was no way back for me. In some ways it was a slow build-up over many years, but at the end, it was like falling off a cliff. I lost control as my body forced me to slow down. One day I was operating at full power, and the next day my battery was dead and could not be recharged.

Recovering From Burnout

Burnout recovery is a multistage process that will take at least a year. For many, recovery may take two to four years, and some individuals may never fully recover from the impact.[7] Recovery begins with acknowledging there is a serious problem and taking immediate steps to stand back from all work responsibilities. This can be hard for school leaders, most of whom experience an overdeveloped sense of responsibility towards their school community and feel uneasy about burdening others with additional work. It is, however, unavoidable if the individual is to stand a chance of recovering.

At this initial stage, it is important that a leader discloses what has happened to their supervisor, HR, and their team. Fear, guilt, and stigma can make this extremely challenging, but burnout is not something that an individual can manage alone. Support from school will be needed if an individual has any chance of continuing in their role once a break has been taken. It is also crucial to seek personal support from family, friends, and close colleagues. It may be necessary to seek medical support from a GP at this stage.

During time off, emphasis needs to be placed on physical recovery, restoring the body that has become neglected, and allowing stress levels to return to normal. This involves prioritising rest, relaxation, and sleep; maximising nutrition; and engaging in gentle physical activity. Social obligations should be curtailed and resumed gradually as the body recovers. During this time, engaging in relaxation activities, such as those discussed in the previous chapter, can help the leader restore their stress physiology to normal.[8] The individual should look for ways to experience joy in non-work settings. A leader is advised not to make drastic life changes at this stage, as the efforts required to do so may be harmful. This period can last from a few weeks to several months, and there is a danger of relapsing back into crisis if an individual returns to work too soon.

Self-reflection is key to effective burnout recovery.[9] While the physical recovery process takes place, individuals will inevitably find themselves reflecting on what has happened to them and why. Researchers recommend that a full process of self-inquiry, supported by a professional psychologist, counsellor, or coach, should not take place until physical recovery is well underway, as it may hinder recovery if undertaken too early. It is crucial, however, that, when the time is right, the leader engages in supported self-inquiry to build awareness around the factors that have caused them to burn out.[9] This involves understanding their drivers, emotions, and needs.

Returning to Work

For most leaders, the next stage of recovery involves planning a return to work. Fifty percent of individuals who return to work following a burnout relapse within two to five years.[10] Leaders must identify what needs to change and seek help in making the necessary changes if a relapse is to be avoided. Professional help from a psychologist, counsellor, or coach is invaluable in supporting an individual to plan for the return to work, advocate for their needs with supervisors, and address the workplace demands that have contributed to their burnout.

Regardless of the steps an individual takes to manage stress and support their own recovery, this recovery cannot be sustained unless changes occur in the work environment. Studies show that interventions which focus purely on the individual are likely to have much less influence on burnout recovery than those which involve the workplace. Individuals who work in more flexible environments, those who have greater control over their work, and employees who have strong communication links with supervisors have a better chance of full recovery.

Leaders need to discuss adjustments to their working conditions with their school and ensure they have support in implementing change, to avoid falling back into familiar routines that led to the burnout occurring. This will involve avoiding new commitments or taking on new responsibilities while the individual gets the situation under control. It will also involve delegating as much as possible, even if this means tasks will be done more slowly or not as well. It is vital that individuals work with their school to address their workload, long working hours, the pace and unpredictability of their workday, and the emotional intensity of the work.

In addition to addressing workload, the other five areas of work life that affect burnout will need to be addressed to deal with any major imbalances. This may involve finding ways to improve the quality of community, increasing control over working conditions, resolving issues of perceived unfairness, and reigniting a sense of purpose.

On-the-job recovery requires the full support of supervisors and colleagues if it is to be successful. The nature of the work and the workplace culture in many schools do not allow for the space that a leader needs to fully recover or for the ongoing maintenance of a recovery. There may also be factors contributing to a leader's burnout that are not easy or possible to address. Burnout may have come about because of a poor person-job fit or a poor person-organisation fit. When there is a mismatch between the person and the organisation, the core values and culture of the school may not be aligned with those of the leader, and this may be impossible to resolve. Where this is the case, it will be necessary for the leader to reflect upon their core values and plan for ways to reconnect with them, to allow for full recovery. Returning to work in an environment where values are no longer aligned may lead to a relapse at some point in the future.

While modifications to working conditions are crucial to allow for burnout recovery, it is also essential that leaders take responsibility for their own wellbeing, if they are to fully recover. This involves ensuring appropriate work recovery, setting boundaries between work and home, and seeking social support. It may be necessary to eliminate professional activities or study that take place outside of school. It may also be helpful to monitor stress levels by keeping a stress diary or taking a regular stress inventory. Leaders will find professional support helpful in ensuring they remain on the path to recovery.

Not every school leader who experiences burnout leaves their job or walks away from their career, but many find it impossible to recover while continuing to operate in the same environment that was responsible for their burnout. Where there is a poor person-job fit, it may be enough for the leader to change roles within their current school. While this is uncommon, I know of leaders for whom this has been successful. Allowing a leader to move sideways, into a role more suited to their skill set, or making provision for them to move into a less demanding role provides opportunities for them to restore their balance, while keeping a valuable individual within the organisation. It is much more common, however, for leaders to move schools, sometimes taking a less demanding role, or to leave the profession completely.

Despite my prior decision to work for only two more years, my crisis forced me to acknowledge that I had to take my health more seriously. I realised I could only manage another year and decided to announce my upcoming retirement on return to school. After a nine-week summer break, I felt ready to commit myself to the role for a final year and then move away from the school environment completely. While I felt well and eager, the symptoms of burnout began to return within days and quickly escalated, finally leading to the panic attack I described in the preface.

I feel very grateful for what happened next. After two days spent at home, I met with my head of school to discuss the situation. We barely knew each other, as she was new in her role, but she was a headteacher of 30 years' standing and gave the impression she had seen it all before. She showed great compassion and concern about my capacity to make it through to the end of the year. She demonstrated a genuine desire to support me and, without prompting, suggested that I work from home two consecutive days each week for the remainder of my time at the school, without a reduction in salary. She called HR into the meeting to make sure that the arrangement was immediately formalised. We discussed who would take the acting principal role on my working from home days and how they would be compensated, and we also brainstormed projects that I could work on while away from campus.

It is hard to express how relieved I felt and the effect that two days away from the school environment each week had on me. Little did we know, in August 2019, that within a few months we would all be working from home. I cannot say that I recovered from burnout during this period. The challenges of leading an international school through the Hong Kong pro-democracy protests and then the global pandemic did not allow for recovery, but I was able to keep my head above water despite the unprecedented demands of the time. This would not have happened but for the compassion and foresight of my supervisor and the care and generosity of my team, who stepped up to fill the gap I left behind during the most challenging of times.

Due to our close working relationships, the lower school leadership team witnessed the effects of my burnout more than others did. They were shocked and genuinely concerned for me. They understood that I could no longer cope with the daily stresses of the job. I had become fragile and needed to be protected. They did everything they could to keep the hard stuff away from me, even as we entered the uncharted territory of the pandemic. The community needed my leadership during this time, and my team made it possible for me to continue to offer this.

Post-Burnout Growth

Post-traumatic growth is a well-documented phenomenon that involves positive change resulting from a challenging life crisis. Research has found that around half of those who experience trauma develop new understandings of themselves, the world they live in, and their relationships with others.[11] This can bring greater self-efficacy, personal strength, and more positive attitudes than before the trauma.[12]

Recent studies into post-burnout recovery have found that surviving and healing from a burnout can be a catalyst for growth that can bring similar positive changes for individuals.[13] Post-burnout growth can lead to a new appreciation of life, clearer priorities, and new possibilities. Individuals have reported experiencing stronger relationships, based on increased vulnerability and intimacy, greater personal strength, and an increased capacity to deal with difficult situations. Many have also reported having more fully developed philosophies on life and experiencing more presence.[8]

In the course of my work as a researcher, coach and consultant, I have encountered many school leaders who have burnt out and taken the decision to move school or leave the profession. Two to three years down the line, the vast majority are now happier and more fulfilled than they were prior to burnout. One international school leader moved to a new school, in a new country, in a lesser leadership role. She now enjoys a slower pace of life and the opportunity to enjoy, with her family, everything that the host country has to offer. She is fulfilled by her new role and takes great pleasure in having time to build relationships with staff and become an integral part of the community. The role is still stressful, but she works with her head of school and team to ensure it is manageable. She also now has a strong understanding of how to set boundaries between school and home to ensure she can recover from work.

Another former leader left his role as a UK deputy head to set up a business coaching and supporting school leaders. While self-employment brings its own stresses, he can achieve the kind of work-life balance that was unthinkable when he was working in schools. The experience of burnout has given him the opportunity to re-evaluate his life goals, spend more time on his hobbies, and be more present for his partner and children. He has been able to channel his burnout experience into supporting struggling colleagues and is really making a difference in their lives.

For myself, the period of two and a half years since I left the profession has provided precious time to reflect and heal. It has been more than three years since my burnout, and I finally feel that I have mended. During this time, I have developed a new professional opportunity, which is both interesting and rewarding. I have fulfilled a lifetime ambition to become an author and have had time to conduct my own research and read widely. This satisfies my natural curiosity and hunger for knowledge. I also work with amazing school leaders and their teams all over the world. While I no longer feel broken, I must accept that I am now more prone to experiencing the negative effects of stress than in the time before my crisis. I must manage my workload carefully to ensure it remains enjoyable and sustainable. It has taken time to understand this, and I have made mistakes along the way. I am now careful to examine every work opportunity that presents itself and consider its impact on my health and wellbeing before I accept.

Post-burnout growth has brought me many gifts. I now understand how important it is to work in alignment with my core beliefs. In both of my previous careers, I observed how unhappy I became if I was employed by an organisation that did not uphold my value system. My happiest times in the workplace, both as a lawyer and a school leader, have been when I believed deeply in what we were doing as an organisation and felt a sense of belonging. These were never the best paid jobs, but they were, without question, the most fulfilling. They are the jobs that I smile about when I look back on my former careers, and they fill me with a sense of pride and achievement. Working independently provides me with the opportunity to choose the work I accept, and the organisations I work with, to ensure I am always operating in line with the things that matter to me. I now understand that professionally this is more important to me than anything else.

I have also had time to acknowledge that I am essentially an introvert. While I enjoy working with others, and I am told others enjoy working with me, interacting with others on a daily basis can be highly draining. While I love working with large groups of school staff, I am also very content sitting at the computer, analysing research data, or writing an article for publication. Although rewarding, I found the intense people-centric nature of school leadership to be challenging. While on the surface I was performing to the expected level, the amount of people-work was taking a lot out of me. I sometimes think that the level of human interaction and the emotional demands involved in school leadership were never going to be something I could sustain over a period of decades. Now I work independently, I can choose how much I interact with others and when. This means that I can give 100% to those I do interact with and can fully enjoy collaborating, knowing my wellbeing is not being jeopardised.

Finally, I have come to understand that I was not meant to live life in the fast lane. I think I made a pretty good job of it for two or three decades, but part of me always sensed it was not for me. Throughout my working life, I made a point of taking a sabbatical every ten years, to get away from work, to study, travel and experience something different. I always hated returning to normal and often felt a deep longing to be somewhere else, growing vegetables or pitching a tent in the mountains. I had a strong sense that there was another version of me that I was suppressing so I could live the life I had chosen. I was never sure if I had chosen well. I don't feel like that anymore. There is only one version of me now, and that version is living life as I feel it should be lived. I go to bed each night feeling grateful for the day that has ended and excited for the day to come. My life is simple. I find I do not need much to be happy. I don't miss the life that I had. My priorities have completely shifted.

While it was frightening and disorientating, I am grateful for my burnout experience. Without it, I would never have had the courage to walk away from what was making me unhappy and unhealthy. Without burnout, I would not have found what I have now – peace of mind.

Chapter Summary

- Unlike short-term stress-related illness, recovery from burnout can take many months or years.
- The initial stage of burnout recovery involves resting to allow for physical recovery, as the body heals from the effects of exhaustion. During this stage, it will be necessary to take time off work and eliminate all professional commitments. It is essential to seek the support of employers at this stage.
- The next stage of recovery will include a process of reflection to determine how the burnout occurred and establish how a relapse can be avoided. This should ideally be facilitated by a mental health professional.
- Avoiding relapse will only be possible if significant changes are made to working conditions. Leaders should seek the support of a mental health professional to help them plan a return to work and reflect upon the changes that will be necessary. They should approach employers with honesty and openness.
- While it is natural to focus on reducing workload, leaders will need to review and address possible imbalances in all six areas of work life when considering their return to work.
- Although it is possible to return to the same role following a burnout, most school leaders find it necessary to change role within their school, move to another school, or leave the profession completely.
- Many leaders experience post-burnout growth, gaining greater clarity and tapping into new possibilities following burnout.

Notes

1 van der Klink, J.J., Blonk, R.W., Schene, A.H. and van Dijk, F.J., 2003. Reducing Long Term Sickness Absence by an Activating Intervention in Adjustment Disorders: A Cluster Randomised Controlled Design. *Occupational and Environmental Medicine*, 60(6), 429–437.
2 Bakker, A.B. and de Vries, J.D., 2021. Job Demands – Resources Theory and Self-regulation: New Explanations and Remedies for Job Burnout. *Anxiety, Stress, & Coping*, 34(1), 1–21.

3 Weber, A. and Jaekel-Reinhard, A., 2000. Burnout Syndrome: A Disease of Modern Societies? *Occupational Medicine*, 50(7), 512–517.

4 McEwen, B.S., 2007. Physiology and Neurobiology of Stress and Adaptation: Central Role of the Brain. *Physiological Reviews*, 87(3), 873–904.

5 Martínez, J.P., Méndez, I., Ruiz-Esteban, C., Fernández-Sogorb, A. and García-Fernández, J.M., 2020. Profiles of Burnout, Coping Strategies and Depressive Symptomatology. *Frontiers in Psychology*, 591.

6 Kahill, S., 1988. Symptoms of Professional Burnout: A Review of the Empirical Evidence. *Canadian Psychology/Psychologie Canadienne*, 29(3), 284.

7 van Dam, A., Keijsers, G.P., Eling, P.A. and Becker, E.S., 2012. Impaired Cognitive Performance and Responsiveness to Reward in Burnout Patients: Two Years Later. *Work & Stress*, 26(4), 333–346.

8 Fjellman-Wiklund, A., Stenlund, T., Steinholtz, K. and Ahlgren, C., 2010. Take Charge: Patients' Experiences During Participation in a Rehabilitation Programme for Burnout. *Journal of Rehabilitation Medicine*, 42(5), 475–481.

9 Salminen, S., Mäkikangas, A., Hätinen, M., Kinnunen, U. and Pekkonen, M. 2015. My Well-being in My Own Hands: Experiences of Beneficial Recovery during Burnout Rehabilitation. *Journal of Occupational Rehabilitation*, 25(4), 733–741.

10 Karlson, B., Jönsson, P. and Österberg, K., 2014. Long-term Stability of Return to Work After a Workplace-oriented Intervention for Patients on Sick Leave for Burnout. *BMC Public Health*, 14(1), 1–10.

11 Parikh, D., De Ieso, P., Garvey, G., Thachil, T., Ramamoorthi, R., Penniment, M. and Jayaraj, R., 2015. Post-traumatic Stress Disorder and Post-traumatic Growth in Breast Cancer Patients: A Systematic Review. *Asian Pacific Journal of Cancer Prevention*, 16(2), 641–646.

12 Linley, P.A. and Joseph, S., 2011. Meaning in Life and Post-traumatic Growth. *Journal of Loss and Trauma*, 16(2), 150–159.

13 Semeijn, J., Van Ruysseveldt, J., Vonk, G. and van Vuuren, T., 2019. In Flight Again with Wings That Were Once Broken: Effects of Post-traumatic Growth and Personal Resources on Burnout Recovery. *International Journal of Workplace Health Management*, 12(5).

Conclusion

We live in an increasingly complex and fast-changing world. Society needs the best qualified, most skilful, and experienced individuals to take responsibility for educating the next generation of workers, leaders, and parents. Yet data from around the world shows we are facing a spiralling crisis of mental ill health and poor wellbeing among school leaders. This is affecting their job performance and causing many to burnout. It is also creating a looming headteacher and principal shortage.

In April 2022, new UK government statistics on school leader retention were published. Figures show that the number of headteachers leaving their posts has significantly increased since 2015. More than one in three secondary school leaders in England, and one in four primary leaders left their jobs within five years of appointment between 2015 and 2020.[1] The National Association of Head Teachers (NAHT) has described leadership supply in England as "teetering on the brink," blaming the government's failure to address low pay, high-stakes accountability, crushing workload, long hours, and inadequate school funding.[2] Similarly, the US National Association of Secondary School Principals (NASSP) released new data in February 2022, showing that four out of ten principals intend to leave their posts within the next three years.[3] School leadership is highly challenging, yet many talented and dedicated leaders are being lost to a profession that is becoming increasingly unattractive to potential replacements.

The growth in headteacher and principal turnover is also increasing the number of disruptive leadership transitions, negatively affecting school performance. Schools that serve disadvantaged populations are particularly vulnerable as they experience chronic leader turnover and serious levels of disruption.

Ultimately, these factors make schools less effective. They are unable to provide students with the high-quality academic learning and pastoral care that they need. This potentially affects outcomes for all students, but particularly those from marginalised communities and low socio-economic backgrounds, who are disproportionately affected.[3]

Deteriorating school effectiveness has wide-ranging implications for the economy but also for social cohesion. It affects the whole of society. This is why school leaders matter. They are a vital societal resource. Headteachers and principals should be valued and nurtured, but instead they are being exploited and their potential wasted.

The go-to solution for governments and schools is to implement reactive, piecemeal approaches to support school leader wellbeing, or place the onus on leaders themselves to manage stress and build resilience. This approach is quite simply ineffective.

Headteacher and principal burnout is preventable, but schools must start being proactive if a crisis is to be averted. This involves treating school leader stress and burnout as psycho-social risks that need to be managed in the same way as other health and safety hazards.

In this book, I have discussed a clear set of solutions to avert a mounting crisis. They include a raft of government measures, but they also involve a strategic approach by schools to address the real issues. Yes, there is often financial outlay involved, but it represents a fraction of the cost of continuing to ignore the problem. The current situation is unsustainable, with many leaders in survival mode, unable to maximise their performance, planning their escape route, or being forced out by ill health. It is time for a significant shift in thinking to create real and lasting change.

Notes

1 Department for Education (DfE), 2022. *School Leadership in England 2010 to 2020: Characteristics and Trends*. London: DfE.

2 Weale, S., 2022. School Leader Retention Rates in England Declining, DfE Data Shows. *The Guardian*, 26 April. Accessed online https://www.theguardian. com/education/2022/apr/26/school-leader-retention-rates-in-england-declining-dfe-data-shows

3 National Association of Secondary School Principals, 2022. NASSP Survey Signals a Looming Mass Exodus of Principals from Schools. Accessed online www.nassp.org/news/nassp-survey-signals-a-looming-mass-exodus-of-principals-from-schools/.

Index

Note: Page numbers in **bold** indicate a table on the corresponding page.

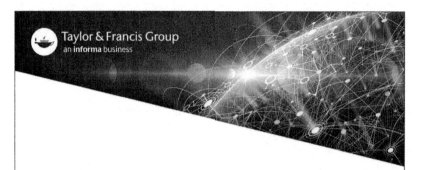

Printed in Great Britain
by Amazon

18819801R00142